HUMBOLDT

THE LIFE
AND TIMES OF
ALEXANDER VON HUMBOLDT
1769–1859

HUMBOLDT

THE LIFE
AND TIMES OF
ALEXANDER VON HUMBOLDT
1769–1859

BY

HELMUT DE TERRA

OCTAGON BOOKS

A DIVISION OF FARRAR, STRAUS AND GIROUX

New York   1979

© Helmut de Terra, 1955

Reprinted 1979
by special arrangement with Alfred A. Knopf, Inc.

OCTAGON BOOKS
A DIVISION OF FARRAR, STRAUS & GIROUX, INC.
19 Union Square West
New York, N.Y. 10003

This reprint was reproduced from
an original in the Brown University Library

Library of Congress Cataloging in Publication Data

De Terra, Helmut, 1900-
    Humboldt: the life and times of Alexander von Humboldt,
1769-1859.

    Reprint of the ed. published by Knopf, New York.
    Bibliography: p.
    "Bibliography of the most important works of Alexander von
Humboldt": p.
    Includes index.
    1. Humboldt, Alexander, Freiherr von, 1769-1859. 2. Scientists—
Germany—Biography.
[Q143.H9D4   1979]   500.9′2′4[B]   78-27653
ISBN 0-374-92134-2

Manufactured by Braun-Brumfield, Inc.
Ann Arbor, Michigan
Printed in the United States of America

TO MY CHILDREN
NOEL AND NIELS

H U M B O L D T *was one of those wonders of the world, like Aristotle, like Julius Cæsar, like the Admirable Crichton, who appear from time to time, as if to show us the possibilities of the human mind, the force and the range of the faculties,—a universal man.*

—RALPH WALDO EMERSON (1869)

Preface

THIS month of May, one hundred and fifty years ago, a man stepped off a sailing vessel in Philadelphia to pay his respects to the young American Republic. A few weeks later he had endeared himself to President Jefferson, Madison, and many other historic Americans, and had returned to Europe a staunch believer in the future of democracy. Half a century later Alexander von Humboldt had come to be a legend and a household word in the United States, memorialized by place names and monuments, then to be forgotten in the rush of an age that he, as one of the founders of science, had helped create. To remember him is to recall the embodiment of the widest possible range of human faculties, a mental prism with facets sparkling on all sides. And he had good reason to call himself "half American." In him a sense of grand adventure was joined with a deep concern for the utilization of knowledge as a common good. If he could but see this continent now, its natural resources scientifically harnessed and its social consciousness directed toward wide dissemination of knowledge, he would stand aghast and feel concerned, lest such fabulous development be endangered by misuse of human power.

With all the humility becoming a scholar he would be the first to admit that much of his scientific labor appears to us outdated, as the ripe ear of Indian corn outdates its seed. Yet he might agree that his long and fabulous life holds much of the human stuff dreams are made of, and that its triumphs, compromises, and sufferings are in a sense as modern as is any life lived ably and vigorously.

It was this human element in Humboldt's life that prompted me to write this portrait of an extraordinary man whose long-forgotten trails I crossed on some of my own wanderings in America, Europe, and Asia. In the Himalayas I have camped in places where Humboldt's pupils had explored, and earlier still student excursions led me to mountains in Germany where Humboldt worked as a mining official. But it was in Mexico that I found the Humboldt tradition truly alive, for there students are brought up in remembrance of his pioneering spirit, officially honored as a benefactor of their nation. If there were temples of science in Latin America, Humboldt's image would undoubtedly be worshipped there as a patron saint, as indeed he was honored all over the Western World as the grand interpreter of nature. These encounters with the Humboldt tradition finally added up to the desire to sketch Humboldt's life in a perspective more modern than previous biographers had been able, or willing, to give.

Tempting as was this task, I soon came to realize that it could be done under two conditions only: by relegating the scientific mass of Humboldt's labors to a place less prominent than a full-scale biography of a scholar might call for, and by not feeling discouraged over the lack of documentary materials concerning certain phases of his private life. Naturally the former condition was inherent in the project of a popular biography that might appeal to others than scientists. As for the incomplete preservation of Humboldt documents, especially those relating to his childhood and student days, I cannot now see how a more voluminous documentation might have materially altered the essential outlines of my portrait. True enough, it might have strengthened—or occasionally detracted from—the force of my interpretations, but I doubt that it would have evoked character traits essentially different from those I was able to detect.

Nothing, of course, is more fascinating to a biographer than to know that his subject deliberately destroyed certain mementos, as Humboldt did. Among these were his letters to Georg Forster, his friend and traveling companion, and to numerous others with whom he maintained intimate friendships, many of them marked by considerable passion and anguish. The mystery that surrounded these relationships betrayed the existence of secrets in the life of this extraordinary man, prompting previous biographers to invest Humboldt with motives whose true nature was revealed for the first time by Albert Leitzman in 1915. As if fate had meant to continue this self-willed destruction of Humboldt documents, many were destined to perish in a warehouse fire in London, while others were scattered through auctions to hundreds of private autograph-collectors and institutions, never to be published. Worst of all, many of Humboldt's portraits and diaries were lost at the close of the Second World War when the Humboldt family seat at Tegel, near Berlin, was pillaged. There, in the fall of 1953, I was personally introduced to the shell of what had once been a showplace of the finest German and European traditions. Sad as was this irretrievable loss, I could hardly leave the place without an added incentive to continue in my task, seeing, as I then did, how imperishable is the heritage of gifted personalities. The Humboldt trail led me to many libraries in this country, France, and Germany. Thereafter I settled down to sifting my notes and documents. Fortunately, there was enough for me to proceed with the story of a man whose life spanned a politically turbulent phase of history, one immeasurably rich in the progress of science. And Humboldt's pleading for a grand synthesis and philosophic orientation of all scientific endeavors, largely forgotten in an age of scientific specialization and moral confusion, made it seem timely to sketch the life of a man who dedicated his genius with rare devotion to the study of man's place in nature.

Grateful acknowledgment is owing to a number of institutions and persons that aided me in my work: the New York Public Library; the Westdeutsche Bibliothek at Marburg; the Library of the Jardin des Plantes in Paris; the Library of Congress in Washington, D.C.; and the files of the American Philosophical Society. To Frau Marie-Agnes von Heinz at Tegel I owe much useful information, as well as personal guidance through the former Humboldt mansion. Others, like Señor Carlos R. Linga in Mexico City and Mr. Francis R. Stoddard in New York City, contributed pictures and unpublished documents. To Mr. Herbert Weinstock, of Alfred A. Knopf, Inc., my warmest thanks for his helpful comments and the experienced aid of his editorial pencil.

HELMUT DE TERRA

Contents

Illustrations

PUBLISHER'S NOTE: Because wartime destruction made unavailable actual photographs of some of these portraits and other illustrations, a few of them have been reproduced from unsuitable printed copies. They have been included here because their documentary interest overrode the objection that clear, handsome reproductions could not be made.

HUMBOLDT

THE LIFE
AND TIMES OF
ALEXANDER VON HUMBOLDT
1769–1859

1

Privilege and Sorrow

THE LUTHERAN BAPTISM of the Humboldt infant was a dignified affair. Not showy, but solemn and simple, with the touch of brilliance added by the presence of the reigning Duke of Brunswick. Acting as godfather to the child, he listened attentively as the boy was christened Friedrich Wilhelm Heinrich Alexander von Humboldt.

This name must bide its time to ring with fame; it must wait for history to ripen until Jefferson can be President and Napoleon crowned Emperor. Then people in Lima and Washington, in Paris and Berlin, would know Alexander von Humboldt as a flame of knowledge on the threshold of a new age.

The youngster would develop by outgrowing his family tradition. He would react strangely to emotional undernourishment by seeking nature's solace, toss aside a promising career, and sail for South America. The steaming jungles of the Amazon and the Andes of Peru would reveal to him in a most original fashion the orderly grouping of living things in their association with climates and with mountains whose tallest summit he must climb, thus establishing the altitude record of his time. To him nature would be a grand orchestration, its strains a harmonious interplay of people and plants with earth and atmosphere. The forgotten world of the ancient Incas, their knowledge of fertilizers, the healing properties of quinine bark, volcanoes and earthquakes, would be surveyed and pondered. And Mexico's riches in minerals and historic traditions would be revealed by his insatiable thirst for knowledge, and this knowledge be generously handed out on his visit to Thomas Jefferson and James Madison. A staunch friend of the young American Republic, he would go to Paris, there to spend his best years, engulfed by ambitious scientific labors, a lonely man craving for intercourse with nature, but constantly seeking the friendship of distinguished men, relishing French intellect and culture. Shaken by political turmoil and financially ruinous publications, he would then accept a King's offer to become a power near the throne. At sixty one could follow him to Russia and Siberia and back to his native Berlin. Torn between his duties at court and his scientific labors, this amazing man would outlive his friends Goethe and Jefferson and a host of eminent collaborators, among them Gay-Lussac and Gauss, often to shine with his liberal convictions, and always striving for completion of his masterwork, *Cosmos,* which was to reveal mankind's orientation in the universe. The substance of this man would leave the memory of a seeding wind.

The child was born on September 14, 1769, in his parent's town house, a modest-looking brick structure in the center of Berlin. That his baptism was witnessed by a reigning Duke was not so much a deliberate act of social staging as a gesture of friendship. In his early days the boy's father, Major Alexander Georg von Humboldt (1720–79), had been the Duke of Brunswick's adjutant, accompanying him on his travels, fighting with no conspicuous enthusiasm in the wars of Frederick the Great. He served as an officer, dreaming of the delights of peace, of women's love, of hunting, and of nature. When appointed court chamberlain at forty-two, he became at-

tached to the suite of one of the King's relatives, hoping
all the while to find his fortune in the vigorous life of the
city that Frederick the Great had embellished with an
opera and a scientific academy. In the King's pleasant
château of Sans Souci, near Potsdam, the major mingled
with foreign celebrities. There he was often a bit bored,
standing in candlelight to listen as the King performed
his compositions on the flute.

Within a short time the major had made a modest fortune, profiting from the leasing of lotteries and from tobacco sales. Among foreign diplomats he was known as a
man of good standing and estimable character, who, ac-
credited to the court, had every chance for a ministerial
appointment under the monarch who would succeed the
great Frederick. Yet this could hardly have suited his
tastes, for he was extremely fond of nature, a man who
might be seen any day strolling with a forester through
copses and woods. This love for the country prompted
him later to spend much time on the estate of Tegel, near
Berlin, which his future wife had inherited with all its vineyards and mulberry plantations. One of the King's projects
was to encourage that cultivation of silkworms which the
descendants of Huguenot refugees from France had
started with considerable skill. For a time everybody
talked of lucrative investments to be made in mulberry
groves. Work with trees had always been to the major's
liking, and while his hopes of large profits at Tegel had
not been fulfilled, he managed at least to plant some exotic
trees and bushes, a gift from the Duke of Brunswick's
botanical gardens.

The major's ancestors had not belonged to the titled
gentry. In fact, his family's nobility was of rather recent

date, being barely a generation old. The Humboldts had lived as bailiffs and magistrates in the northern provinces, especially Pomerania, where chronicles commended them for substantial contributions to local churches as far back as the sixteenth century. No reliable record survives of the title of baron having been conferred on any of them, so that its use, as in the case of the major's son Alexander, was merely a pleasant courtesy, after the fashion of the times. The major was a simple and affable man, not given to snobbery, but shrewd in the choice of his friends.

To him good fortune appeared in the guise of Madame Maria Elisabeth von Hollwege (1741–97), *née* von Colomb, a good-looking woman of character and wealth. Experienced man that he was, he may have found comforting assurance in the fact that she had borne a son to her first husband: he might expect to have children by her. Her inheritance—a town house from her mother and an estate from her deceased husband—would supplement his own landholdings to good advantage. It was a good match all around. Soon after his marriage his wife bore him a daughter, who died in infancy. Later they had two boys, Wilhelm and Alexander.

Frau von Humboldt was a well-educated woman from the noble Colomb family. Her ancestors had left Burgundy at the close of the seventeenth century in a stream of distressed refugees, many of whom found asylum in Prussia. Under the Grand Elector of Brandenburg, Prussia had produced the Edict of Potsdam, that humanitarian gesture which admitted the homeless, wretchedly persecuted Huguenots to its poorly equipped land. There they settled, most of them owning nothing more than a title of nobility, an officer's rank, or the skills of provincial silkweavers.

Frau von Humboldt's son by her first marriage turned out to be a troublesome youngster. He is little mentioned in the family annals, a fact that may account for her ambition to make the most of her younger sons. A letter written in 1785 by her friend Caroline de La Motte-Fouqué described her as "somewhat pale, with finely drawn features that on no occasion betrayed emotion." She spoke, the letter continues, in a low voice, and appeared cool but sincere. Her hair was always the same, worn smooth and simple, and by contrast with her lively husband she displayed a reserved and quiet nature. Everybody knew her as a conventional woman lacking in warmth and heartiness. In her household nothing much was allowed to change. After an absence of ten years a visitor might find it the same, with the old dog snoring on the couch, and Frau von Humboldt much occupied with ailments.

What she was temperamentally unable to offer to her sons by way of affection, her husband might have given. He was a warmhearted, friendly man, known to everybody as a generous benefactor of people less fortunate than himself. An avowed lover of nature, he took the boys into the woods on many occasions, thus arousing their feelings for natural beauty. Tegel was pleasantly situated among pine woods and meadows extending to a lake surrounded by tall reeds and sandy beaches where the boys could find nests of waterfowl. The park was dotted with centenarian oaks, and on one side was flanked by forested hills with natural sandpits to play in. On the southern slopes the forest had been cleared to make way for grapevines and mulberry trees. From a vantage point one could see far across a smiling landscape, bright with lakes and little islands, fields, farmhouses, and windmills. In the distance

rose the spires and contours of the small fortress town of
Spandau, and on clear days one could see the northern
gate of Berlin. From the city it was less than a two-hour
coach ride to the Humboldt country place. Here the family would spend their summers, frequently in the company
of guests, some of whom would ride or drive by coach
from the King's palace. In the fall or spring the major invited his friends for duck-shooting or deer-hunting, and
he would return to his townhouse refreshed by their gay
company. From Tegel it was only a few hours' coach ride
to the King's residence at Potsdam. Alexander von Humboldt would recall in his old age how his father had taken
him there to be presented to the great man of whom it
was said that he could improvise on a theme by Bach
as cleverly as he could turn a military defeat into vic-
tory.

In those days Berlin was one quarter the size of Paris,
being a provincial town of about 150,000 inhabitants. Like
other eighteenth-century towns, it was a smelly, noisy
place, its streets littered with refuse, full of clattering carriages, beggars, and vagrant musicians, its nights noisy
with brawling drunks and the wailing hourly songs of
nightwatchmen. Frederick the Great had done his best to
provide Berlin with a nucleus of culture, French or Italian
according to his preferences for either French letters and
science or Italian music. He was distrustful of German culture. As first president of the Academy of Science, the
King had installed Pierre-Louis Maupertuis, a Parisian
physicist and mathematician who had determined the
flattening of the earth at the poles. To the man in the street
it mattered little that this Francophile on the throne preferred the company of foreign eccentrics as long as he

stuck to his plan to make Berlin a manufacturing center for woolens, cottons, and silks.

With his free and roaming manners, Major von Humboldt could hardly have had much in common with his wife. In fact, her restraining influence must have been a never ending source of irritation, a situation of which the boys may not have been aware, considering that they were mostly in the company of tutors and servants. With the major's premature death in January 1779, the boys, Wilhelm and Alexander, then respectively twelve and ten, had to turn to a mother who could see in them only objects for duty and ambition. Naturally, she would give them the best education to be had; already before her husband's untimely death she had engaged tutors—"house chamberlains," as they were then called.

The influence of this ménage turned out to be unfortunate for both boys, more intensely for Alexander than for Wilhelm, who was a bright, jolly youngster, likely at any time to raise laughter with his boisterous ways. But for Alexander, the more delicate and sensitive boy, his mother could only fail during that most important time which called for special warmth and loving affection. He would always remember her and his boyhood with the pain and anguish that, at twenty-two, he expressed movingly in a letter to his friend Karl Freiesleben:

I passed most of that unhappy time here at Tegel, among people who loved me and showed me kindness, but with whom I had not the slightest sympathy, where I was subjected to a thousand restraints and much self-imposed solitude, and where I was often placed in circumstances that obliged me to maintain a close reserve and to make continual self-sacrifices. Now that I am my own master, and living here without restraint, I am unable to yield myself to the charms of this prodigal nature because I am met at every turn by painful recollections of my childhood, which even the inanimate objects around me are continually awakening. Sad as such memories are, however, they are interesting for the thought that it was just my residence here which exercised so powerful an influence on the formation of my character and the direction of my tastes to the study of nature, etc. But enough of this. I shall weary you with so much about myself.

Humboldt obviously was capable of analyzing in retrospect the conditions to which he had been subjected. The restraint with which he wrote about them to an intimate friend shows a good deal of the tact that he could exercise in later years when it pleased him. He could never be quite himself with his mother. Forced to play a role with her because of the differences in their temperaments, he found it restful to go back into the woods. There he found the desired acceptance.

Alexander and Wilhelm grew up like twins. They were inseparable. Wilhelm was alert in every way, the favorite with tutors and servants. Alexander was known as the *"petit esprit malin,"* possibly because he found it necessary to act the "good boy" role with all manner of tricks and excuses. The tutors, complaining to Frau von Humboldt about Alexander's slowness in learning, praised Wilhelm for knowing his Latin verbs and his history. But the younger boy was so talented in drawing and painting that his mother allowed him to exhibit his art on the walls of her bedroom.

The tutors had to take the place of the father, and one may suspect that they really tried their best, each in his own way, to substitute for both parents. One of them,

Joachim Heinrich Campe (1746–1818), who had tutored the older stepbrother, returned in 1775, when Alexander, at the age of six, had already learned to read and write. To us this may seem like premature forcing, but in the Humboldt home it was considered slow progress: Wilhelm had learned to read at three. If the tutors found reason to complain about Alexander's slow progress in learning, they may have overlooked his frequent headaches and bad moods. But how did they explain his frequent turning away from them to nature, that comforting source of enjoyment and intimate vision?

Alexander might have turned to Campe, full of learning and already known as the translator of *Robinson Crusoe*. But how hard it must have been for the boy to reconcile a pedantic manner of teaching with the much more exciting adventures of the man who, by sailing away to a tropical island, had really done things right! Many a boy has wished to run away from his schoolroom and plunge into adventures. Alexander took his boyish dreams and longings very seriously. At last he too would sail forth, a new Columbus, to dive into the unknown jungles of the Amazon.

After Campe came Gottlob J. Christian Kunth (1757–1829), who was to play an important role in the Humboldt household, not only as a tutor, but also as a confidant of its head and owner. Frau von Humboldt took a liking to this learned and gracious young man, the son of a Protestant minister, and immediately requested him to attend to her correspondence and social affairs. In 1777, when only twenty, Kunth turned down a legation secretaryship, preferring a tutor's position. He brought to it no special gifts as a teacher, but he had executive ability and a general knowledge of languages, history, and economics. His gracious, lively manner showed to excellent advantage at parties, and he soon gained the complete confidence of the mistress of his new home, who entrusted him with the management of her estates. There is no reason to believe that this bond between Alexander's mother and his tutor was anything but correct, for to be correct was the axiom of her life, no matter what emotional strain it might entail. She must have been delighted with her new acquisition, for here, at last, was a capable and trustworthy young man. Now she could relax a bit from the strain of her manifold burdens—the household, parties, and visitors, the correspondence with the overseers of her estates, and their accounts. Only four years after Kunth's arrival she made this poor son of a pastor more secure by presenting him with an annuity of four hundred gold florins. Years after her death, he would become an influential civil servant in Berlin, a champion of free trade and of a tariff union for Germany. He would remain as manager of the Humboldt estate, and long after Wilhelm and Alexander had inherited it, he would—reputedly at his insistence—be buried on the family estate of Tegel.

Campe, on the other hand, Alexander did not remember with much kindness, even alluding to him in a tone of ridicule. Writing to the anatomist Samuel Thomas von Sömmering in January 1791, he referred to Campe's plan of going to America:

Not that he may enchant the intelligent youth of that country by the introduction of his children's books, his Robinsoniade, etc., not that he may disseminate among savages his new proof of the immortality of the soul, not that he may regulate dancing in Philadelphia according to the laws of chastity—no, but that he may closely study the Constitution of the United States, so as to publish within a year (for Europe must even be deprived of him for that long) the result of his observations on the New World, in order that truth and freedom may be extended to all mankind. Can you fancy anything more truly absurd?

The boys received their lessons together except when supplementary teaching was deemed advisable. In addition to German, French was obligatory and most necessary for a home and age in which it was *de bon ton* in refined circles. The boys learned their classics by reading and translating passages from Vergil and Horace, and from that classic Greek historian and naturalist Strabo, to whom Alexander must have taken a very special liking. History should have come easily to these pupils. The drama of Frederick's exploits was close at hand, the smoke of cannon hardly having drifted from his battlefields. And they could draw maps on which the campaigns of the illustrious namesake of one of them, Alexander the Great, were outlined in colors chosen for their pleasing brightness. Campe had given the boys an inkling of botany, a smattering of Linnæus's great system of classification.[1] How comforting for Alexander to name his favorites in the park and forest!

Kunth, on the other hand, insisted on languages. It was he who inspired Wilhelm to acquire that linguistic knowledge by which the older brother would outshine his contemporaries and become one of the founders of compara-

[1] "Linnæus had a passion for classification. His *System of Nature* included not only the orders of the various animals and plant species, but also of minerals and diseases. He even classified past and contemporary men of science according to military rank with himself as the general." (S. F. Mason: *A History of the Sciences*, 1953, p. 268).

tive philology. But Kunth, with his pedantic methods, must have given his pupils a hard time. "I remember scenes," Wilhelm wrote to his bride years later, "which will shake me forever. He [Kunth] guided my entire childhood. What I am now I did not become through him, but with him and under his supervision." [2] Much later he told of Kunth's painful rambling when teaching history: "His lectures on history made one almost wish to have been Adam, when history had only just begun."

Both tutors, and especially Campe, were under the influence of Rousseau's writings when they insisted that a certain measure of nature study should go hand in hand with history and the classics. Rousseau's ideas on education were much in vogue at the time among families of distinction. The great evangelist of the age of reason had been given protection by Frederick, whose brother, Prince Henry of Prussia, had at one time invited the French rebel to Potsdam.

To mention Rousseau to the pupils and to explain his philosophy in simple terms was one thing, but it was another to keep the effects of such experience within reasonable bounds. With Alexander this was difficult, for at an early age he showed uncommon perseverance in nature studies. Already he was known around the house as the

---

[2] How great Kunth's influence was over the Humboldt boys is evident from Wilhelm's letter to Caroline, his future wife, dated May 22, 1789: "You must praise the Lord for having preserved my nature in the face of the many difficulties and adjustments I had to make in my childhood." And in another letter to Caroline, of April 12, 1790: "As long as I lived with Kunth, I lived a woman's life." According to information given to me by Dr. Charlotte Weidler, of the Carnegie Institute, Pittsburgh, such unhappy childhood experiences led to disturbances in Wilhelm's character, the true nature of which can for the moment not be ascertained ᵇecause of the unavailability of Wilhelm's unpublished diaries.

"little apothecary," a nickname that both acknowledged his special concern with nature and showed a slight contempt for this peculiar interest, peculiar because of the traditions of his home environment. Yet "interest" does not quite express what the younger Humboldt boy must have felt when he returned from his field trips laden with little boxes of butterflies, plants, flowers, and insects. Most children are avid naturalists for a time, finding bright toys in fields and woods, wanting to enjoy them until something else diverts their attention. With Alexander it was different, for he collected such things not for temporary pleasure, not as mere toys, but for their enduring companionship. He would classify and arrange them, write out a label for each specimen collected, and place them on exhibit in the room he shared with his brother. Wilhelm undoubtedly collected too—he could scarcely have helped it, watching his younger brother run for a flower here, a lizard there. But it was Alexander, not Wilhelm, who was nicknamed "the little apothecary," possibly in ridicule, but in any event for something singular.

Would it have needed a Rousseau to teach the lonely boy a concern with nature, really the only realm in which he could feel at home? Surely not, for in the company of trees, birds, and flowers he felt himself accepted, uncriticized, and unrepressed. Merging with nature's beauty, he found with a sure instinct the security and happiness that his mother and the tutors could not provide.

Such deep concern with nature assuredly was not a "gift" or a "talent." Rather it was a moving and desperate necessity for a boy so impressionable and in need of affection. In the child's predicament is to be found a key to the man who would have to roam the world to discover the affirmation of an ideal motherly love speaking the pagan language of rocks, plants, and stars. From this child's singular love of nature would grow the exploring naturalist, who for the rest of his life aspired to that artistry which we call romanticism, but which in him produced a singular blend of thinker and artist, of explorer and sensitive observer.

Fantasies accompanied Alexander to woods and lakes. There he could dream about the adventures life might hold. Undisturbed, he could imagine the exploits of historic personages, of heroes of classical mythology, and of Robinson Crusoe. To sit by a lake, waves glittering and splashing, on a summer's afternoon, and perhaps follow a bulging sail for a while, was like merging with distant, desirable things. Suddenly the world was full of boundless possibilities. Unhappily, most of us are stripped of such dreams by educational methods that give us too little chance for inspirational moods. But for Alexander they would come again, many times, both in the steaming jungle and on the snowy heights of the Andes. They would lend his thinking a very alluring touch and a singular way of recognizing harmony in the physical diversity of nature. With him the extraordinary capacity for synthesizing often came as if in a dream, lending wings to his scientific observations. These early moods were mentioned in his later writings. In his *Narrative of Travels* he wrote:

From my earliest youth I had an intense desire to travel in those distant lands which have been but rarely visited by Europeans. This impulse is characteristic of a certain period in our existence when life appears as a boundless horizon, when nothing so completely captivates the fancy as the manifestations of physical danger and the excitement of sensational emotion. . . . The study of maps and the perusal of travel books aroused a secret fascination that was at times almost irresistible, and seemed to bring me into close relationship with distant places and things. The thought that I might possibly have to renounce all hope of seeing the splendid constellations that shine in the Southern Hemisphere invariably sent a pang to my heart.

And in *Cosmos* he remarks:

The pleasure I derived as a child from the contemplation of the form of continents and seas as outlined on maps, the yearning to behold those southern constellations which never appear above our horizon, the pictures of palms and cedars of Lebanon in a pictorial Bible, may all have contributed to excite in me the desire to travel in foreign lands.

Continuing in the vein of such rationalizations, Humboldt finally stated in *Views of Nature:*

The tastes first awakened by the impression of childhood and molded by the circumstances of later life often become, when imbued with the deep earnestness of later years, the incentive to scientific labor or to undertakings of vast import.

This was an age of daring explorations and exciting discoveries. Between 1768 and 1779 Captain James Cook on two voyages had explored the whole extent of the Pacific Ocean, lifting a curtain of ignorance that had concealed half the world. Educated Europeans had begun to follow with breathless excitement the courageous example set by Cook and his companions, Banks and the two Forsters, and by Vancouver and Flinders, who sailed along the coasts of Australia and New Zealand. The tropical splendor of South America was revealed by La Condamine and by Bougainville, whose name became familiar in association with the bougainvillæa vine. Contemporary writers were Bernadine de Saint-Pierre and Buffon, who introduced geological perspective in his *Épochs de la nature* (1778). Such was the inflammatory substance that in a mind like Alexander's required only mental fanning of a spark of fantasy to be kindled and aroused to a grand conflagration.

And yet the boy must have suppressed much of his imagination and smoldering desire, for he wrote to his friend Marc-Auguste Pictet in 1806:

Until I reached the age of sixteen, I showed little inclination for scientific pursuits. I was of a restless disposition, and wished to be a soldier. This choice was displeasing to my family, who desired that I should devote myself to the study of finance, so that I had no opportunity of attending a course in botany or chemistry. I am self-taught in almost all the sciences with which I am now so much occupied, and I acquired them comparatively late in life.

It was not surprising that this boy, torn by all manner of conflicts, was often stricken with ailments. His brother Wilhelm said: "Alexander could master his daily tasks only by dint of extraordinary effort," undoubtedly because his inner conflicts weakened his health. Such psychosomatic symptoms were to stay with him for many years. He was critically ill time and again, until complete liberation came with the momentous opening of his own age of exploration.

At Tegel the boys were introduced to distinguished visitors, among them Goethe, who paid his respects to the Humboldts in 1778. He stayed for lunch and then continued on foot to Potsdam. Later he was to recall the story of the Tegel gamekeeper's ghost in the First Part of *Faust:*

ALEXANDER VON HUMBOLDT (above)
and WILHELM VON HUMBOLDT (below),
ca. 1784, from crayon drawings

ALEXANDER VON HUMBOLDT as a young man,
after a charcoal drawing (*Bettmann Archive*)

> *Vanish at once! We've said the enlightening word.*
> *The pack of devils by no rules is daunted:*
> *We are so wise, and yet is Tegel haunted.*

The ghost of Tegel! Goethe would meet him later in another form. Not a spook, but a "fountain of knowledge"— the young Alexander, a man who would incite the aging poet to grand expectations of an America controlling its two flanking oceans by means of an interoceanic canal.

The passing of Frederick the Great in August 1786 diminished the influence of French culture and the efficiency of government. Berlin, in which the Humboldt boys grew up, came to be known for corruption and loose living. Yet there were some whose intellectual charms stood out like beacons of culture in the drab wastes of mediocrity. Into their homes we must follow the young Alexander to share his excitement over the first meeting with the enlightened.

One bright morning in the autumn of 1785 the blue-eyed boy, his adolescent mind restless under a crop of unruly brown hair, stepped into the home of the botanist Karl Ludwig Willdenow. Tutor Kunth may have told him about the author of the *Flora of Berlin,* a botanist unrivaled in all Germany for his profound knowledge. Was it not Willdenow who had inquired into the meaning of plant forms and their geographic distribution? Reaching beyond the confines of Linnæus's classification, he had coined such terms as "tropical" and "boreal" flora, being the first to differentiate between central European and Mediterranean plant life. Alexander, unwrapping his parcels, entrusted his treasures to Willdenow: flowers and pine cones, rock and mineral specimens. He had waited all

these years for this supreme moment when their names
and origins could be revealed with greater authority than
Campe's. They had always been friends waiting for a
learned man like Willdenow to come along and tell Alexander why plants grew the way they did, why some minerals sparkled and others were dull. Willdenow knew
something about rocks. He could explain Abraham Gottlob Werner's system of classifying, which made it easy to
recognize and name the most ordinary pebbles. How marvelous this first authentic gleam of order, this realm of
names and definitions, this newly discovered intimacy with
natural objects!

At Tegel, Alexander had made little sketches of flowering plants and scenery, which he felt prompted to show
to Daniel Chodowiecki, director of the Academy of Arts.
These so delighted the famous etcher that he enrolled the
boy as his pupil and taught him the rudiments of drawing
and engraving. In Chodowiecki's class Alexander made a
pencil copy of a Rembrandt painting which found a place
in the Berlin art show of 1786, the first occasion on which
his talents were presented in public. He must have been
thrilled beyond measure by this event, as every boy of
his age would have been, but especially because of that
inner uncertainty which had wormed itself into his nature.
Probably this chance to exhibit was partly engineered by
himself: records make it obvious that Alexander needed
praise and public acclaim as if in need of affirmation of his
inner nature. To draw was almost a prerequisite for nature studies, photography not yet having been invented.
But aside from this, Alexander would always be partial to
art, especially in Paris, where he would come to move in
art circles. Yet his talent for drawing should not be mis-

taken for the creative compulsion of an artistic tempera-
ment. With him it would always remain a visual aid, a
pleasing mode of synthesizing pictorially what could not
be expressed easily in words: the æsthetic concept of nature's harmony.

At sixteen, one might say, the caterpillar began to burst
its cocoon, twisting and turning as if excited by a strange
light from without and by the promise of new nourishment. Such sustenance came from an unexpected source,
astonishingly unorthodox in view of the prejudices of the
youth's social caste. With his brother Wilhelm he attended
lectures in physics and philosophy which the physician
Marcus Herz presented at his home. As Willdenow had
given Alexander his first grounding in botany, Herz first
acquainted him with physics, and especially electricity. In
the Herz home he was shown the epoch-making experiments of Benjamin Franklin and Count Alessandro Volta.

No sooner had the boy understood the mechanism of
the lightning-rod than he implored Kunth to permit its in-
stallation at Tegel. But what would the local clergy say
to this? A wanton trespassing against God's will, an unheard-of interference with divine providence, perpetrated
by an adolescent whose mother was a respected pillar of
the church! A few weeks later Alexander had his will.
Soon everybody knew that after Göttingen University the
Humboldt home at Tegel was the next place in the land
to be protected by Franklin's invention. There it was, a
symbol of Alexander's craving for science, hoisted on that
old house in defiance of outmoded prejudice. We can only
guess at his feelings and excitement over this achievement,
elated as he must have been with this deflection of a fright-
ening element.

Men like Franklin were pointing the way, and so was Immanuel Kant, the philosopher at Königsberg, with his new theory of planetary origins. Captain Cook was navigating uncharted lands again, and Maupertuis had measured geographic latitudes in Lapland. A Frenchman, Antoine-Laurent Lavoisier, had recognized the importance of oxygen in the transformation of chemical elements, and James Watt in England was rumored to have perfected a steam engine. In the learned circle of Dr. Herz it seemed to young Alexander that the world was being re-created with boundless horizons.

Equally momentous, more challenging to mind and body than the crackling sparks from instruments, was his meeting with Henriette Herz, the beautiful young wife of the doctor. As hostess she managed to turn Alexander's head by a devastating combination of feminine charm and wit, until he wanted to please her by learning Hebrew and English. To her he would write "dreadfully long letters" in English to impress her with his industry and devotion. She wrote of him in later years:

In those days, whenever Alexander von Humboldt wrote to me or any other member of our intimate circle from the family seat at Tegel, he usually inscribed his letter from "Castle of Boredom." This occurred chiefly in the letters he wrote in the Hebrew script, in which I had given him and his brother some instruction, and which, with the additional help of our friends, they wrote very successfully. It was not to be thought of that a young nobleman should confess in letters that could be read by anyone how much more entertaining was the society of Jewish ladies than a visit to his ancestral mansion.

This, indeed, was unheard of in times when even the most enlightened leaders of the Jewish community in Berlin required special protection and a license for them to move in the social circles to which they rightfully belonged. The Jewish intellectual community gave Berlin in those years a cultural glamour it would otherwise have lacked. Its leader was Moses Mendelssohn (1729–86), grandfather of the composer Felix Mendelssohn-Bartholdy, and himself immortalized in Lessing's drama *Nathan the Wise*. As the author of *Phædon*, a widely read book on man's immortality, Moses Mendelssohn was regarded not only as a peer among European philosophers, but also as an emancipator of European Jewry: his translations of Hebrew Scriptures into German made possible a subsequent acceptance of Jewish traditions in Western culture. This apostle of enlightenment was reported to have spent his morning hours walking about the garden in company with the young Humboldts, giving them liberally of his visionary mind.

The thought of it makes one wonder how much they may have absorbed from the forceful idealism of this man whose intellectual greatness contrasted so brutally with his licensed social status. Even though the injustice of enforced Jewish segregation was then generally accepted as an established tradition, it could hardly have failed to impress the sensitive Alexander by its mixture of human greatness with oppression and hostile isolation. Did he not feel isolated in his own home environment, shackled as he then was by its boredom? That Alexander, at this impressionable age, should have identified himself with men of spiritual authority is quite understandable considering that he lacked a father. But that such an authority spoke from behind a curtain of segregation must have been disturbing enough to determine Humboldt's attitude toward oppressed minorities for the rest of his life. It is as if in those years of contact with the Jewish circle his sense of justice had received a blow from which he strove to recover by championing the cause of the underprivileged. This attitude became all the more pronounced in later years in his adherence to the ideals of the French Revolution. Yet the essential impact of these circles on the Humboldt boys was the intellectual ferment and the everlasting memory of these champions of liberty, which led to the exponents of German romanticism, Klopstock, Wieland, Goethe, and Schiller. One brilliant member of that Berlin circle, the young girl Rahel Levin, was to meet the Humboldts time and again in Paris, Vienna, and Berlin and, after many a romance, was to marry Alexander's cherished friend Varnhagen von Ense.

Yet at this time neither of the boys was the intellectual hothouse product of a privileged home. Both kept their engagements for dances, Alexander instructing Madame Herz in the latest *minuet "à la reine,"* sporting a gleaming watch-chain, and corresponding with his dance partners. He had grown into a slim lad of medium size, his pinched adolescent face, with its large nose and keen eyes, like a falcon's. From his sensuous mouth torrents of words flowed, with occasional quick, hard-hitting flashes of irony, as if the world owed him something that so far he had missed. He was restless on his parental perch, eager to alight he knew not where.

2

A Student Takes to the Road

THE TIME HAD come for the Humboldt boys to start their training in earnest. The choice of a university had been discussed at some length between their mother and Kunth, the tutor. There being none in Berlin, the nearest was a day's coach ride to Frankfurt an der Oder, not far from the Polish lands. This nearness determined Frau von Humboldt's choice. It permitted the close supervision essential to a woman who suspected moral dangers at every turn. Kunth would naturally remain in charge of her sons, and from Frankfurt it would be easy to recall him at a moment's notice. On no account must her boys be allowed to sow their wild oats. She had spent effort and money on a carefully planned education and would not jeopardize her sons' future by exposing them to contaminating contacts with unruly classmates. With Kunth's advice, plans had been made. Her sons would enter official careers. They must become dutiful servants of the state that Frederick the Great had built up with such amazing ability. Considering the corrupt condition of the world, her country, she concluded, would be in dire need of honest citizens.

So off tutor Kunth and his two charges went, in September 1787, to Frankfurt. It was a drab provincial town where the clatter of a foreign coach was a sensation. As a river port it was lively during the summer. Its university, known as the *Academia Viadrina*, had been founded in 1506, but a university in our sense it assuredly was not. The students, few more than two hundred boys, were taught by a handful of professors. They lectured on law, medicine, philosophy, theology, and history. The "faculty" of medicine consisted of a single professor. In economics the students were instructed to draw plans for a brandy distillery and learned methods of textile manufacture and cheese-making and the art of exterminating caterpillars.

Whether it was as safe a place for the Humboldt boys as their mother thought, only time could tell. But it was not the right academy for two gifted minds. Alexander accepted this first contact with university life like a skipper caught in the doldrums. The teen-age lad wrote to his friend Beer in Berlin:

In Frankfurt everything conspires to facilitate the acquisition of a doctor's degree, for the disputation, if it can be so called, is nowhere easier. . . . If it were not for the friendly intercourse we enjoy here so thoroughly, Frankfurt would indeed be a dull place to both of us. It requires but a very small amount of philosophy, however, to be convinced that mankind is created for every spot upon the earth, consequently for the icebound bank of the Oder. What more exalted aim can the Goddess of Science (who certainly has no temple here) propose to herself than to make mankind contented?

What was the friendly intercourse referred to in this letter? Was Alexander in love? That he was starved for affection anybody might understand who knew how his mother had failed him, forcing him to seek for it elsewhere, in nature, there by the lake, and under the trees at Tegel. Departing from Berlin, he had left good friends behind, and while his brother's company was comforting, it was not what he was looking for: a human being identified with happiness.

A classmate of Alexander's, a student of theology named Wilhelm Gabriel Wegener,[1] reported in his autobiography that the older Humboldt boy was too aloof and studious ever to give freely of his friendship. The younger, on the other hand, attached himself with such warmth and kindness as nobody had offered Wegener before. They may have met in Professor Hartmann's philosophy class, thereafter going home together to Wegener's attic room to discover their friendship. From then on they were inseparable. Wegener was Alexander's chosen friend. Now he no longer had to feel lonely or greedily snatch fleeting affection from strangers.

Since that February 13, as we swore eternal brotherly love to each other, I feel that none of my other acquaintances can give me what you have for me. . . . Those glorious days [Alexander continued in a letter to his friend from Berlin] are gone forever, for such happiness can never be again. Nevertheless my fervent love and sincere friendship for you are as imperishable as the soul that gives them birth.

And again Alexander wrote to Wegener:

When I measure the longing with which I wait for news from you, I am certain that no friend could love another more than I love you. When I recall all the signs of your friendship, I feel tormented in the thought that I don't love you as much as your sweet impressionable soul, your attachment for me, deserve.

Entire pages were filled with such reflections, with expressions of ailing desire and descriptions of dreams symbolizing the union with his cherished friend. Wegener was

[1] As minister and administrative official, Wegener had a career of little significance in comparison with Humboldt's. The friends lost track of each other a few years after the Frankfurt episode.

implored to share Alexander's interests, study botany, collect plants and minerals, travel and explore exotic lands
with him. The devotion to Wegener had kindled what was
parched in Alexander; it had aroused feelings that he had
never known before.

The eighteenth century was full of romantic friendships
and idealizations, but this experience of Alexander von
Humboldt seems to have been of a different order, especially when seen in the light of his total life. This ardent relationship with a boy his own age was only one of many
similar relationships. He never married, because women
never played an important role in his emotional life; his
mother had failed him. His friendships would always be
ardent. Not infrequently one of them would last only a
few years, to be replaced by another, as, in fact, his relationship with Wegener was replaced. His character was
marked by a distinctly homosexual leaning.[2]

No sooner had the warm breezes of late spring begun to
thaw the icebound fields around Frankfurt than the Humboldt boys returned to Berlin. Had their tutor Kunth perhaps realized the inadequacy of Frankfurt's academy, or
had their mother insisted on firmer direction of their training? Her older son Wilhelm seemed to her the more prom-

---

[2] I was privileged to discuss Humboldt's homosexual nature with
Dr. Erich Fromm, the well-known psychologist and author. Dr. Fromm
suggested tentatively that Humboldt's unhappy relationship with his
mother may account for a tendency to identify himself in later life with
an ideal mother, as evinced by strong protective motives in his friendships, but more so by a philosophic orientation toward cosmic creative
processes—a universal mother, as it were—with whom a union was consummated on a spiritual plane. While it would seem hazardous to explain
genius by psychological formulas, Dr. Fromm's suggestions are all the
more striking because it would seem that Humboldt's "abnormality"
actually gave to his nature a haunting longing for fulfillment, and an unusual force of mental creativity.

ising of her boys. Kunth had reported favorably about his progress in law studies, for which reason he would be allowed to enroll at the University of Göttingen, famed for its excellent faculty. As for Alexander, she would have to see whether his restless mind could be captured by a practical schooling in economy and finance. His private tutoring would have to be continued and supplemented by regular visits to manufacturing plants, potteries, textile mills, and salt works in Berlin. Not that her son Alexander minded this, for he was interested in everything new, always seeing things in a most original and novel light. How delightful for him to return to the Mendelssohn household, to his art class, and especially to Willdenow, whose profound knowledge of botany had inspired him! [3]

To Wegener he wrote from Berlin in 1788:

I am collecting materials for a work on the various properties of plants, medicinal excepted. It is a plan requiring great research and such a profound knowledge of botany as to be far beyond my unassisted powers. Therefore, I am endeavoring to enlist the co-operation of several of my friends. Thus far I have been working at it only for my amusement, and in the course of my studies I am constantly meeting with things that set me gasping with astonishment. Pray do not imagine that I am going to appear as an author forthwith. I don't intend that to happen for the next ten years, and by that time *I trust I shall have discovered something startling, new, and important.*

How little does he know himself! He would be known as an author within two years, and shortly later as an inventor

[3] As a pioneer in botanical science, Willdenow was no doubt acquainted with the significant advances made in plant classification and physiology by Antoine-Laurent de Jussieu (1748–1836), whose work was assisted and continued by August and Alphonse de Candolle at Geneva. All of these men came to be influential in Humboldt's botanical studies.

of sorts in the technology of mining and a pioneer in electrical therapy.

For over two years Wegener and Humboldt exchanged letters very frequently. The former reported on one occasion that he had taken up botany—news that elicited in Alexander a special longing for a friend who so obviously wanted to please him by this hobby. Berlin had excitements in which the distant friend must share. In the fall of 1788 the French balloonist Blanchard exhibited his novel machine there.

The sight of the enormous machine, twenty-six feet in width, the appearance of the man who, with superhuman boldness, dared in such a contrivance to cross the ocean [meaning the English Channel], the majestic movement of the balloon as it soared aloft—but mainly the thought of the rapid march of human civilization whereby the third element has thus been brought under control—all this conspired to produce a most powerful impression that stirred me to the heart. . . . The stories told of him [Blanchard] that he gambles and has three wives are complete fabrications; they are nevertheless believed by everyone in Berlin.

In another letter Alexander wrote that censorship of the press would not allow him to publish some innocent couplets on a pair of garters (a customary wedding present in those days) without having the garters laid before the Court of Censorship!

In the spring of 1789 Alexander prepared for his departure for Göttingen, where he was to join his brother Wilhelm and a few classmates from Frankfurt, and whence Wilhelm had been sending glowing reports to his mother. The thought of increasing the distance from his friend Wegener was a bitter pill to swallow. As in his boyhood days, an unhappy mood made necessary the secure solace of nature studies.

How happy, how inexpressibly fortunate should I be if I had a friend like you by my side! . . . I am persuaded that no strong passion will ever sway me with an overwhelming power. Serious occupation and the *calm induced by an absorbing study of nature* will preserve me from the temptations of life . . . you can judge by yourself whether I am strong enough to walk alone on this world's slippery path.

This is the theme familiar from his younger days, but in a variation: to preserve calm through nature's company lest he become lost in human entanglements.

Amply equipped with letters of introduction, Alexander presented himself most dutifully, en route to Göttingen, at the court of his godfather, Duke Ferdinand of Brunswick. On his way he visited the potash works near Magdeburg and, near Helmstedt, a botanical garden containing the oldest and most extensive plantation of American trees in Europe. Then he paid his respects to Germany's eminent mathematician Johann Friedrich Pfaff, who must have read with some astonishment in the letter of introduction that "if he [Humboldt] had been able to devote his attention exclusively or even partially to mathematics, he would have become a distinguished mathematician." So as not to disappoint Professor Pfaff, Alexander wrote to him a few weeks later from Göttingen that he was working on a new system of logarithms and equations, "for how can mechanics accomplish anything without the aid of higher analysis?" Twenty years later the problems touched upon in this letter to Pfaff would be successfully solved by the great mathematician Friedrich Gauss at

Göttingen. There Alexander was enrolled on April 25 as a law student.

At Göttingen the Humboldt brothers took common lodgings in a good bourgeois home and were joined by a young man destined to play an important, if somewhat dubious role in European politics: Count (later Prince) Klemens Metternich (1773–1859). Among their classmates were two English princes of royal blood, Ernest August, later King of Hanover, and Adolph Frederick, Duke of Sussex. Alexander took a special liking to a young mathematics student, Jabbo Oltmanns, who in later years would collaborate with him on the results of his American travels.

Founded in 1737 by George II of Hanover, Göttingen had come to be the foremost university in Germany. Here, Albrecht von Haller had lectured on his epochal discoveries about the evolution of the animal egg (1757), and Johann Friedrich Blumenbach (1759–1840) had presented the first system of comparative anatomy and the races of mankind. Philology, until then confined to the study of languages, enlarged its scope through Christian Gottlob Heyne's studies in classic archæology and sociology. Half of the university's eight hundred students were enrolled in the law school, where new courses in government and German law attracted budding state officials and diplomats. Among European universities, Göttingen ranked high. Its rapid development responded to an upsurge of intellectual life throughout Europe. Only a few years before Humboldt's matriculation, Henry Cavendish in England had found the chemical constitution of water, and William Herschel had discovered the planet Uranus. In Italy, Alessandro Volta had discovered the first electric condenser, and Jan Ingenhousz in Holland had revealed the respiration of plants. The highest mountain in Europe, Mont Blanc, had been scaled (1787) by the geologist Horace Bénédict de Saussure, and the English geologist James Hutton had presented, in 1785, the gist of his challenging *Theory of the Earth*, stressing the geological processes of the earth's internal heat over and above the action of running water. In Paris, George Buffon denied the existence of classes, orders, and genera in nature.

The Göttingen professors had long felt the need for assembling this new exciting knowledge. Various departments published learned magazines, with reviews of foreign publications. By so doing they broke the traditional confines of higher learning, until then restricted to scattered academies. Such visions of a wider exchange of knowledge originated in cramped, ill-heated, and poorly lit quarters, enthusiastically supported by a tightly knit academic community in which students worked on a graduate level, with little time and inclination for organized drinking parties. These came spontaneously, to celebrate a monarch's or a professor's birthday, with torchlight parades and oratorical display. Such hilarious student parties seemed to have had little attraction for the young Alexander, known, as he then already was, for his all-consuming preference for learning. In Berlin his mother and former tutor Kunth had mapped his career in finance; he must make the most of this precious privilege of attending courses in natural science.

How prodigious Blumenbach's knowledge was, and how clarifying his systems of anatomy and anthropology! First to have presented a new classification of animals on the basis of anatomical relationships, and first to have outlined the principal racial divisions of mankind as we still know them today, Blumenbach may be credited with Humboldt's interests in anatomy and anthropology. And Blumenbach, having experimented with the effects of electrical currents on animal bodies, must have inspired his pupil to similar research, prompting Humboldt later to make an important contribution in this field.

Small wonder that the student became a member of Göttingen's distinguished Philosophical Society, an organization that, in the fashion of the times, aimed at a broad advance in higher learning. Once a member of this group, Humboldt was able to reach the most eminent naturalists of his age, a small European circle that struggled for scientific enlightenment amid incredible ignorance and prejudice.

From Blumenbach's class Alexander went to the lectures of Christian Gottlob Heyne, "undoubtedly the most clear-headed man and, in certain branches of knowledge, the most learned professor in Göttingen. His delivery," Alexander wrote to Wegener, "is labored and hesitating, but he is in the highest degree philosophical in his turn of mind and logical in the sequence of his ideas." Heyne, who lectured on the history of civilization, an encyclopedic survey of the advances and institutions of mankind through the ages, was an original interpreter of classical mythology and art. Alexander wrote in later years that Heyne "was undoubtedly the man to whom this century is most deeply indebted." The time would come when Alexander would remember Heyne for possessing knowledge obviously necessary to the solution of archæological problems. With Woltman, his Greek and Latin professor, Alexander spent from nine until eleven at night reading Plautus and Petronius. On one occasion he was treated to an ex-cathedra criticism of Prussia, whose royal house was likened to "an ancient oak under whose shadow a free German people delight to cast themselves"! Such freedom of thought and academic expression was to breed liberals and scholars. One wonders how they accepted the startling news of the French Revolution, which broke out during that fateful summer of 1789. While feudalism was being guillotined in Paris and crowds danced madly to Revolutionary tunes, Alexander went touring along the Rhine with his geologist friend Van Geuns. A note to Wegener reported little time for letters, what with the incessant labors of packing mineral and plant specimens and the writing of a diary.

The observations made during this trip piled up material for additional studies. Back at Göttingen, Humboldt asked for permission to work in the library on Sundays. There he sweated over an essay on the loom in use among Greeks and Romans ("quite a prodigy of learning, and its compilation has therefore been quite distasteful to me"). Inspired by Heyne, and because of earlier acquaintance with textile-manufacturing in Berlin, Alexander was determined to publish something about it. But this first manuscript needed so much editing that it would be published only much later, and then through the aid of his brother Wilhelm. To satisfy Blumenbach, he worked over his notes on the geology of the Rhine country. What a lot of questions came to his mind! Did the geological terms used by classic writers like Pliny and Strabo fit current geological terminology? What Strabo had called "basalt" actually answered to the description of granite rocks. What precisely was the origin of basalt rock? Was it volcanic or water-laid?

With this question Humboldt had touched upon a hotly debated scientific issue whose importance was keenly felt by all the eighteenth-century naturalists who had begun to challenge Biblical traditions. If minerals had originated from liquids, as Werner maintained, rocks should be regarded as precipitates of primordial oceans and of solutions in the earth's interior. This "neptunist" concept of Werner was challenged by James Hutton, who ascribed the formation of minerals and rocks to deep-seated volcanic ("plutonic") forces. To what fantastic errors this debate led is evident from a contemporary publication suggesting that the Egyptian pyramids were remnants of volcanic craters! Among the adherents of the plutonist school was the French Abbé Giraud-Soulavie, who maintained that the inhabitants of basaltic regions were prone to insurrection, as in Germany, where they had spread the heresy of the Reformation. "There can be no question," Alexander wrote, "that the inhabitants of a mountainous region differ very decidedly from dwellers on plains, but an attempt to determine what particular influence upon people is exerted by special rocks must be regarded as a wanton trespass beyond the boundaries of our knowledge."

The experience of his short excursion to the Rhine country had taught him that theories should rest on sound observations and that natural objects should be seen as interrelated. Rocks should be studied in their relationships to soils and the plants they produce. To us this may seem commonplace, but in Humboldt's time it was a concept of nature so novel and revolutionary that through him it would fertilize many branches of science. For who but Aristotle had looked at nature as an integrated design whose component parts revealed their special order through interlocking relationships? Who among naturalists of that period envisioned, beyond the nearest tasks of registering and classifying, this interrelatedness of living things with the earth, its rocks and surface forms? This visionary ability to walk into a cave or quarry and not merely observe a few minerals and rocks, but see them related to types of soil and plants, perhaps even animals and people, would make Humboldt into a new sort of explorer and a unique interpreter of nature. There would always be many to do the classifying and labeling, but few like him to reach for the laws and ideas that make for nature's orchestration.

As for the problem of the origin of basaltic rocks, Alexander felt tempted to side with Werner's theory. Humboldt's incomplete grasp of his subject made him conclude this first geological essay [4] with an equivocal statement: "Whatever hypothesis one may applaud . . . with Dolomieu regard it as erupted lava or with Werner as dried substance (for all is equally impressive and incomprehensible), one cannot but be everlastingly impressed by the sight of the rock cave of Unkel."

Oddly enough, this first publication was destined to be quoted as supporting Werner's ideas long after its author had repudiated the tenets of the neptunist school. It was Campe, his former tutor, who had had Alexander's first scientific essay published in his bookshop at Brunswick.

The first two manuscripts out of the way, Humboldt could devote more time to correspondence. To Wegener he entrusted his observations on Göttingen professors. His teacher in modern history, Kästner,

---

[4] *Mineralogische Beobachtungen über einige Basalte am Rhein* (Braunschweig, 1790).

has unfortunately a very indistinct delivery because of the loss of his teeth. He is very humorous, and always saying something witty, but as he invariably laughs at his own jokes before he is through with them, this kind of humor is not always appreciated. . . . I have also attended lectures on moral philosophy given by Less, and certainly never heard anything so miserable. On one occasion he inquired whether it was lawful for a Christian to play at a lottery. It might well be asked: ought a Christian to be allowed to play cards and chess? . . . The English princes are condemned to listen to such trash for a couple of hours every day, and the unfortunate youths are obliged to write out each lecture, an exercise that is afterwards corrected by Less. Such is the folly actually demanded by that detestable English orthodoxy."

One day Professor Heyne introduced Alexander to a visiting celebrity, his son-in-law, Georg Forster. Everybody knew Forster as an intrepid explorer and the author of wonderful travel books. He had accompanied Captain James Cook on his memorable second voyage. Now librarian at Mainz, he was taking a brief vacation in Göttingen. Here was a personality to Alexander's taste, a naturalist explorer fabulously gifted in languages, and a master stylist. Travel literature, until then steeped in tales of piracy and ribald fiction, had in Forster's books reached a level on which exotic peoples and landscapes came to life under the pen of a humanist and scholar.

For Forster, trained in zoology and botany, was both scholar and explorer. He had made valuable scientific collections and had studied exotic peoples in their natural habitat. He realized the value of multiple researches with geographic objectives. That through his influence Humboldt decided in favor of a career in exploration and science was possible only because of Humboldt's receptiveness. For it is quite evident that Humboldt's tutoring and science courses had transformed his sentimental interest in natural objects into meaningful symbols for decipherable laws. In their knowledge one could be secure, and feel less dependent and exposed to the kind of tormenting anguish which the separation from Wegener had produced. In Forster's company he would surely not feel rebuffed when it came to expressing his powerful longing to understand the meaning of rocks and fossils and plants. And yet he was to have a career in finance, for his mother insisted on it. Was there any career for one so addicted to an understanding of nature? If so, Forster might be his right guide.

Forster had appeared like a comet in Göttingen's academic firmament, and young Humboldt was quick to grasp its tail. Invited or not, he decided to accompany Forster on a trip to England. What if his mother should object? He could go, she wrote, if on his return, he would continue with his schooling in commerce in Hamburg. She and her adviser Kunth clearly did not foresee what this trip with Forster would do for Alexander.

Forster returned to Mainz, whence he wrote his father-in-law at Göttingen about the objectives of his journey. He intended to collect data on "pithecology," a science treating the relationship between apes. Forster held this to be of great promise because of certain fossil human remains that he had seen in the museum at Bonn. It would seem that this traveling companion of Humboldt pondered the possibility of man's descent from apes.

In the spring of 1790 Forster and Humboldt traveled down the Rhine. Nothing was allowed to escape their attention, whether churches, museums, factories, botanical gardens, or observatories. In *Sketches of the Lower Rhine* Forster relates how greatly impressed he was by Humboldt's comments on Cologne Cathedral.

In all earnest, with his sensitive disposition and restless imagination, I should have been sorry to have watched there alone through the night. I have never yet been able to determine whether it is more satisfactory to derive our ideas directly from the world around us, or better to receive them through the medium of an intelligent mind, which, by selecting and arranging an infinite variety of impressions, obtains an idealized concept more in harmony with our nature.

From Cologne, they took the diligence to Liége in Belgium, sharing their contrivance occasionally with eleven passengers, and from there they proceeded to Dunkerque, where Alexander had his first view of the sea. In Forster the sight of ocean and waves invoked exciting memories of his Pacific voyage with Captain Cook, and his companion listened eagerly to every detail. In the evening, Alexander sat by the stove, drying plants and seashells. Haversacks shouldered, they tramped across Flanders, dodging military campaigns of the French Revolutionary army and witnessing the insurrection in Lille.

At last they arrived in London, "finding among other things to interest us the trial of Hastings before the parliamentary tribunal, the war with Spain, the music at Westminster Abbey, elections for a new Parliament, and various exhibitions in museums and scientific institutions." In Parliament, Humboldt heard speeches by Edmund Burke, Pitt, and Sheridan all on the same night. They visited Oxford, Blenheim Castle, and Stratford-on-Avon. Then they traveled across Lancashire, where Humboldt took meticulous notes on textile fabrics and wool prices.

In his first long letter to Wegener, dated June 15, he begged indulgence for not having written in three months. "I am quite unstrung and very tired, for I have spent most of the day below the ground in the Peak Cavern, Eldon Hole, Poole's Hole, and among mines." Five days later he wrote to his friend that Forster was writing a narrative of their trip, and warned him to accept Forster's opinion as his only, "for we look at everything from very different points of view." His health was not so good as it had been the preceding winter at Göttingen. Forster alluded to this illness in a letter to his father-in-law, stating how ill Humboldt was and that he had admitted having been ill often during the preceding five years. "Undoubtedly," he continued, "such frailty is caused by an overexertion of the mind to which Humboldt had been led by *certain people in Berlin.*" At about the same time Wilhelm mentioned in a letter to his bride that at Göttingen his brother had been subject to hypochondriac moods and unhappiness.

The pace of this English journey had surely been too much for Alexander. He would never relax. A demon was whipping him constantly to rush from one place to another. What was he so restless about? Perhaps it was a final realization of the incompatibility of his own intentions and his mother's. She and Kunth appeared to be bent on diverting him from becoming what he really wanted to be: an explorer and naturalist. The trip with Forster had been a kind of test, a probing into his own capacities. How much did he really know about botany, geology, and physics? To find out, he must visit every museum, mine, cave, and factory that came his way. On top of such anxieties came the exertions of constant travel. His mother no doubt expected him to shine at the Hamburg School of Commerce, so he took notes on sheep-breeding, fluctuations of wool prices, statistics on exports. He observed with great satisfaction that the industrious English had managed to extract a dye from a lichen so common in Germany that for a similar commercial purpose one need only collect it. One never knew how handy all this diverse information might be!

Forster, much disappointed by contemporary English art, and complaining about English reserve and how incredibly reticent the English were to accept foreigners in their midst—the explorer and author Forster had followed eagerly reports about the progress of the French Revolution. Those Frenchmen seemed to have unloosed a flood, and Forster secretly desired to be swept away by it. Equality and liberty—how precious they must have appeared to one who knew from personal experience the grace and ease of life among natives in the Pacific! Europe seemed rigid and corrupt by comparison. A human-made earthquake was needed to correct what had gone wrong in society. The people of Paris were making one. He must see it with his own eyes to believe in it, and he may secretly have hoped that young Humboldt would come to share his views.

In July 1790 the two travelers arrived in Paris just in time for the celebration of a grand national festival on the Champ-de-Mars. The city was full of dancing and shouting crowds. Forster would have loved to stay on. Already he was convinced that Paris was the spearhead of a political movement about to create a new Europe. He was swept off his feet, determined to devote himself body and soul to the Revolution. And Humboldt? Naturally he felt shaken and must have visualized the tempting prospects for a society free at last to develop what was inherently good in mankind. But the concern about liberty, implanted by French literature and the contact with the Mendelssohn circle, was for him a much more personal thing: Forster's allegiance was to the Revolution, Humboldt's to learning and to himself. The journey to England had clearly revealed his devotion to the study of nature. Humboldt's sympathy with the lofty aims of the Revolution would always remain his fundamental political orientation, but he would never allow it to divert him from his singular aim. He clung to this dedication in the face of the greatest political unheaval Europe had witnessed since the Reformation, and it made him secure amidst the swirling tide to which his friend Forster would entrust his fate. It swept Forster away and later prompted him to return to Paris as a deputy from his town. There he was caught up in political intrigues and died in complete misery.

When Forster's furlough was at end, the travelers were obliged to return posthaste to Mainz. There they parted, never to see each other again. But Humboldt remembered his friend, whose name he would never mention without feelings of the most heartfelt gratitude. In his *Cosmos* he eulogized Forster's eminence as a writer and character. There he says:

I was more than ever reminded of the remarkable resemblances and contrasts existing between Forster and myself. . . . We held, in fact, the same political views. . . . It was in the company of this circumnavigator of the globe that I first beheld the sea. . . . The companionship I enjoyed on

this journey, the sudden passion that seized me for everything connected with the sea and for visiting tropical lands,
all exerted a most powerful influence on the formation of
projects that, however, could not be carried out during my
mother's lifetime.

It was as if in that hour of remembrance the aging
Humboldt had seen the ghost of his distinguished traveling companion arise to remind him of a lasting service
that he had never been able to reciprocate.

3

The Brief Career in Mining

THE JOURNEY WITH Forster was a prelude during which the dominant strains of Humboldt's character were uniquely revealed: boundless energies, an unusual capacity for observation, deliberate harnessing of his powers for a life of study and travel, and much restlessness. Suddenly he had gained more confidence in himself: a weapon of persuasion in the conflict with his mother. If she continued to insist on his going to the Hamburg School of Commerce, well and good, but that should not prevent him from preparing the next step in his life. At all costs he must apply for permission to enter the famous Mining Academy at Freiberg. Freiberg offered the finest training to be had in Europe for a young man dedicated to exploration.

Humboldt had hardly shaken the dust off his travel outfit when he sat down, in Forster's home, to write to the director of the Mining Academy at Freiberg, Abraham Gottlob Werner (1749–1817). To do that took courage and nerve for Werner was a man of awesome knowledge, a principal founder of the science of geology. It goes without saying that Alexander had sent him the geological essay in which he had sided with Werner's theory on volcanic rocks. "Your theory," Alexander wrote to Werner, on July 25, 1790, "never seemed to me more reasonable. . . . I shall no doubt be severely censored for this opinion by many of our geologists." Continuing in that flattering vein, he acknowledged that Werner had "ren-

dered to the science of mineralogy as great and important a service as that given by Linnæus to botany.[1] . . .
Various circumstances have until now prevented me from
visiting your admirable institution, but perhaps I may
be so fortunate at some future time as to enroll myself
among your pupils." In concluding, he placed himself most
humbly at the mercy of the great Werner by reminding
him of his youth and deficiencies, which he was eager to
repair under Werner's expert guidance.

The writer of this letter, one suspects, felt considerable
anxiety about his future. He was prostrating himself before a scientific authority who had the power to make his
plan succeed or fail. And was this plan not at bottom
a plot against his mother's authority, launched spontaneously without her knowledge?

A few weeks later, Humboldt was safely enrolled in the
Hamburg School of Commerce, there to study political
economy and business procedures, subjects for which the
school was famous. Almost half of its students were foreigners—Englishmen, Scots, Frenchmen, Russians, and
one American. In a long letter to Wegener, Alexander mentioned that he had visited an exhibit of marine life containing the most fascinating specimens.

The desire to own them overwhelmed me. . . . I embarked in
a sailboat and accomplished in eight days a stormy voyage of
45 miles to the North Sea island of Helgoland. . . . Since
then I have had to content myself with looking at ships in the
harbor. I am not happy here, but reconciled. I had just begun
to feel satisfied with myself at Göttingen. There I worked so
hard—yet, for all my efforts, I realized how much needs to be

[1] Werner had provided the first classification of minerals and rocks
to be used widely in Europe and the Americas.

done. My health has suffered considerably, though it improved somewhat on the trip with Forster. Here too I am frightfully busy, so that I cannot spare myself. *There is a drive in me which, at times, makes me feel as though losing my mind.* Yet this energy is essential to arrive at good ends.

With customary zeal he attended his classes punctually, though to him they must have seemed like a waste of time that he would rather have spent in scientific studies. He must prepare himself for Freiberg. Fortunately, the school library was reasonably well stocked with books on botany, mathematics, travel, and geology. On occasions he mixed with the "purse-proud" circles of Hamburg society, which gave him a taste of the common-sense attitudes of its business people. Through such contacts he may have foreseen what he wrote to Wegener: "The common sense of our western neighbors will triumph in this century, while Germany will yet for a long time look on with astonishment, try, prepare, and still postpone the decisive moment."

During his stay in Hamburg he kept up a lively correspondence with Georg Forster, probably entrusting to him impressions and ideas that he did not care to have read by his executors—for when Forster's friends returned the letters to Humboldt in his ripe old age, he destroyed them all. Yet a period of emotional strain such as he experienced in Hamburg left traces that escaped the destruction he would no doubt have meted out to them.

In November 1790, Wilhelm von Humboldt confided to his bride, Caroline von Dachröden:

His [Alexander's] is a lovable nature, yet he maintains very peculiar ideas for which I really don't care. . . . He is a busybody, full of enterprise that to others necessarily must seem like vanity. He peddles the wares of his knowledge with much ado, as if he desperately needed either to dazzle people or to beg for their sympathy. . . . All this wanting to impress others really stems from a desire to impress oneself. The concern about oneself should pass in silence, and unassumingly.

The girl to whom such brotherly criticism was entrusted was the daughter of a noble landowner, a beautiful brunette who had made Alexander's acquaintance before his Hamburg days. In January, Alexander wrote her a letter that made her believe that he would lose his mind. "I honestly think he is screwy and may go mad any time," she wrote to Wilhelm.

Alexander has much beauty in him, but his entire being lacks grace and delicacy. Such qualities cannot be acquired merely by mingling with society; they stem from within and should pervade a person quite naturally. . . . Besides, *Alexander will never be inspired by anything that does not come through men.* Time, I believe, will tell that I am right.

Caroline's instinctive judgment was not sidetracked by Alexander's efforts at humor. On one occasion he wrote to her that he was in love with a woman forty years his senior, an expert on jewelry, who might well appreciate the ruby-like polish of his nose! Coming from one who craved the company of intellectual men and obviously aspired to fame, this makes us suspect how self-conscious and insecure he must have been among discerning women. Yet Caroline was charmed by his "lovely youthful warmth." All the more regrettable that he should want to mislead people by his droll mannerisms. If only later, after her marriage to Wilhelm, this charming brother-in-law could live with them! Her instinctive wish was to shelter one so precious and yet so clearly destined for exposure and loneliness. How different was the man of her choice! Already in that winter of 1791 Wilhelm was safely installed as Apprentice Justice and Legation Secretary in Berlin. The letters between Wilhelm and his bride, testifying to their great love, ultimately found their place in classic German literature.

Meanwhile, in Hamburg, Alexander was preparing for his next move. Whether or not his letter to the geologist Werner was answered, we do not know. Werner never was a letter-writer, which explains why, in later years, his foreign correspondence remained unopened until his dying days. His executors reported that in an unopened envelope they came across Werner's nomination to membership in the Institut de France! Answer or no answer, Alexander sat down to address Werner a second time. With equal eloquence and flattery he begged again for admission to the Mining Academy. The letter stated with some emphasis that he would be able to remain for only six months before entering official employment, and boldly inquired whether he would be welcome for so short a time. "I should be greatly obliged if you would send me a few lines at once in reply." One may assume that Werner did not like this prospective pupil to limit the training period to six months. Indeed, young Humboldt must have been pressed for time. Could it be that Freiberg and the ensuing official employment were meant to be but temporary stops en route to a destination still unselected?

At Easter 1791 the trying interval at Hamburg came to an end. Alexander joined his brother in Berlin. A few days later he wrote out his application for a position in the Ministry of Industry and Mines. It was addressed to the Minister, Heinitz, a man who had previously acknowledged Alexander's geological essay in the most gratifying terms. Heinitz not only had founded the famous Mining Academy at Freiberg, but also had won considerable fame as Frederick the Great's mining expert and geologist, a man whose industry had helped to win campaigns and improve the country's output in minerals. The tenor of this letter had much self-assurance, disclosing what Alexander planned to do with his life:

I have now reached an age when I cannot help wishing to be settled in some kind of occupation. . . . I want to complete my education by obtaining Your Excellency's commission to work in the various departments of your office. . . . It would greatly relieve my mind were I to arrange something definite about my future career in life. . . .

At the end of May the reply arrived. He was to proceed with his training at Freiberg; upon completing it, he would receive a suitable position in the Department of Mines. What wonderful prospects! His mother must have felt proud that her youngest son was starting life in earnest. Surely he could be expected to climb the ladder of a civil-service career diligently until he reached the top. Such a fine recommendation from the Minister could hardly fail to impress Werner.

But Wilhelm was worried. On June 3, 1791 he wrote to Caroline how bitter it was for him to see Alexander leave. His brother was such a fine person, and yet had turned out so differently from what he had expected.

Alexander is undoubtedly vain and has his own way of seeing and admiring greatness in others where he believes he can find it. I cannot discern anything really significant in him, yet he has more than average warmth, a capacity for sacrificing himself for others and for forming quick attachments. Happy he will hardly ever be, and never tranquil, because *I cannot believe that any real attachment will steal his heart.* . . . He will never be satisfied with himself because he seems to sense his incapacity to grow fully into his own. Now and then he admitted that much to me, though generally a veil hung over our innermost feelings which neither of us dared to lift.

At Freiberg, Alexander took temporary lodgings in the building of the Mining Academy under the same roof as Werner. The place was swarming with students from all over the world, many of whom were to occupy important positions in their own countries or contribute to the growth of the new science of geology. There was Manuel del Río from Spain, whom Alexander was to meet again as director of the Mining Academy in Mexico; and Leopold von Buch, notable Werner pupil, destined to outdo Alexander in the pursuit of regional geology. Another student was Fischer de Waldheim, who would come to be honored as one of Russia's eminent men of science. But it was to Karl Freiesleben, an instructor in surveying, that Alexander gave his friendship as wholeheartedly as to other chosen friends. It was he who replaced Wegener and Forster for a while. Two years Alexander's senior, Freiesleben recognized in the younger man a brilliant mind and a fabulous capacity for detailed observation and synthesis. Werner immediately appointed Freiesleben to act as special tutor and guide to his new and highly recommended pupil.

From then on, Alexander's new studies became all-absorbing. The morning hours from six to noon were spent underground studying rocks, minerals, and mining methods. The afternoons were given to classes, as many as six a day. Werner taught Alexander his system of classifying rocks and rock formations, while others instructed him in geologic surveying. Here was true rock-bottom science, the world of stones and fossils, where eternities were locked up as in ocean depths, their silent histories so soothing and yet so challenging to the imagination. In their guarantee of timeless laws Humboldt found, at last, a kind of security for his restless nature.

Evenings he often went "moss-hunting"—botanizing—or read in his apartment, surrounded by piles of books on geology, botany, and chemistry.

The work was fascinating but fatiguing. The cold dampness of mines, drafty rooms, and mental overexertion caused him to suffer from occasional colds and rheumatic pains. His best friends had reason to complain of his sudden lack of attention. Brother Wilhelm married his Caroline, and Alexander excused himself for not being present at the wedding. Forster continued to write to him for a while, but then gave up for lack of response. Even Wegener's letters remained unanswered. The reason is obvious. In February 1792 Alexander wrote to a friend at Hamburg:

I wish you would bear in mind that during the nine months I have been here I have traveled nearly seven hundred miles on foot and by carriage through Bohemia, Thuringia, Mansfeld, etc.—that I am daily in the mines from six till twelve (nearly two hours are occupied by survey work, which in the snow is very fatiguing). . . . I have never been so busy in all my life.

My health has suffered in consequence, though I am on the whole very happy. I have a profession that must be followed passionately to be enjoyed.

On February 26 he celebrated with his classmates the successful end of his studies. A week later he received their congratulations on his first appointment: as an Inspector of Mines. This was the civil-service position Heinitz had promised him. It called for inspection of various mining enterprises in the districts of Bayreuth and the Fichtel Mountains, which had just then been added to the Prussian state.

Advancement to so responsible a position at the age of twenty-three should not be viewed only in the light of Humboldt's talents and industry. After the death of Frederick the Great, Prussian officialdom had lapsed into mismanagement and impotence. Young men of Humboldt's caliber were at a premium; a Minister of Mines might consider himself very fortunate to obtain such services. Even Alexander may have seen it this way. In the spring of 1792 he wrote to Freiesleben: "It seems as if everything is as in a chess game. . . . The olfactory nerves are finally rendered insensitive from the incessant burning of incense so unmerited!"

Yet no mining official could have been more conscientious and more energetic than he. Under his management the annual revenues from mining in the district increased very substantially. Within one year, production of gold ore rose to almost as much as the total output for the preceding eight years. "I possess the confidence of the men, who think I must at least have four arms and eight legs, which is doing pretty well in my position."

The confidence of the miners in his management was

based not only on recognition of his superior knowledge, but also on the fact that he had proved himself deeply concerned with their welfare. He believed that the terrific hazards of their underground labor should be somewhat compensated for by assistance to them in understanding up-to-date methods and the worth of their work. This idea induced him to establish in 1793 the first training school for mine labor, at the village of Steben in the Fichtel Mountains. It was unheard-of for a government official to bother about the laborers. To Minister von Heinitz he reported in March 1793:

In a mountain region so rich in ores, where the people often, out of sheer prejudice and ignorance, pursue foolish projects damaging to their interests, it is doubly important to disseminate clear and reasonable concepts of mining. . . . When, last September, after visiting several mines, I found the necessary leisure, I resolved to open a school for common miners for the winter season (even if I had to give the classes myself). Whoever learned of my plan advised against it. . . . Such arguments could not scare me, so I decided to defray the costs for such an institution out of my private purse. . . .

Continuing his report, he stated that it seemed only prudent to engage a local foreman for the task, one with sufficient imagination, knowledge of local conditions, and enthusiasm, a man who might learn while teaching. With him Alexander discussed the manner of instructing:

I proceeded immediately to work out my own suggestions, gave him books for his own benefit, and did everything in my power to attain my purpose. . . . The plan of the Royal Mining School at Steben is twofold: first, to educate the young miners of the Neila District to turn into capable and informed laborers, and second, to plant in them, from childhood on, a real love for and sense of the value of their profession.

The Minister in Berlin was delighted. When he offered to reimburse Humboldt, Alexander replied that it might be better to distribute the money among miners who had helped to make the school a success. The Minister's mood would be benevolent, so Alexander added a request for a speedy consideration of a pension plan for miners.

It was there at Steben [he later recalled] that I formulated many of my most significant plans by abandoning myself so utterly to my feelings that I almost dread the prospect of see-ing it again. During my stay there in the autumn and winter of 1793 I was constantly kept in such a state of agitation that I could never see the lights of cottages, shining as they were through the mist of night, without much emotion.

His was the direct approach, personal action at the risk of official censorship. That was how he managed to estab-lish this first training school for labor, a royal institution without charter and permission from his government. It came to serve as an experimental model for others that Humboldt inaugurated in the same region, and it no doubt inspired social improvements for miners in later years.

Humboldt's social conscience gave him no rest. The miners were badly in need of a relief fund to be used in emergencies arising from accidents and sudden destitu-tion. One day when he had just emerged from a mine shaft, he wrote to Freiesleben:

I have ridden nine miles, and spent three hours in the Prince's mine. Don't be surprised, therefore, if my letter shows signs of confusion. I got on faster than expected with my operations. The preliminary organization is nearly complete.

The office of administration is open, every arrangement made
for the miners' relief fund, and now there remains the question
of appointments. . . . The universal confidence shown in me
by the miners makes me enjoy my occupation. Otherwise my
position is strange enough. I am really doing the work of a
foreman, not of a superintendent of mines. The heat is unbearable and the atmosphere of the mines enervating.

But this mine inspector was of a very special sort. At
Freiberg he had surprised everybody by his extraordinary
talent for seeing things in their natural association, including mosses and lichens growing without sunlight on
the walls of mine shafts and tunnels. He would emerge
with an armful of mineral and plant specimens. In fact,
there were times when he seemed to be much more fascinated by botanical problems than by minerals. What physical agencies made plants grow in darkness, and what
made them keep or lose their green? Was it a special life
force inherent in plants or just a matter of chemical in-
gredients? Puzzled, Humboldt began to investigate. The
underground plants were subjected to various tests, grown
in different types of soil, some rocky and some clayey,
treated with phosphate of lime or moistened with other
carefully diluted chemicals. The green coloring matter,
known to us as chlorophyll, seemed under failing sunlight
dependent on the release of oxygen that might induce
light-conduction invisibly. He was on the track, if not the
right one, of one of the most puzzling processes of nature:
the release of special energies in plants when struck by
light (photosynthesis). He observed spontaneous motion
of plant filaments under varying temperatures and studied
germination under controlled conditions.

Minerals were interesting, and useful besides, but with

plants it might actually be possible to reveal something extraordinary, a mysterious life force to which all living matter might owe its puzzling variety of organization. The discoveries piled up on him, and by searching for clues in the learned writings of a Priestley or an Ingenhousz, Humboldt suddenly discovered how novel his experiments were. He must publish them immediately so that others could repeat them, check his observations, and, incidentally, learn about the author. In 1792 he mentioned no less than half a dozen different notes on his botanical studies to be published in the *Annals of Botany,* the *Journal of Physics,* and *Crell's Annals.* A year later his first important scientific work appeared: the *Freiberg Flora,* in which he summarized his studies of plant physiology.[2]

As was customary with botanists, the *Freiberg Flora* was published in Latin, no mean task for this Superintendent of Mines who had covered thousands of miles inspecting mining enterprises all over the land. The problem of plant growth without light, and the manner in which he dealt with it, produced a sensation he could hardly have foreseen. Not only did the Elector of Saxony honor him with a gold medal in recognition of a study carried out in his own realm, but scholars in Paris and Stockholm felt inspired to acknowledge Humboldt's contribution. A Swedish botanist honored the work by naming a new species of East Indian laurel after its author. It prompted Goethe, poet and naturalist, to inquire after Humboldt so that he might discuss with him his own studies on the metamorphism of plants.

As an official of the Duchy of Weimar, Goethe, like

[2] *Floræ Fribergensis, accedunt Aphorismi ex Doctrina, Physiologiæ Chemicæ Plantarum* (Berlin, 1793).

Humboldt, had inspected mines and was well versed in geology and mineralogy. But Humboldt doubtless knew of Goethe's other scientific contributions: his discovery of the intermaxillary bone in the human skull, his studies on plants and on light-refraction. And when, in the winter of 1794, Alexander went from Bayreuth to visit his brother at Jena, he was overjoyed to meet the extraordinary Goethe in person. Here was genius at its most sublime, a mind to illumine all, the nature of man and of all creation, serene, but receptive to every advance in knowledge. "All of us," reported Goethe in his *Annals*, "walked with friend Mayer in the deepest snow so that we might partake in the demonstration [of the anatomist Loder], which took place in an almost empty auditorium." This momentous meeting led to a friendship which deepened with every visit of Humboldt. "The Humboldt brothers were present," Goethe wrote in the late fall of 1795, "and I discussed with them all that is of philosophic and scientific interest in nature. I outlined the metamorphism of insects. . . . The sketches of rock formations in the Harz Mountains led to geologic discussions. Humboldt showed some galvanic experiments."

In the winter of 1794 Humboldt suffered from intermittent fever, but did not allow it to interfere with his crowded schedule. Constant travel as far as the Baltic, Poland, Austria, and the Tyrol had furnished him new data on rocks and geologic structures and on plants found associated with particular types of soils. Whatever spare time there was he must have used for another type of research concerned with experiments on the excitability of nerves and muscles. This new interest, so far removed from geology and botany, was to produce an astonishing publication. The first mention of it to Freiesleben, in January 1794, was coupled with the statement: "You are aware that I am quite mad enough to be engaged on three books at once"—not all of which saw the light of day. At the same time he wrote about his new appointment as a Counselor of Mines (*Bergrat*), with an annual salary of fifteen hundred thalers, almost four times his initial compensation. A startling statement concludes the letter: "My former plans remain undisturbed. I shall resign my post in two years, and go to Russia, Siberia, and I don't know where."

At last the secret was out. His final destination was elsewhere. Freiberg and the successful three-year start of an official career were what he had secretly meant them to be: temporary stations. Now that he had proved his worth to his mother and his superiors, he would lay claim to a free and wandering life. What might an official career have meant to him? Already he could foresee the end, a ministerial position, with all its conflicting responsibilities and restrictions. Too easy, really, to climb this ladder away from his most cherished dreams. His Excellency the Minister of Mines in Berlin may have sensed that something was afoot with young Humboldt, for in February 1795 he offered him a still better appointment as Director of Mines for the smelting and salt works in Silesia, the southeasternmost province of Prussia. Humboldt declined this gratifying proposal by putting his cards on the table.

"I am considering a complete change in my mode of life," was his honest reply, "and I intend to withdraw from *any official position with the state.*" His health, he claimed, had suffered. All he had wanted was to prepare himself for a scientific expedition by a practical employment in the mines. "As I have a deep conviction that such an expedition is highly important for increasing our knowledge of geology and physical science, I am exceedingly eager to devote my energies immediately to this end."

The perplexed Minister renewed his offer and employed every means at his disposal to bring this young man to his senses. It needed the intervention of the Minister of State, Hardenberg, to induce Humboldt to accept, temporarily at least, the position of Counselor at the Upper Court of Mines, with the special provision that he might follow his plans for foreign travel as chances might arise. It was Hardenberg who had summoned him in the preceding summer to act as his private secretary in the settlement of the negotiations between Prussia and Revolutionary France. It had been a most flattering distinction, one that he would remember in later years when one of his friends suggested that he claim French citizenship on the legal basis of a special provision forming part of that very Treaty of Basel to the negotiation of which Humboldt had been summoned. He may have felt obligated to Hardenberg, which could account for the length of the time before his resignation became effective (February 1797). Meanwhile Minister von Heinitz was left with the hope that a vacation tour in Italy would restore Alexander's health sufficiently to enable him to resume his official duties.

4

The Unfolding of Genius

THE DECISION TO abandon a promising official career
for an uncertain life of travel and private studies was as
momentous as it was inevitable. Humboldt's claim for
travel as a way of enlarging knowledge appeared quite
logical on the face of it, though none of his former teachers would have regarded it as very pressing. If anybody
had a right to speak of travel as a gateway to knowledge
it was Werner at Freiberg. A geologist of his standing
might well have advanced claims more justified than
Humboldt's for the necessity of exploring. Heyne and
Blumenbach at Göttingen could have walked out of their
classrooms to inspect the outside world. Neither of these
distinguished men felt the urgent need to do what Humboldt claimed as his privilege. His need for travel, at least
at that time, was not based on strictly professional necessities.

The records prove quite clearly that his was a restless
disposition. He lacked the common instinct for social and
domestic roots; in fact, he had led an uprooted life ever
since his Frankfurt days. The atmosphere of his mother's
home was not to his liking, and he could not have wished
for it. Such a person had little to carry but a weight of
rather self-centered interests. This does not mean that
he lacked the deeper passion for knowledge. On the contrary, his interests made it easier for him to bear what in
later years would be the much heavier burden of growing
loneliness and isolation. As a student at Göttingen he had

already rationalized his self-centered existence. From there he had written to his former tutor, Campe: "A man should early accustom himself to stand alone. Isolation has much in its favor. One learns thereby to search inwardly and to gain self-respect without being dependent on the opinions of others, which are likely to be too favorable." To rationalize and even camouflage his innermost motives, especially those he feared might elicit unfavorable comment, came to be a necessity to Humboldt. Had he admitted that his resignation was motivated by anything but failing health or the desire to serve science, he might well have risked a complete and lasting break with the influential officials who had shown him an extreme measure of sympathy and had recognized his talents.

He might learn to stand alone in the world, but when it came to travel, companionship was necessary to him. His active and impressionable mind could function best in the company of a friend. In May 1795 he wrote to Freiesleben:

> One of my heartfelt wishes is to take you with me, not only to Switzerland, but to Sweden. I shall relieve you of all expense in either journey, as I have a thousand thalers at my disposal. I depend absolutely on you to accompany me. Your wishes shall be to me as commands, and you shall not repent going. You must, if you please, consent to make one in a trio with me and a friend of mine. . . .

This friend was a young army officer, Reinhard von Haeften, whom he had met at Bayreuth. His description of Haeften to Freiesleben was ardent and full of extravagant praise, and must have contained a passage that was later torn away from the original letter. An earlier biographer of Humboldt, Karl Bruhns, assumed that this missing part "*probably* contained a confession of an attachment which, according to a distinct and circumstantial statement by Kunth, the botanist, existed between Humboldt and Haeften's sister. Although faithfully cherished for upward of ten years, it was never consummated by the union so ardently desired."

Bruhn's remark appears to be a deliberate misinterpretation of Humboldt's nature and motives, an unnecessary romanticization of an important personality, and an untruthful one. To cover up Humboldt's homosexual nature by fictionizing will not do in the light of such information as even Humboldt himself was unable to erase from his records. How greatly indebted Humboldt felt to Haeften may be seen in excerpts from his letters, first published by Leitzman in 1915, at a time when Freud's psychoanalytic concepts had not yet become household goods. The truth is that Humboldt's relationship to Haeften was at least as passionate as his friendship with Wegener, if not more so.

On December 19, 1794 Humboldt wrote to Haeften:

I always keep my promise, my dearly beloved Reinhard. In a few hours I leave and will ride to Lauenstein tomorrow, on the 21st to Steben, so that I may embrace you on Christmas Eve. . . . I had hoped to meet with young Freiesleben, whom I had asked to join me here, yet I failed in this pleasure. He will be at Freiberg for the holidays, using this as an excuse. It hurts me greatly, for he interests me more than my brother. I prefer him any time. . . . Goethe insisted on my returning with him to Weimar, where he was wanted by the Duke. Much as I like to be with Goethe (he really is my favorite here), I would have lost the holidays. It would have meant seeing you six days later, and such a loss cannot be made up by anything in the whole world. Other people may have no understanding of this. I know that I only live through you, my good precious Reinhard, and that I can only be happy in your presence.

This Haeften was the friend Humboldt had invited for a trip to Italy, and he did not conceal from Freiesleben that he "would rather neglect some of the scientific aims than not be entirely at his [Haeften's] disposal during the first part of the journey."

That Freiesleben declined to share the experience of the pair is obvious from his desire to join Humboldt for the second part of the journey, after Haeften's furlough was over. Humboldt reported to Freiesleben faithfully upon the trip through the Tyrol, to Venice and the Italian Alps, carefully emphasizing his geological and botanical observations, and tactfully avoiding the mention of his traveling companion. When they separated in Switzerland, Humboldt sat down to write a moving letter to Christiane, Haeften's betrothed:

Nothing could really have happened to our dear Reinhard, but you know yourself how deep is my indescribable and wonderful attachment to this precious person, sufficient for me to worry over the merest possibility of mischief. . . . I can well imagine and jointly measure with you the feeling of bliss you must have felt when you saw him again. . . . Tell Reinhard how much I loved the lakes of Lucerne and Sarnen. For me they make the most wonderful scenery in the whole of Switzerland, and if we cannot go to America, that is where we should go, removed from all so-called educated people, to live a harmonious and happy life together.

For Humboldt to have dreamed of America can only mean that he discussed certain travel plans with Haeften. Had the glamorous harbor of Venice perhaps incited Humboldt to sail away in the company of a young couple just for the sake of enjoying happiness? If so, it suggests a reckless mood evoked, no doubt, by the bliss of friendship. Who among us has not felt moods when we meant to perpetuate happiness, to flee the world by living on an island or by the smiling shores of a lake?

On the second part of this journey, Humboldt tramped with Freiesleben through the Bernese Alps and visited such outstanding naturalists as the physicist Marc-Auguste Pictet (1752–1825) in Geneva, who with his brother had founded the Bibliothèque Brittanique (later the Bibliothèque Universelle), which was to make known to French readers outstanding literary and scientific works of England. Pictet was trained in geology, and took a great interest in atmospheric physics. His encyclopedic mind and professional contacts with English and French scholars were sufficiently important for Humboldt to invite his friendship.

Freiesleben was impressed with Humboldt's aptitude for travel. "His zeal for science and his unexampled industry have led him from boyhood on to employ every moment in some useful or instructive occupation. Even his night's sleep was never allowed to extend over more than a limited number of hours." According to Humboldt's own statement, he could do with half the amount of rest normally required by active minds, a habit to which he ascribed his unusual capacity for leading a studious life in a constant stream of other occupations.

In the fall of 1795, Humboldt was back at Bayreuth,

ostensibly for the celebration of Haeften's wedding. There
he invited the whole wedding company to a grand ball in
a castle, celebrating the event with magnificent abandon
as if he, not Haeften, had pledged marriage vows. If his
friend had contemplated a honeymoon, none was recorded, but Humboldt remained in the vicinity for almost
a year, unable to separate himself completely from the
happy couple. He visited the mines in the Fichtel Mountains, where he had spent such fruitful times, checking
on projects he had inaugurated earlier. Sooner or later he
was bound to lose sight of Haeften, and when such a terrifying prospect appeared close at hand, he wrote, in
January 1797, what must be considered one of the most
moving and tragic letters in his vast correspondence:

Two years have passed since we met, since your fate became mine. I still bless the day when you confided for the
first time in me, telling me how soothing it was for you. I felt
better in your company, and from that moment I was tied to
you as by iron chains. Even if you must refuse me, treat me
coldly with disdain, I should still want to be with you. . . .
Never would I cease to remain attached to you, and I can
thank heaven that I was granted before my death the grand
experience of knowing how much two human beings can mean
to each other. With each day my love and attachment for you
increase. For two years I have known no other bliss on earth
but your gaiety, your company, and the slightest expression
of your contentment. My love for you is not just friendship, or
brotherly love—it is veneration, childlike gratefulness, and
devotion to your will as my most exalted law. I will vow to
die if in this festive night an untrue word should flow from
my pen.[1]

[1] I own an autograph poem dedicated to Humboldt in 1793 by his
friend L. Cettzet, in which reference is made to the ruining of their

Once again Humboldt begged his friend to accompany him on a trip to Italy. The Haeftens agreed, and would have followed him south if political events had not interfered. Or was it rather that the trio found life together impossible? From Jena they traveled to Dresden, there to separate forever. When Humboldt received the news of Haeften's death six years later, his memory had been drowned in a flood of adventurous explorations and replaced by other friendships. Yet one may surmise that the remembrance left a wound from which he never quite recovered.

The winter of 1795 passed into the spring and summer of 1796. Suddenly news reached Humboldt from Berlin that his mother was gravely ill. Wilhelm had written that she could not possibly last beyond the fall. Coming on top of his torments over the separation from Haeften, the news struck Humboldt with dreadful forebodings of death. Back in Berlin, he felt so depressed that he filed his own last will and testament at the Municipal Court in Berlin. Did he perhaps contemplate suicide? Certainly it was not he who lay on the deathbed, stricken down by cancer, but his mother. To have given away his beloved in marriage to a woman, and then to experience the torturing memories of his relationship with his mother and the prospect of never repairing this most natural of human ties—all this may have hurtled him into a pit of despair. When his mother died, in November 1796, he wrote to Freiesleben:

friendship by slander. A forget-me-not was attached to it. After receiving the death notice of this friend, Humboldt wrote under the poem: "This noble friend of my youth has gone; how impoverished life becomes when friends pass away."

I was long prepared for this, yet I feel not stricken, but calm, as she suffered little. She passed away quietly. You know, my dear friend, that my heart could not have been much pained by this event, for we were always strangers to each other. But who would not have been much moved by her suffering?

Much as Humboldt had succeeded during the preceding years in acting independently of his mother, he had felt her influence like a clamp to be resented and loosened. But the unhappy memory of his mother would continue to torture him. Schiller reported to a friend, when visiting Jena in 1797, that Humboldt repeatedly suffered from apparitions of his mother. Her ghost may have remained with Alexander for long, but outwardly he could feel free at last, and financially secure, for his inheritance was considerable.

According to his own statement of June 16, 1797, it amounted to the sizable sum of 95,000 thalers, yielding an annual income of 3,476 thalers. This was six times the salary of a Superintendent of Mines, which a civil-service official could generally not hope to attain short of twenty years' service. Alexander's share was a country estate and a portion of real-estate mortgages in Poland. His brother Wilhelm inherited the family place at Tegel, in addition to a half share in the Polish mortgages. Tegel would remain a permanent haven, for Wilhelm would occupy it later with his family. Complete independence for the Humboldt brothers meant that each would follow his own interests. This led to Wilhelm's resignation from a government position that left too little time for his studies in classic philology. For Alexander it meant that he could devote himself with greater fervor than ever to his scattered scientific interests.

In those times a discerning mind like Humboldt's might have made scientific discoveries almost anywhere. The temptation to spread one's light was overwhelming, especially in one so bright, intuitive, and visionary. The dimness of the scientific field in which he moved was bound to produce a scattering effect on his interests, though he had a clear tendency to explore the impact of various physical factors on organic, and principally plant, life. To be sure, his academic training in science had been woefully brief, amounting to no more than two semesters. Yet if this had left professional deficiencies, none was evident. He was, as he himself stated later, an autodidact who had managed to inform himself fully about physics, chemistry, and mathematics. He worked on the composition of gases in mines, of carbonic and phosphoric acids, and of soil waters. He made contributions to various scientific journals, sent occasional notes to the Institut de France, and a sequence of letters to Pictet in Geneva dealing with atmospheric physics and related subjects. Time and again he mentioned in his letters to Freiesleben plans for publishing his observations on rock structures. Although nothing came of this plan at that moment, it was nevertheless obvious that he had been working all along on a subject to which he might at any time give preference above all others.

While on a trip to Vienna in 1792, Humboldt had read about Galvani's [2] experiments in animal electricity. If the nerves and muscles of animals could be excited artificially to involuntary actions, it would be of great interest,

---

[2] Luigi Galvani (1737–98), the Italian anatomist who in 1789 demonstrated electrical conductivity by the contact of metals with animal nerves and muscles.

thought Humboldt, to probe into the electric responses of animal and human organs. Might such studies not reveal a special "life force" peculiar to all living things, and if so would it not help in the treatment of functional disorders? Whatever might result from such researches, he was bound to decide the issue raised by Volta, who argued against the existence of animal electricity, saying that the frog legs of Galvani's experiments merely acted as an electroscope under contact with metals. But how on earth was Humboldt to carry out such experiments, busy as he then was with his other duties? He must equip himself with a traveling kit of scalpels, pincers, bottles, chemicals, and a microscope and make the best of his spare time.

And so, between visits to mines and coach rides, Humboldt started to dissect frogs and other animals, testing systematically the effects of galvanism on various organs. He brought muscle fibers under the microscope and observed their contraction when electric contact was made. Amazing how the heart responded to the electric shock, how blood vessels contracted, and how the blood of wounds started to secrete a serous liquid! Then he proceeded to watch the influences of certain chemicals, like oxygen and carbon dioxyde, on heart pulsation. He found that in hibernating animals nervous irritability was heightened, thereby disclosing for the first time what neurophysiology would confirm much later: that nervous weakening leads to increased sensibility. By tying together alternately moist muscle fibers and thin metal plates he unconsciously discovered the principle of Volta's column. But the supreme test came with the experiments on his own body, no doubt undertaken for therapeutic ends, which convinced him of the galvanic effect on the function of human blood vessels and blood-secretion.

In June 1795 Humboldt described in a letter to his former teacher Blumenbach the gruesome details of one such experiment:

> I applied two plasters to my back, each the size of a thaler coin, covering the trapezoid and deltoid muscles respectively. Meanwhile I lay flat on my stomach. When blisters appeared, they were cut, and contact was made with zinc and silver. I then felt a violent, painful throbbing, so severe that the trapezoid muscle swelled considerably, the throbbing sensation being conducted to the base of my skull and the spinal processes of my vertebræ. . . . Frogs placed on my back hopped about even when the nerve was not in immediate contact with the zinc, but separated from it half an inch . . . my wound serving as conductor. My right shoulder was until then principally affected. It pained considerably, and the lymphatic serous liquid, produced with ever greater frequency by the irritation, was red. As in the case of bad sores, it turned out to be so corrosive as to inflame my skin in red streams where it ran down my back. . . . After being washed, my back looked for many hours like that of a man having run the gantlet.

Similar experiments were repeated upon various wounds on the hands; and a tooth extraction served to apply them to a cavity in the jaw. An attempt to anesthetize the exposed nerve by galvanization proved unsuccessful. In the spring of 1797 Humboldt wrote to Freiesleben: "I begin to feel persuaded that such experiments might well form the basis of a practical therapy whereby I might establish a new science (*vital chemistry*)." But a few months later a cautious weighing of the results induced him to announce publicly in the *General Literary Intelligence of*

Jena, that he was careful to separate the observed facts from explanatory statements "because it would grieve me no end to discover later that these studies, which were carried out with such extreme efforts, could be forgotten on account of incorrect hypothetic conclusions." [3]

On the occasion of his Italian journey he had discussed his studies with the Italian physicists Volta and Scarpa. Encouraged by their interest, Humboldt continued his experiments, but the attending physician became so alarmed over the effects on his health that he advised their discontinuance. The results of five years of research were published in 1797 in two volumes, with many illustrations and tables.[4] This work was based on some four thousand experiments, and created a sensation. It has its assured place as the pioneer effort in physiological research.

A mining geologist and plant-collector had turned physiologist! A genius no doubt, but what would the members of his profession say to this? They were amazed at such mental versatility, and accepted the unique values of this man who felt at home with gold ores, plants, and muscle fibers. Nobody fired Humboldt from his job; nobody criticized him for his daring. The thought of it makes one wonder how such a genius could succeed in our age, which regards specialization as an imperative prerequisite to professional recognition and success.

Although the impulse to conduct such painful research

[3] The French physicist Antoine-François Fourcroy thought that Humboldt was a bit hasty in his conclusions and predicted that he would be obliged to abandon some of his views. Later he hailed Humboldt's work as an epoch-making contribution to science.

[4] *Versuche über die gereizte Muskel- und Nervenfaser nebst Vermutungen über den chemischen Prozess des Lebens in der Tier- und Pflanzenwelt* (2 vols. Posen and Berlin, 1797).

had been philosophic, Humboldt very soon began to have doubts about the existence of a "life force," an assumption that he had the courage to abandon altogether in later years. More lasting and more impressive for posterity is the humanitarian aspect of his studies, his passionate concern for the suffering part of mankind. The same trait of his personality prompted him to invent a safety device for miners which he hoped might alleviate fatal accidents and diseases. His frequent mine-inspections had given him much opportunity to observe the effects of noxious gases known to cause mine explosions and ailments of the pulmonary tract. By analyzing the chemical constituents of various gases, and by careful study of their distribution underground, he finally developed a new type of respirator. In his publication on the subject [5] he not only carefully stated the modes of its construction and application, but also outlined the principles of subterranean meteorology. Nobody had ever done this before, so this work may justifiably be regarded as the beginning of the science of caves (speleology). The respirator, on the other hand, though actually in use for a few years, was ultimately (1816) replaced by Davy's safety lamp, which operates on similar principles. Again, Humboldt's researches exposed him to mortal danger when he went alone into mine shafts filled with poisonous gases. On one occasion he lost consciousness and was saved only by the rapid action of a foreman. In one of his letters of this period he remarked that he "experienced a deep satisfaction in devising methods for the preservation of health and well-being among laborers."

[5] *Über die unterirdischen Gasarten und die Mittel ihren Nachteil zu verhindern* (Berlin, 1799).

Such cases of extreme devotion refuted the charges that Humboldt scattered his interests uselessly and that he worked solely for such gains as his vanity dictated. Criticism of his personality and work emerged from a source from which it could have been least expected: the august literary circle of Weimar. Schiller wrote of Humboldt to his friend Körner on August 6, 1797:

I am afraid that despite all his talents and restless activity he will never contribute much that is important for science. There is a little too much vanity in all his doings, and I cannot see a sign of purely objective interest in him. Absurd as it may sound, yet I experience through him, with all due respect for the tremendous wealth of his subject matter, a poverty of meaning which in his profession is the worst of all evils. He is the undisguised dissecting intellect that measures nature shamelessly . . . and with such impudence as I cannot conceive. His are empty words and narrow concepts. . . . He has no imagination. Nature should be contemplated with feeling. . . .

Schiller's friend Körner could not quite agree with such severe criticism. In his answer to Schiller he remarked that "people of this type are much too preoccupied to be bothered by what goes on outside. This gives the impression of their being insensitive and heartless."

But Goethe was deeply impressed by young Humboldt. They met again at the end of February 1797, when Alexander had followed his brother's family to Jena, where the university provided the liveliest intellectual and social contacts. Besides Schiller and Körner, there were Fichte, the philosopher, and Loder, the anatomist. Loder's lectures and anatomical demonstrations were at that time of special interest to Alexander, who was finishing his book on nerve and muscle fibers. Loder's course gave him a more thorough grasp of a subject that could be expected to fit into his plans for an expedition. He attended these lectures in Goethe's company, which led to frequent visits to the poet's home at nearby Weimar. In Goethe's home he found collections of minerals, rocks, and plants, besides copies of antique sculptures and a well-stocked science library. There they sat on many occasions discussing problems of geology, the metamorphosis of insects, the physics of light. "He is a true *cornu copiæ* of natural science," reported Goethe enthusiastically to his monarch and friend Karl August, Duke of Saxe-Weimar. "His company is exceedingly interesting and stimulating. Within eight days one could not learn as much from books as he imparts in an hour." To his friend Knebel, Goethe wrote: "The presence of the younger Humboldt would suffice to render an entire lifetime interesting and to stir up everything that could possibly be exciting in chemistry, physics, and physiology, so that I find it sometimes extremely difficult to retreat into my own circle." A month later Goethe admitted to Schiller that his scientific studies had been rekindled by Humboldt's visits, "if only they will not sink into a spring slumber!"

Goethe wanted Alexander's company on a tour in Thuringia, but there was his sister-in-law Caroline to attend to. She had become indisposed in her husband's temporary absence. That Alexander should have declined Goethe's invitation on such grounds suggests how much he enjoyed her company. It may be presumed that she mothered her brother-in-law, whom, we should remember, she desired to draw into her household. Wilhelm had gone to Berlin to attend to a final settlement of the Humboldt estate.

Soon he would return to Jena to complete a translation of a Greek drama by Æschylus and finish a collection of classic choral poetry. The young Haeften couple were there with their young children, so Alexander had a full taste of family life at frequent gatherings in his brother's home. It was planned for all of them to join in a trip to Italy. This "caravan," as Goethe called it, consisting of two mothers, Caroline and Frau von Haeften, their five children, Alexander, Reinhard von Haeften, two maids, and a man-servant, was to leave on the first lap of the journey for Dresden, where Wilhelm was to join them. This ménage, crowded into two coaches, proved a bit too much for Alexander's taste: he left them at Dresden, going on alone to Vienna.

The political horizon began to be darkened by Napoleon. His armies had invaded Italy, and the ensuing political turmoil upset all plans for further travel. Wilhelm wrote from Dresden that he was about to take his family to Paris, where Caroline managed to find suitable quarters a few weeks later. These she was quick to offer to her esteemed brother-in-law, should Alexander want to join them.

In Vienna, Alexander worked feverishly on his manuscripts and pondered over his chances for travel. A young Russian and former fellow student from Hamburg was the first to learn about Alexander's plans. He would go via Spain and the Canary Islands to the West Indies, and the Russian friend agreed to go along at his own expense. With such prospects in mind, Alexander left Vienna for Salzburg and the Tyrol, there to try out surveying and astronomical instruments that he would need for his explorations. Leopold von Buch, a former fellow student from

Freiberg, joined him for a while. As a team, the two succeeded in correcting previous determinations of the latitude of Salzburg and other towns.

Winter passed into the spring of 1798. The political news was disturbing. France appeared to be in open warfare with England, and a British naval blockade against Napoleon threatened to close off Alexander's projected route to the West Indies. Might he go to the Orient instead? On April 20 he wrote to Freiesleben from Salzburg that Lord Bristol, an old Englishman ("half mad and half genius") who enjoyed an annual income of sixty thousand pounds, had offered him a trip to Egypt. In August the noble Lord would embark at Naples in his own ship, which was to carry armed guards, cooks, servants, and artists. If Humboldt went as a member of this motley party, the journey would not cost him anything. In the spring of 1799 they would return via Istanbul to Vienna. Humboldt was quick to accept. This might be his great chance. From Egypt he could go to India and farther east! Yet there were disquieting rumors of an impending French occupation of Egypt. The shadow of Napoleon lengthened over the Near East. Humboldt must go to Paris to find out how the political situation might affect his plans. If Lord Bristol's expedition should fail, Alexander might yet leave by himself for the Orient, provided the Turks kept peace with the French.

Humboldt had spent five strenuous months in astronomical observations, meteorological studies, and occasional visits to mines in the Tyrol. There was so much to be completed: an essay on the composition of the atmosphere and another on subterranean gases and the respirator. This would be done in Paris. But before he left for the

French capital to join his brother Wilhelm, he answered
some of the critics who had difficulty in checking his experiments with nerve and muscle fibers. He announced
with some irritation that his reply was to be published at
once as a newspaper article. "It is peculiar," he wrote to
the director of the astronomical observatory at Gotha, "to
expect to produce within five days, often within hours, all
the phenomena that another investigator had the good
fortune to observe over a period of five years on hundreds
of individuals." Did people expect him to travel all over
Germany to demonstrate sundry experiments single-
handed?

Arrived in Paris, he learned of Napoleon's invasion of
Egypt and that Lord Bristol had been arrested in Milan
on the suspicion of preparing an intervention against
France! It had become urgent to look around for other
travel prospects.

Alexander's arrival in Wilhelm's new Paris home was
greeted with much joy, especially by Caroline, who now
could see another chance of giving him some home life and
a stabilized existence. What a good-looking young man
her brother-in-law had come to be! His light brown hair,
as unruly as ever, the high forehead and blue lively eyes,
and that large mouth of his with the strong chin below!
He was of medium size like her husband. Too bad that his
forehead should have smallpox marks, but then so many
people had them that it really mattered little. She must introduce him right away to her circle of friends: the French
painters David [6] and Gérard,[7] the young German poet

[6] Jacques-Louis David (1748–1825), for three decades the most influential leader of the French official school of painting.

[7] Baron François Gérard (1770–1837), favorite pupil of David, and
founder of the classicist school of French painting.

Ludwig Tieck, and many others. It was, as she proudly expressed it, a *"point de raillement,"* and presumably one of the few salons in Paris, if not the only one where Alexander could mingle easily with a distinguished group of French and German people. Mornings, as Alexander's springy gait echoed in the hall, Caroline knew that he was off for his appointments. He would return for lunch, leaving his coach waiting downstairs ready to carry him off again to the Jardin des Plantes or the Observatoire.

Anyone who has experienced the delicious excitement of Paris as a center of culture and tempting diversions can imagine how Humboldt must have felt in this first prolonged contact with it. Delambre was just about to complete a prolonged survey of the exact location of the Paris meridian.[8] Alexander was invited to witness the final measurements, which he could expect to be useful for his own explorations. At the Jardin des Plantes, half museum and half natural-science laboratory, he met the aging Captain Bougainville, with his botanical collections from South America and his firsthand accounts of that exciting continent. There he was also introduced to the zoologist George Cuvier (1769–1832), who, as it turned out, had gone to school with Schiller near Stuttgart. And Étienne Geoffroy de Saint-Hilaire (1772–1844), later a brilliant protagonist of the theory of the functional unity of organisms, could engage Humboldt in a discussion of Goethe's views on science. With Alexandre Brongniart he could marvel at fossils of plants and animals, and with the Abbé René-Just Haüy, the mineralogist, discuss theories of the origin of volcanic rocks.

[8] This work led to the establishment of the *meter* unit as one forty-millionth of the Paris meridian.

On the Seine embankment stood the National Academy, the fabulous home of science, of Cardinal Mazarin's making. The Institut de France, as it came to be known, was conveniently close to the Latin Quarter. Here at a single session Humboldt could meet the famous mathematician Joseph-Louis Lagrange, author of *Analytical Mechanics* and *A Theory of Analytical Functions*, the astronomer Pierre Simon Laplace, and the chemist Claude-Louis Berthollet. Yet a few illustrious men were missing: the chemist Antoine Lavoisier, who, with Malesherbes, had been guillotined. Napoleon, another member of the Institut, was in Egypt dreaming of Alexander the Great's trail to the East.

How much Humboldt felt at home among these peers of science, and how reassuring it was for him to be received as one of them! Many of them had read his contributions to French scientific journals, and welcomed him as a valuable collaborator. Humboldt was asked to advise a commission on the study of galvanism; he lectured at the Institut on nitrogenous gases and on the possibility of analyzing the atmosphere. A few days before his departure from Paris, he presented an address on the relationships between chemistry and agriculture.

Bougainville urged Humboldt to accompany him on a voyage around the world, perhaps to the South Pole.

Just then [Alexander wrote to Willdenow in Berlin] I was engaged in magnetic studies, and it occurred to me that a journey to Egypt might be less attractive than an expedition to the South Pole. Of such grand hopes I had my full share when suddenly the Directoire made the momentous decision not to send the seventy-year-old Bougainville around the world, but Captain Baudin. All national collections were opened to me to select the instruments I might want. They asked me to advise on the choice of personnel and equipment. Many of my friends showed discontent at my wanting to be exposed to the hazards of a voyage lasting over five years, but my decision was firmly made. I would have despised myself if I had turned down such a chance to be useful. The ships were rigged. Bougainville wanted to entrust me with his fifteen-year-old son, so that he might get accustomed to the dangers of a seafaring life. The choice of our expedition staff was excellent, all young, husky men, and well trained. How carefully they scrutinized each other as they met for the first time, thinking that they would have to spend five years in each other's company!

The expedition would go to various countries in South America, also to Mexico and California, then to the South Pacific and Africa.

What an unspeakable pain when, within a fortnight, all, but all of these hopes came to naught! A miserable 300,000 livres and the threat of open warfare were the reasons. Paris, all excited over our voyage, thought us already on the way. The Directoire delayed the departure until next year.

"But men," he concluded at the end of his letter, "must act, and not indulge in lamentations." How could he act, now that the cannon of his knowledge was charged? Where precisely was its target? Perhaps it would be Egypt, after all. He planned to join Napoleon's expeditionary force. From Marseille he would sail to Algiers, and from there go overland by the annual pilgrim caravan in the direction of Egypt and Mecca. Fortunately, he had found his travel companion, a capable young botanist by the name of Aimé Bonpland (1773–1857), who also had been chosen for the Baudin voyage, and who, like Alexander, had been left stranded in Paris. Alexander took an instant liking to him: he was cheerful and well trained.

On October 20, 1798 the two took the diligence for Lyon and Marseille. Everybody knew that they were off, though God knew whither. Wilhelm and Caroline were in despair. "We had shared," Wilhelm wrote a couple of days later to a friend in Germany, "the same house for the last months, we took our luncheons together, accepted the same invitations—in short, we lived in close friendship. Now, after this enjoyable close companionship, comes this separation, which to all accounts will be anything but short." How right he was! For many years he and Caroline would have to rely on letters written in jungles and other strange places that seemed to be of another world. There would be disquieting rumors of Alexander's death, and accounts of incredible adventures would fill them with sinister forebodings. Was it for this, a sudden departure for the Great Unknown, that Caroline had planned and labored to make him a home? Her scheme to keep him anchored in their midst had come to nothing. Her secret hopes for him had been torn like a sail in a squall—and for what? To be famous, perhaps to shine as the century's greatest naturalist!

The passport issued to Humboldt in Paris in 1798 described him as "five feet eight inches tall, light-brown hair, gray eyes, large nose, rather large mouth, well-formed chin, open forehead marked by smallpox." On the envelope in which this document was kept, the owner wrote at a later age: "big mouth, fat nose, but *menton bien fait*"— well-formed chin. Judging by Charles Willson Peale's portrait of 1804, Humboldt's eyes were blue, and they were described as such in later years by the American writer

Bayard Taylor. The pencil sketch by Gérard shows him a good-looking young man with a frank, appealing expression, and with much leaner features than in Peale's painting.

In Marseille, Alexander learned that the Mohammedan tribes in North Africa were in revolt against the French invasion of Egypt, with the result that the authorities refused him permission to sail for Algiers. As a last hope he and Bonpland might catch a Swedish frigate, but then the ship suffered heavy damage on the coast of Portugal and could not be expected to arrive. What should they do? The travelers decided to go to Spain to try their luck once more.

They tramped along the Mediterranean coast, collecting plants for Willdenow in Berlin. "Arrived in Madrid," Humboldt reported later in his travel account,[9] "I soon had reason to congratulate myself on having decided to visit Spain. Baron Forell, Minister of Saxony at the Spanish court, treated me in a manner most favorable for my purposes. Endowed with a good knowledge of mineralogy, he maintained a most active interest in all scientific enterprises." Forell spoke to the Foreign Minister, Mariano Luis de Urquijo, about Humboldt's plan to travel at his own expense to the Spanish colonies in America. In March 1799 Alexander was presented at court, where he succeeded in interesting the King in his project, though it was actually the Foreign Minister who received the memorandum relative to his expedition. "The enthusiasm with which he incessantly supported my intentions had no other motive but his love for science."

[9] *Personal Narrative of Travels to the Equinoctial Regions of the New Continent* (London, 1852), Vol. I, p. 6.

The specifications for Humboldt's and Bonpland's passports mentioned as destinations Cuba, Mexico, New Granada (Venezuela), Peru, Chile, Buenos Aires, and the Philippines. Political circumstances might make it desirable to return via the East Indies. The passport would have to mention a permission to carry out all manner of explorations, collect plants, minerals, and animals, measure mountain heights, make astronomical observations. The same document would serve as instructions to governors and magistrates to aid in every possible way, as Humboldt had been asked to collect scientific objects for the museum and gardens of His Catholic Majesty. Finally, it would give specific permission to travel in all His Majesty's vessels.

"Never," Humboldt acknowledged in the same travel book, "had a traveler been granted greater concessions and never before has a Spanish Government placed greater confidence in a foreigner." To fortify him against all unpleasant eventualities, in which the Spanish colonies in America were said to be richer than other lands, he received two passports, one from the Secretary of State and another from the Council of the Indies. In return for such courtesies he promised to deliver copies of his reports to the governor and to present several geological collections to the museum in Madrid. "I can state with joy," he wrote in his travel account, "that we never had reason to complain, under the most trying deprivations, about unjust treatment, struggling as we were with a savage nature." In the middle of May the travelers left Madrid for La Coruña, where they expected to embark for America.

At last the great moment had come when dreams and plans would materialize. To sail forth to the New World and explore the unknown! Until now life had been a prep-

aration, a schooling- and testing-ground. Its last retarding
elements had been like a final charging of energies. Napoleon's power politics had prevented Humboldt from sailing eastward, had shattered all hopes of seeing the Pyramids and India. Here at La Coruña a shadow reappeared.
Outside the harbor three British men-of-war lay in wait
for the Spanish packets. The naval blockade of Europe's
coast, which England had imposed in answer to Napoleon's threat, loomed like a last barrier. Would Humboldt's ship succeed in escaping the watchful eye of those
British seadogs?

Those he had left behind trusted in a benign providence.
His brother Wilhelm comforted himself with the thought
that the dangers of Alexander's voyage might, after all,
not be so bad as they seemed. Writing to Schiller, he re-
joiced in his brother's good fortune and reassured himself
by stating that the ocean crossing to Havana was considered very safe. In South America neither yellow fever nor
any other epidemic illness was to be feared! Moreover,
Alexander would travel under official protection, and his
manner would enable him to escape the Spanish jealousy
experienced by other travelers. "Hence I can see nothing
that could stand in his way. He has asked me to send his
best regards to you and Goethe." A month later, when
Humboldt was about to sail, Goethe asked Wilhelm to
wish his brother a happy journey. "What with his genius,"
he wrote, "his talent, and his energy, the advantage of his
journey is altogether incalculable. Yes, one might say that
he himself will come to be surprised at its riches, from
which the profits are bound to be great."

5

Into the Amazon

IN THE HARBOR of La Coruña the Spanish frigate *Pizarro* lay under sail. Humboldt and Bonpland stood on deck looking across the bay. They could see the Castle of San Antonio, where the Marqués de Malaspina, the famous explorer, languished in jail. A commodore of the Spanish Navy, he had, in 1789, been put in command of a fleet to explore the northwest coast of America. His surveys completed, he had then set out to discover a passage through Arctic waters to the Atlantic and had been beaten back by ice. Six years later Malaspina had returned to Spain to find himself arrested for alleged political intrigues. The thought of how fickle fortune was reminded Humboldt of the ups and downs of his own travel plans. Only a month before, he could not have been sure of his fate. A banking house in Berlin had refused to send him a letter of credit unless he furnished guarantees of his securities. From this calamitous situation he had been saved, on the brink of his departure, by the banking firm of Mendelssohn and Friedländer in Berlin, which guaranteed and remitted the desired sum to its correspondent in Madrid. The banker Mendelssohn must have recalled with some emotion how proud his father had once been to count the young Alexander among his gifted pupils.

"What good fortune has come to me!" Alexander wrote to Freiesleben on the eve of embarkation.

My head is dizzy with joy. I am sailing on the Spanish frigate *Pizarro*. We will land on the Canary Islands, and on the coast of Caracas in South America. . . . More from there. Man must strive for the good and the great! Within a few hours we sail round Cape Finisterre. I shall collect plants and fossils, and with the best of instruments make astronomic observations. Yet this is not the main purpose of my journey. I shall endeavor to find out how nature's forces act upon one another, and in what manner the geographic environment exerts its influence on animals and plants. *In short, I must find out about the harmony in nature.*

On June 5, 1799 the ship weighed anchor. Soon after, it was battered by a gale, and the fore-topgallant mast was broken. For moments it was in danger of being thrown on the rocky coast. But misty weather and rain screened the *Pizarro* and its precious load as it slipped through the British blockade.

The ship's company was agreeable, Alexander reported to Wilhelm from Tenerife. A portion of the afterdeck had been reserved for his and Bonpland's labors. There they made astronomic and meteorologic observations, sampling ocean water, measuring its temperatures and analyzing its chemical constitution, watching the nets that dragged up the life of the sea with its ever fascinating wealth of specimens.

The nights were magnificent. In this clear, tranquil atmosphere it was quite possible to read the sextant in the bright moonlight.[1] And then the southern constellations, Lupus and

[1] At that time there was real need for travelers like Humboldt to improve upon sailing charts and maps, the method for measuring geographic longitude at sea having been perfected only in 1756. This was made possible by two men: Tobias Mayer, Director of the Göttingen Observatory, who had won the prize of the British Board of Longitude with his tables of the moon's motions relative to the fixed stars, and by the clockmaker Pierre Le Roy, who built the first improved chronometer. As for geographic maps of the Americas, no explorer as conscientious as

the Centaur! What splendid nights! . . . The sea was phosphorescent every night. As we neared Madeira, some land birds appeared to accompany us throughout the day.

The captain had given strict orders for a blackout so as to avoid the watchful eyes of British naval vessels. What incredible luck for their ship to have escaped these men-of-war right at the entrance of Tenerife! Humboldt's first objective was to climb the highest peak of the island.

What a remarkable spectacle was presented to us at this height of 12,500 feet! [he wrote to his brother]. Overhead the dark-blue vault of heaven, ancient lava-flows at our feet, and on either side the scenes of volcanic devastation. Three square miles of pumice bordered by groves of laurel. Beyond, vineyards that stretch to the sea, wonderfully interspersed with banana trees. Pretty villages dot the coast. Around us the ocean with all the seven islands. . . . I am in ecstasy at finding myself at length on African soil, surrounded by coconut palms and bananas.

A postscript follows:

I could almost cry over the prospects of leaving this heavenly place. I should be quite happy to settle here, and yet I am scarcely out of Europe. Could you but see these luxuriant fields, these laurel forests, the growth of a thousand years, these vines and roses! They actually fatten pigs here on apricots. All the roads are lined with camellia bushes.

Humboldt was in his element. In climbing the island's highest peak he had for the first time noticed the effects

Humboldt could have relied on any of them. Hence the necessity for constant astronomic observations involving the determination of fixed stars in relation to the traveler's actual position. Within five years Humboldt carried out 201 astronomic determinations of geographic positions and over 500 barometric measurements.

of elevation on plant distribution, the gradual change from subtropical to temperate flora, with oak and pine. The sight of the volcanic landscape loosed a torrent of novel thoughts. There, among burned-out craters and lava-flows, doubts arose in Humboldt's mind as to Werner's ideas of the origin of volcanic rocks. Everywhere he noticed the unmistakable signs of fiery eruptions: the black, twisted masses of lava issuing from a central cone. If Werner could see this, he would hasten to correct his views on the aqueous origin of such formations. In geologic age the Canary Islands appeared to Humboldt to be relatively young. If this was so, how could anybody in his right senses claim that they were remnants of the legendary lost continent, Atlantis? Humboldt noted that Strabo had referred in his report on Atlantis to a strip of land that formerly had joined Europe to Mauretania, the northwest coast of Africa. Also, the archæological evidence appeared to argue for historic migrations of the Guanche people from Africa, for their mummified remains were shown to him in certain caves. They bore no trace of such an antiquity as had been claimed for the mythical Atlantis.

The *Pizarro* pursued its westward course. Still within sight of the islands, Humboldt and Bonpland stretched their necks to watch the trunk of an American cedar float by—the first exciting proof of an ocean drift from the New World. Columbus had reported on two corpses of American Indians which had drifted to the Azores at the end of the fifteenth century. It was exciting to think of Columbus's faith in the New World sustained by such an observation. And had not James Wallace later learned of Eskimos who had been stranded on the Orkney Islands in a canoe? To Humboldt these were clear indications that ocean cur-

rents were capable of spreading the races of mankind
across oceans.

The *Pizarro* sailed on Columbus's route. Night after
night Humboldt was on deck with sextant and telescope.
Once already on approaching Tenerife, he had been able
to correct the captain's reckoning. To improve upon existing navigation charts was imperative, in view of faulty calculations of longitude. "For three centuries," Humboldt
wrote in his narrative, "the entire coast of Terra Firma
[America] has been laid down too far southward. This was
owing to the current near the island of Trinidad, which
moves northward, so that navigators are led by their dead
reckoning to think themselves farther south than they actually are." For Humboldt to make such corrections, reliable instruments were needed and the energy to use them
properly on every occasion.[2] No island or coastal promontory, no mountain peak or river bend, not even eclipses of
the sun or moon must pass unobserved. Humboldt, like so
many explorers before and after, came to be sentimentally
attached to his instruments. Through them he could feel
safe in the vastness of ocean and jungle. They brought him
closer to a familiar order of things, helped him forget the
dreadful hazards and lurking dangers of his existence. At
first, as the ship's course turned toward the tropics, the appearance of new constellations was a sad reminder of the
ever growing distance from familiar scenes. "Our joy," he

---

[2] Humboldt's instrumental equipment was the most up-to-date of its
kind. Among the more notable instruments were: a chronometer by Louis
Berthoud; large Ramsden and Bird sextants; Troughton's small sextant;
two telescopes; a Borda theodolite; barometers; compasses; thermometers;
hygrometers. Humboldt took great pains to check these instruments for
their accuracies throughout his journey, and subjected them to final
control on his return to Europe.

wrote later, "evoked by the appearance of the Southern Cross was shared enthusiastically by those members among our crew who had lived in the colonies. In the silence of oceans one is likely to greet a star as a friend from whom one has been separated for so long."

As the ship approached the West Indies, its sails flapping now and then in the mild swells of a calm sea, disturbing news came from the crew's quarters: several of the men had been stricken by fever. Typhoid had broken out on board, and nobody was safe. It took the life of the youngest crew member, the son of a poor Spanish widow who had meant to find riches in the New World and thereby to support his mother. The captain foresaw the loss of his crew and passengers if he should pursue the course for Havana. During the night of July 15 he changed his course, making for the port of Cumaná, on the coast of New Granada (Venezuela). "We would never have reached the Orinoco and the frontier of Brazil," Humboldt wrote later, "had it not been for this sudden change of plan." Incidents like this would frequently occur to change the plans of the two travelers, whose ultimate destination would remain as unpredictable as was the long chain of their adventures.

As the *Pizarro* approached the coast, two dugouts appeared, each carrying eighteen Guayqueria (Guayaqui) Indians

naked to the waist, and very tall of stature. They had the appearance of great muscular strength. . . . Seen from a distance, standing motionless against the horizon, they might have been taken for bronze statues. We were all the more struck by their appearance because it did not correspond with the accounts given by some travelers who reported on their [the Indians'] extreme feebleness. . . . The master of one of the canoes offered to remain on board the *Pizarro* as coastal pilot. He was an Indian of excellent disposition, well acquainted with sea animals and plants.

His name was Carlos del Pino, and Humboldt was so impressed with this first Indian that he engaged him on the spot for the expedition to the Venezuelan coastal region. With Bonpland, Humboldt sat on deck all night talking to the Indian, questioning him, and listening breathlessly to his description of his land, the leafy dome of the virgin forest, and the giant mimosa trees in his garden. It all sounded wonderful to one who had waited since his childhood for such a moment: to sit with an American Indian in the tropical night aboard a Spanish ship off the coast of America!

The scented darkness of the night hid a continent. Amerigo Vespucci and Bougainville had navigated its shores, La Condamine [3] and Bouguer had surveyed streams and mountains in the Amazon regions and Peru, but none of these men had known that exploration can mean other things: plants and creatures related to climates and mountains, and rocks to earthquakes and the thunder of volcanic explosions. Because nature operated by integration of its parts, its life was held tightly by a web of physical elements. Just as there were new stars in this southern sky to guide Humboldt, so was his mind uniquely equipped for the adventures to come.

On July 16 the passengers landed. Humboldt insisted on

[3] Charles-Marie de La Condamine (1701–74) had joined with Louis Godin and Pierre Bouguer for an expedition to Peru to determine the length of a meridian and then to survey parts of the Amazon. Louis-Antoine de Bougainville (1729–1811) sailed round South America on his voyage around the world (1776).

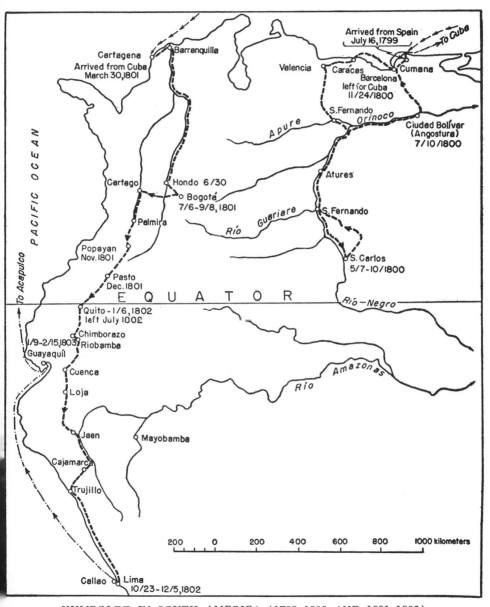

HUMBOLDT IN SOUTH AMERICA (1799–1800 AND 1801–1803)

seeing the Indian's home. The captain reminded Humboldt that he must present his credentials to the Governor first, but in so doing the ship's master talked to deaf ears. In big strides they went off, the two travelers and the Indian, walking briskly through a native settlement to the straw-thatched hut of their native guide. To sit in the shade of a giant mimosa tree, the air scented by tropical flowers never seen before, and watch the Indian with his family was infinitely preferable to visiting a governor's palace. Shortly afterward they walked into the town of Cumaná, or what was left of it after the terrible earthquake that had leveled most of its houses a few years before.

The Governor, Don Vicente Emparán, was delighted by so unexpected an arrival of two distinguished naturalists. IIis province, known as New Andalusia, was then part of the Spanish crown colony of New Granada, second in South America only to the Vice-Kingdom of Peru. Don Vicente was eager to introduce the strangers to cotton fabrics dyed with native plants and to fine furniture made exclusively of native woods. Luckily for the strangers, Señor Emparán was a lover of science, "and the public marks of consideration that he gave us during a long abode in his government contributed greatly to a favorable reception in every part of South America."

"We run around here like mad," Alexander wrote to his brother.

In the first three days we couldn't proceed with any scientific work. We would pick up an object and within seconds reject it for a more striking one. Bonpland assured me that he would go stark mad if the excitement didn't stop soon. But more overpowering than single objects is the impression of the entire mass of luscious and joyful vegetation. I know that I shall be most happy here and that these experiences will make me gay ever so often in days to come. . . . I entered a native hut. As we at home sit on chairs, the mother sat with her children on blocks of coral cast out of the sea. Each ate fish from coconut shells. . . . How bright is the plumage of birds, how colorful are the fish! Why, even the crabs are sky-blue and yellow!

Soon enough the intoxicating impact of this tropical wealth gave way to more sober studies. How stupendous and how taxing to their knowledge and endurance was this meeting with the tropical forest, considering that no botanist before them had explored this wilderness! They must name and classify each plant that excited their interest, search for their flowers and fruits, and then label them, and press them between sheets of paper after a day spent in the steaming jungle. To Humboldt and Bonpland the forest must have seemed like an army of recruits, each plant waiting for its assignment to be ranked among families, orders, genera, and species. Soon the system of that famous Swedish botanist Linnæus would overflow with new plant categories. And that same forest, teeming with myriads of insects and brightly plumed birds, seemed to have waited out its existence through countless ages for this moment, to be valued and fitted into a scientific order of things.

In Humboldt's first reports of this fabulous scenery one senses a kind of relief as he turned from the wilderness of plants to the solid order of rocks and minerals. Among them he could recognize many geologic features already seen in similar associations in central and southern Europe. In this exotic environment they struck him like old friends, his mind fascinated by the relationships of geologic structures and formations for the first time seen on American soil. Limestones and shales, seemingly so analogous on both sides of the Atlantic, must have originated in similar earth periods, and in similar structural associations, as Werner had classified them. And this Venezuelan coast exhibited uniquely the subterranean forces responsible for these geologic structures: Cumaná's houses wrecked by an earthquake, and the islands offshore clinging like torn fragments to the fringe of a continent. No one before Humboldt had seen the drama of geologic change in this land, no one had speculated on a scale that permitted him to see America in its geologic relationship with Europe. In years to come the Andes and Mexico would furnish evidence for his theory that "earthquakes indicate the action of elastic fluids seeking an outlet to diffuse themselves," and that the upheaval of the American cordilleras had released vast subterranean reservoirs of lava.

By November, Humboldt reported to the Director of the observatory of the University of Jena that within three months he and Bonpland had collected more than 1,600 plants and had found 600 new species. He had made sixty drawings of plants, and other sketches to illustrate the comparative anatomy of shellfish. With Berthoud's chronometer and Troughton's sextant he had determined the latitude of fifteen localities in preparation for a map of the interior, and had measured the height of the coast ranges.

The oppressive and almost unbearable heat did not prevent me from observing the solar eclipse of October 28. On the same day I took altitudes of the sun with Bird's quadrant. I give you the results below, and I should be glad if you will kindly look them over and correct them. . . . When, on November 4, a severe earthquake shook our region I was surprised to notice that the dip of the magnetic needle was reduced by 1.1 degrees. . . . On November 12 we had a regular display of fireworks. From two till five o'clock in the morning large fire-balls passed incessantly across the sky. Of some which we measured, the movement was almost perpendicular and upward. Some of these "aerolites" were thousands of feet high and gave out a brilliant light. . . .

He had seen the great shower of meteorites famous in the annals of astronomic science.[4]

In his *Narrative of Travels* he referred to a mineral that in our time has provided Venezuela with fabulous riches. "In crossing the arid hills of Cape Cirial, we noticed a strong smell of petroleum, which the first historian of this country, Oviedo, called 'a resinous, aromatic and medicinal liquor.' . . . Near Cape de la Brea the petroleum covers the surface of the sea more than a thousand feet from the coast."

At the end of November 1799 the travelers took a coastal boat to New Barcelona, where Bonpland left the ship in order to proceed overland to Caracas, while Humboldt proceeded to pay his respects to the Governor General of the province. The rainy season forced them to stay at Caracas until the beginning of February 1800, but tropical downpours could not stop Humboldt's surveying work. He and Bonpland were the first to climb the Silla de Caracas, the picturesque lookout. From Caracas they visited the

---

[4] Only after his return to Europe did Humboldt learn of the enormous regional extent of this great meteorite shower. It had been traced from Brazil across Venezuela to central Europe, covering an area of almost one million square miles. His measurements of the meteorite fall at Cumaná and his meticulous observation of associated optical phenomena helped astronomers to recognize the lawful periodicity and nature of asteroids.

shores of Lake Valencia, and from there went on across the mountains to Puerto Cabello.

These wonderful chances for exploration were owed largely to Baron Forell, the Minister of Saxony at the court of Madrid, who had intervened on their behalf.

I need scarcely assure you how often I am reminded to whom I am indebted for the privilege of being here, and to whom the public will owe thanks for the results that may accrue from my expedition to the West Indies. . . . Gratitude is the first law of our being, and the naturalist in studying the law of nature should pay them unhesitating obedience.

Forell in his diplomatic quarters could not possibly know how incredibly prolific Humboldt's harvest had been thus far. As a reaper of knowledge, there was none among his contemporaries to equal him, for he was thorough and diligent in his studies, whether historical, astronomical, botanical, or geological. He was not content with the gathering of facts and statistical data, but related them to one another, earthquakes with vulcanism and land forms, meteor showers with optical properties of the atmosphere, rock formations with soil types and specific plant associations, climatic phenomena with human behavior.

His *Narrative of Travels* is full of curious reports on missionaries, settlers, and Indians, whom he interrogated with an inexhaustible curiosity. There was the meztizo laborer who had nursed his infant boy with his own milk after the mother's illness had deprived the child of its natural source of nourishment. On hearing about this extraordinary case, Humboldt gathered testimony from all the neighbors who, some sixteen years before, had seen the father nursing the child twice a day for five months. So that Humbodt might prove the case to his own satisfaction, father and son were asked to submit to an examination at Cumaná, where Bonpland examined the father's breast and found it as wrinkled as the breasts of a woman who had nursed children in her youth. In the valley of Caripe the explorers entered a cave where nocturnal birds, the guacharos, were killed by the thousands for their fat. There Humboldt was able to supplement his studies of subterranean caverns, a fact that prompted him to sketch the principles involved in their formation and meteorology. His observations on the progessive increase of temperature below the earth's surface helped establish the law of the average temperature gradient of the earth's crust.

In February 1800 the travelers left the Caribbean coast for the Orinoco River. This northern neighbor of the Amazon would provide access to the jungles of the equatorial region, with its immense wealth of tropical vegetation. It was to give Humboldt his long-hoped-for chance to carry his magnetic observations to a latitude where earth magnetism could be expected to differ greatly from that of northern lands. What would give this trip the flavor of high adventure was the chance of discovering the alleged connection between the Orinoco and the Amazon, or Río Negro, river systems.

From Puerto Cabello they proceeded across the coast ranges and llanos to Lake Valencia. The heat was so terrible that it forced them to ride at night. Often the sky was reddened by forest fires carelessly kindled by stray Indians. The relative of a local governor, a certain Don Nicolás Soto, joined the party to keep them company for over a month. So difficult was it for local plantation-own-

ers to convey messages across this endless wilderness that
the party found itself carrying jungle mail. The wife of a
plantation-owner begged the travelers to describe the hair
and the color of the eyes of her newborn child to her husband, who had gone on a trip south. On March 27, 1800,
they reached the Apure River, which they followed in a
pirogue, a large Indian canoe, to its confluence with the
Orinoco.

"Here it is just as it may have been in paradise," one of
their Indian guides remarked, prompting Humboldt to
reply in a laconic vein that "in this paradise of the American forests, as well as elsewhere, experience has taught all
beings that benignity is seldom found together with
power." Alligators, sunbathing on sandbars in the river,
seemed to illustrate the point, for Bonpland gave the
length of one of them as twenty two feet. At night these
primordial reminders of past geologic ages crept ashore,
delighting in staring at the campfire. And nights the jungle
came alive.

Finding no tree on the riverbank, we stuck our oars in the
ground and fastened our hammocks to them. Soon such a
racket arose in the surrounding forest that it was impossible
to sleep the rest of the night. A wild screaming of creatures
terrorized the woods. Among the many voices heard simultaneously the Indians were able to distinguish those which
could be heard at intervals. There came the monotonous wailing of howling monkeys, the soft whistling of the small sapa-
jous, the rasping growl of the striped night-monkey (*Nyctipi-
thecus triviragtus,* first described by me), the staccato howling of the jaguar, of the peccary, sloth, the shrill scream of
parrots and other birds. When a jaguar approached the edge

of the forest, our dog stopped his incessant barking and howling to take shelter quickly beneath our hammocks. At times
the cry of a jaguar came straight out of a tree. At such a provocation the monkeys would sound their complaining whistle as
they attempted to escape the strange pursuit. When I asked
the Indians why there was so much noise on particular nights,
they replied with a grin: " The beasts delight in the beautiful
moonlight. They celebrate full moon." Long experience has
taught us that it is by no means always the celebrated moonlight that creates such disturbance in the jungles. In fact, the
cries appeared to be loudest during a heavy downpour or
when the inner forest was rent by lightning and thunderclaps.
For many months, whenever the forest approached the river
we listened to the same noises. . . . The security evinced by
the Indians inspired confidence, so that we were readily persuaded that the jaguars are afraid of fire, and that they do not
attack a man lying in his hammock.

The jaguar, venerated by their Indian companions, kept
the party in a constant state of suspense. On one occasion
Humboldt had gone off into the jungle, when suddenly
he found himself within eighty paces of the beast. It was
lying under the thick foliage of a ceiba tree.

No jaguar has ever appeared to me so large. There are accidents in life against which we may seek in vain to fortify our
reason. I was extremely alarmed, yet sufficiently master of
myself to follow the advice that the Indians had so often given
us about how we ought to act in such cases. I continued to
walk on without running, and avoided moving my arms. I
thought that I saw the jaguar's attention fixed on a herd of
deer crossing the river. I then started to return by making a
large circuit toward the riverbank. With increasing distance
I felt like accelerating my pace. How often was I tempted to
look back so as to assure myself of not being pursued! Fortu-

nately I yielded very slowly to this desire. The jaguar remained motionless. I arrived at the boat out of breath, and related my adventure to the Indians.

At last they were able to purchase a larger boat from a missionary. A little over forty feet long, and three feet wide, it was large enough so that a small hut could be constructed on a projecting platform at one end of it. The Indian rowers sat in front, pairwise and unclothed, singing monotonously. From aft came the cries of monkeys and birds whose bamboo cages hung suspended from the hut. At night this menagerie was placed near the hammocks, while the instrument-boxes were kept at a safe distance from an outer circle of fires that the Indians were ordered to keep up through most of the night. The boat was a bed of Procrustes which forced them to stretch out so as not to upset its balance. Each time they needed an instrument, they had to land to extract it from the storage space beneath the hut. Each observation, and every plant collected, required special chores. Downstream, the Orinoco widened to what seemed a huge lake, its surface whipped by foaming waves splashing furiously in a stiff breeze. Gone were the flocks of flamingos and cranes which had enlivened the banks of the Apure River. A few large alligators were seen instead, their long tails cutting obliquely through the choppy water. The horizon was bounded by dense forest, its margins forming weird bastions and fantastic towers, floating, as it were, on water.

In the port of Encaramada they met some Carib Indians. Their *cacique*, or chieftain, was going up to the Orinoco in his canoe to join in the annual fishing for turtle eggs.

He was seated beneath a kind of tent constructed, like the sail, of palm leaves. His cold and silent gravity, the respect shown him by his attendants, everything denoted him to be a person of importance. He was equipped like all his Indians. They were naked, and armed with bows and arrows. The chief, his domestics, boat, and equipment were all painted red with a substance they call *onito,* a plant dye. These Caribs are men of almost athletic build. Their smooth, thick dark hair, cut short off the forehead like that of choristers, their eyebrows painted black, their look at once gloomy and animated, gave a singular expression to their faces. . . . They attach a great importance to certain shapes of the body. A mother might be accused of culpable indifference toward her children if she did not employ artificial means to shape the calves of their legs after the fashion of the country.

The Otomaco Indians, at the mission of Uruana, turned out to be an especially curious lot. It fascinated Humboldt to think them capable of overcoming an annual season of famine by eating a special kind of earth. At a time of high flood these Indians found it well-nigh impossible to detect in the muddy stream fish they were wont to kill with bow and arrow.

We spent a day with them, sufficient to learn their way of preparing *poya,* small balls of clay, and to estimate the amount that they consume in twenty-four hours. During the flood period, which lasts from two to three months, they consume unbelievable quantities of this earth. In their huts we found heaps of these balls arranged in pyramids three to four feet high, each ball measuring three to four inches in diameter. Such was their supply for the next season. This earth is a very fine sticky substance of yellow grayish color, which turns red in roasting. Vauquelin [the French chemist] found it to consist mainly of diatomaceous earth and clay, with three to four per cent lime. . . . It does not contain any organic matter. The Otomacos admitted that besides a few lizards, some fern roots, or a dead fish, they eat nothing for two months but this earth, of which they consume from three quarters of a pound to a pound in twenty-four hours. They prepare these *poya* balls in the dry season, when there are plenty of fish, and even then mix a little of it with their food. They roast the balls first, but wet them upon eating.

Reading this strange account by Humboldt makes one think of the serpent in paradise which the Lord condemned to eat earth. In any case, the custom of the Indians fascinated Humboldt so greatly that upon his return to Paris he persuaded two French physiologists to experiment with this strange earth diet. For five days they lived on talc without feeling any the worse for it. In his *Narrative of Travels*, Humboldt cited other such practices from Africa and Java, where native women keep to a soil diet for a while to regain a girlish figure. The Inca messengers in Peru, Humboldt reported, were accustomed to mix powdered lime with coca, which kept them strong for days without any other food. He concluded that geophagy, the custom of eating earth, served to stimulate the flow of gastric juices, which, so he claimed, have a certain nutritive value. But earth-eating was by no means practiced solely by humans: it was even known among animals. Among the Otomaco tribe, alligator fat served as an effective remedy against constipation occasioned by the seasonal earth diet.

Ascending the Orinoco past the rapids of Maypures as far as San Fernando, the party proceeded upstream on its southern tributary, the Atabapo, and at last came within sight of the watershed between the Orinoco and the Río Negro and Amazon basins. From the Río Tuamini, porters carried the pirogue overland for three days to the Río Negro, which the party navigated as far as San Carlos, near the frontier of Brazil. Within two degrees of the equator Humboldt had reached his goal. There was every reason to celebrate the event, yet Humboldt was much too busy with his instrument-readings, astronomic determinations of their geographic position, magnetic observations, plant-collecting, and writing in his diary.

This was the land of the fabled Amazons. Not that Humboldt expected them to emerge from the jungle, and if they had he would no doubt have questioned them at some length about the Amazon stones, which the Indians invested with magic powers. They wore these green stones suspended from their necks as amulets to defy nervous complaints, fevers, and venomous snakes. The beads and pendants were ornamented with strange inscriptions and symbolic figures—vestiges, Humboldt thought, of very ancient traditions, as the natives no longer knew how to carve such hard stones. In former times the Indians had cut the amazonite mineral into very thin disks, "perforated in the center and suspended by a thread, and these ornaments gave a metallic sound when struck by another hard object." As for the legend of the Amazons, Humboldt speculated, on the basis of his inquiries and subsequent historical studies, that the early European explorers had a tendency to invest the newly discovered continent of South America with the features the classic Greek writers had fancied when they described exotic lands. Yet Humboldt did think it quite possible for native Indian women to have organized themselves into a matriarchial society whose members had learned to defend their freedom against the enslavement of men.

Already here, in the thick of the Río Negro jungle, Humboldt was convinced of the great antiquity of Indian traditions, far more ancient than historical records. He had observed petroglyphs depicting animals and hunting scenes. Inaccessible above the river, they persuaded him to the belief that the stream must once have flowed at a much higher, an almost geologically ancient, level for the prehistoric Indians to have carved the inscriptions. This was a feat of observation, considering that other travelers had made no point of this, leaving their European readers under the impression that the jungle Indians were incredibly savage and primitive.

On May 10, 1800, Humboldt and Bonpland embarked to go up the Río Negro as far as its confluence with the Casiquiare River, which they hoped to navigate to the Orinoco. Ahead lay the exciting prospect of verifying the connection between the Río Negro and the Orinoco. Rain and tropical mist obscured their view for days, preventing Humboldt from calculating their progress by astronomic observations. Worrisome as was their situation, it might have been worse if Humboldt had known that the Brazilian government had issued an order for his arrest. One month before their arrival at San Carlos, a notice had appeared in the *Gazeta de Colonia* that

a certain Baron von Humboldt, a native of Berlin, has been traveling in the interior of America making geographic observations for the correction of certain errors in existing maps, collecting plants . . . a foreigner who, under a pretext of this kind, might possibly conceal plans wherewith to spread new ideas and dangerous principles among the faithful sub-

jects of this realm. Your Excellency [the Governor] should investigate at once . . . as it would be extremely injurious to
the political interest of the Crown of Portugal were such the
case. . . .

A posse may have been under way as the Humboldt
party escaped the trap that officials had prepared for him.
The route to Esmeralda turned out to be the most dangerous and difficult of the entire trip. The narrow boat was
barely able to navigate between granite rocks and driftwood. As the river passage narrowed, the marshy banks
offered few camping-grounds, and mosquitoes thickened
into stinging clouds. On the Río Negro it had at least
been possible to find dry firewood, but here on the Casiquiare the equatorial forest was dripping with moisture.
For one month they had not met a single soul, except in
the vicinity of a few missions scattered here and there
on the edge of the forest. The mosquitoes were so thick
that it was hardly possible to write during the day. The
pen trembled in one's hand from their incessant stings.
Once Humboldt and Bonpland jumped with the Indians
into a waterfall to escape the troublesome insects, and
another time they dug themselves into the sand. For weeks
they had eaten nothing but manioc, some rice, dried cocoa,
bananas, and occasionally monkey meat.

On May 20 their canoe slid past steep riverbanks and
masses of drifting wood toward the junction with the
Orinoco. One more night, made sleepless by jaguars, and
the boat entered the great stream below the mission of
Esmeralda. It had taken them one month of incredible
hardships to establish the existence of the Amazon-Ori-
noco waterway and to reach this point. Already Humboldt

could foresee its economic importance: "A country nine or ten times larger than Spain, and enriched with the most varied products, is navigable in every direction by the natural canal of the Casiquiare and the bifurcation of the rivers." He imagined the products of Europe and of the coastal regions traded as far as Peru, and the vast forested Amazon a new cradle for human enterprise, an empire that would surpass the ancient nations of Egypt and Mesopotamia by its incalculable riches.

Weakened by bad food and an exhausting journey in damp boats, Humboldt and Bonpland thought it best to return to the coast. The little hut in their pirogue was swept clean of insects, and on May 23 it was seen drifting into midstream on its way to the river port of Angostura. For twenty-two days they were condemned to remain stretched out in the narrow boat, for twenty one nights to hang up their hammocks under the palms of the Orinoco.

Arrived at Angostura, Humboldt and Bonpland came down with typhoid. The jungle had caught up with them at last. While Humboldt managed to cure himself with a tincture of honey and bitter extract from the angostura tree, Bonpland's condition became alarming. Humboldt had his friend taken to the cooler country home of a physician in the hills nearby. One evening a servant burst into Humboldt's room announcing Bonpland's death. He entered the sickroom to find Bonpland in a coma, but in a few hours he had survived the crisis. Humboldt's anxiety and extreme worry are evident from a letter to his brother:

I can barely describe to you the worry I suffered during his [Bonpland's] illness. Never could I have hoped to meet again with a friend as loyal and devoted as he. I shall never forget how he saved my life in a storm that overtook us on the Orinoco . . . when he offered to swim ashore from the boat with me on his back.[5]

Bonpland's slow recovery forced them to stay until July 10, which gave Humboldt a chance to gather all sorts of information. Angostura was then a town of 6,000, flourishing from a new trade with Spain which had been inaugurated by merchants in 1771. The voyage from Cádiz to the mouth of the Orinoco, at Punta Barima, took from eighteen to twenty days, the return to Spain up to thirty-five days. The rich province exported cacao, cotton, indigo, and sugar, receiving manufactured goods from Europe in return.

No sooner had Bonpland recovered than Humboldt started on the trek back to Cumaná, their original point of departure. When, on September 1, 1800, the travelers reached there, they had covered some 6,443 miles of one of the least-known and most hazardous regions in the Americas. Their scientific bounty was fabulous in terms of scientific data, collections, and instrument measurements. Twelve thousand plants had been collected, of which fourteen hundred had already been classified en route. Nobody would doubt that Humboldt and Bonpland had seen and studied more plant species than any other exploring botanist before them. Had they not laid the first cross-section through the profuse vegetative wealth of the American tropics, and would they not be able to apply Linnæus's system of plant classification to thousands of species hitherto unknown? And yet Humboldt wrote to Willdenow in Berlin:

[5] In his moments of anguish over Bonpland's and his own illness, Humboldt drew up a will in which he left the considerable sum of 50,000 francs to his friend.

We were barely able to collect a tenth of the specimens met with. I am now perfectly convinced of a fact that I would never admit while visiting with botanists in England . . . that we do not know three fifths of all the existing plants on earth! But, alas, we grieve almost to the verge of tears when we open our plant-boxes. The extreme humidity . . . has caused more than one third of our collection to be destroyed. Daily we discover new insects destructive to paper and plants. Camphor, turpentine, tar, pitched boards, and other preservatives so effective in a European climate prove quite useless here.

Annoying as such losses must have been, Humboldt had emerged from this jungle trip with results sufficient to compensate him. For one thing, he had mapped the stream connection between the Orinoco and the Río Negro. He had further observed variations of earth magnetism which would permit him later to establish the law of diminishing magnetic declination between the poles and the equator. He had determined the location of the numerous inland stations, mountains, and streams by astronomic observations. His eyes had pierced the wildest curtain of foliage imaginable, and had observed patterns of stream erosion never before seen on such a scale or with such discernment.

From Cumaná he wrote to his brother:

I could not possibly have been placed in circumstances more highly favorable for study and exploration than those which I now enjoy. I am free from the distractions constantly arising in civilized life from social claims. Nature offers unceasingly the most novel and fascinating objects for learning. The only drawbacks to this solitude are the want of information on the progress of scientific discovery in Europe and the lack of all the advantages arising from an interchange of ideas.

6

An Altitude Record
in Ecuador

HUMBOLDT'S LIFE IN the jungle illustrates afresh that human nature is capable of amazing transformations when liberated from impeding strains. He was a young man of thirty-one who had never felt either really well or happy for any length of time. He landed in the tropics and, from that moment on, led a charmed life. He seemed so perfectly adjusted to his new environment that neither fevers, mosquitoes, wild beasts, nor hunger mattered. He wrote to his brother that in this jungle existence he actually did not miss anything but intellectual stimuli. His emotional wants were happily satisfied by the friendship with Bonpland, who, to all appearances, had accepted Humboldt as leader and protector.

The travel narrative speaks of many encounters with government officials, missionaries, planters, and Indians cast in contrasting roles, which to Humboldt seemed but temporary assignments. The role of the Indians, especially —enslaved and tragically oppressed as they were by colonial wardens—was bound to change one day, Humboldt hoped, considering their ancient and impressive traditions. For these he respected them. He would never cease to point out that they were not mere savages, as Europeans believed, but inherently gifted and spiritually endowed. To be sure, Humboldt loathed their ritual of butchering their own kind, but despite this, one feels that he would have sided with the Indians at any time if given a chance to better their lot. In this attitude he was a true child of the age of reason: all human beings, regardless of skin color, were precious, and capable of improvement if liberated. Unlike the missionaries, the Indians did not pretend to be something else.

The Spanish padres came in for devastating criticism from Humboldt most of the time. With their soul-hunting expeditions and their cruel treatment of aborigines, they emerge from Humboldt's travel accounts as the real savages except on a few occasions when he acknowledged their contributions as explorers. Possibly this experience of seeing the symbol of the Cross wielded with the savageness of gun and whip accounts for Humboldt's disdain for organized religion. The misdeeds of missionaries were reported factually, and rarely with comments of any sort, as if in writing his narrative he was conscious of a censorship that might deprive him of future opportunities to explore. By and large, he held to the belief that a man of science who enjoyed official protection in other lands had better avoid adverse comments on social or political institutions, with one exception: slavery. And precisely this issue came to be all-important during the next phase of his American travels.

Humboldt had missed visiting Cuba on his outward journey from Europe—because of the typhoid epidemic on board ship—and he longed to visit Havana next. It was one of the world's busiest ports, and Cuba was the most developed of Spain's colonial possessions. And beyond Cuba beckoned prospects of visiting Canada and the Great Lakes region. He definitely planned to descend the Ohio and Mississippi rivers to New Orleans, proceed from there to Mexico, and from Acapulco sail for the Philippines and the East Indies. "I wished to make known the countries I had visited, and to gather such information as would elucidate a science of which we barely knew the outline, vaguely defined as Natural History of the World, Theory of the Earth, or Physical Geography. The last of these subjects seemed to me the most important." Others before him had circumnavigated the globe for the sake of geographic discoveries. What was needed was somebody to describe the varieties of the world's physical structure and find out how its component parts functioned in relation to living things. With this vision, Humboldt might well have seen himself as a missionary of sorts, trained in the best manner imaginable, and, what was singularly evident, endowed with a mind capable of deriving general principles from scattered facts.

On November 24, 1800 the travelers left the Venezuelan coast in a vessel so small that it took them twenty-five agonizing days of storms and perils to reach Havana.

"One walked through ankle-deep mud and suffered the stench of salted meat," and the walled town was cramped, with 44,000 people, half of whom were Negroes and mulattoes. With its sprawling suburbs Havana was almost the size of New York, but dangerously infected by yellow fever. Receptions and festivities were held in honor of the two travelers, and leisurely days were spent in the comfortable homes of their titled hosts. The harbor, a pivot of commerce, and the most important strategic base of the Spanish colonial navy, had not been accurately placed on the map. Humboldt set to work with his surveying instruments to correct its geographic latitude.

Then came a trip with Bonpland into the island's in-

A native raft on the Orinoco, after a drawing by Humboldt

Street scene in Lima, after a French lithograph, ca. 1800

terior. For weeks they visited its sugar plantations and factories, its indigo, tobacco, and cotton fields, where the slaves labored in unspeakable miseries. "I wanted to throw light on facts," Humboldt wrote later, "and give precision to ideas by comparing the island's condition with that of South America." From these studies resulted his *Political Essay on the Island of Cuba,* a geographic monograph unique for its thorough treatment of such physical aspects as land forms, geology, and climate in relation to population, commerce, internal communications, and revenues. Its publication in 1828 coincided with the upsurging tide of independence movements in Latin America. It was a timely document for its economic statistics, and even more so for the humanitarian ring of its chapter on slavery.

"If the legislation of the Antilles and the condition of the colored population does not experience some salutary change, and if discussion without action is continued, the political power may well pass into the hands of that class which holds the might of labor, the will to throw off the yoke. . . ." An African federation of states might arise in the West Indies, Humboldt thought, if legislators (meaning those in Madrid) failed to realize that Cuba's wealth could not be maintained and developed without the cessation of slave labor. Cuba inspired Humboldt to advocate an end to the traffic in slaves. Between 1811 and 1825 Cuba received, through licit and illicit channels, some 185,000 African Negroes, of whom 116,000 passed through the Havana customs between 1811 and 1820.

It is for the traveler who has been an eyewitness of the suffering and degradation of human nature to make the complaints for the benefit of the oppressed. On leaving America I retained the same horror of slavery which I had previously felt in Europe.

From Venezuela, Humboldt had described to his brother a scene in the slave market at Cumaná:

The slaves exposed for sale were young men from fifteen to twenty years of age. Every morning coconut oil was distributed among them, with which they rubbed their bodies to give them a black polish. The people who came to purchase examined the teeth of these slaves, to judge of their age and health, forcing their mouths open as we do with horses in a market. This odious custom dates from Africa, as is proved by the faithful scenes drawn by the inimitable Cervantes, who, after his long captivity among the Moors, described the sale of Christian slaves at Algiers. It is distressing to think that even at this day there exist European colonists in the West Indies who mark their slaves with a hot iron, to know them again in case of escape. This is the treatment bestowed on those who save other men the labor of sowing, tilling, and harvesting!

At Cumaná he had taken notes on the slave population, which at that time consisted of 6,000 colored among 110,-000 white and creole inhabitants. The government archives at Havana furnished Humboldt with gruesome statistics. During the 106 years previous to 1786, the English possessions in the West Indies had received more than 2,130,000 Negroes forcibly carried from the coast of Africa. In 1806, the English slave trade involved some 53,000 sales, and that in the United States 15,000.

It would be easy to prove [Humboldt wrote in his travel narrative] that the whole of the West Indies, which now comprises scarcely 2,400,000 Negroes and mulattoes (free and slaves) received from 1670 to 1825 nearly 5,000,000 Africans. These revolting calculations regarding the consumption of the human race do not include the number of unfortunate slaves who perished on the passage or were thrown into the sea as damaged merchandise.

Of all impressions gained in South and Middle America, none was more effective than the sight of slavery in rousing Humboldt to indignation and fury. Time and again, in political congresses and correspondence, he advocated strict enforcement of laws against the slave trade. His great hope was that "the generous principles that for so long have animated the legislatures of the northern part of the United States will be extended southward and toward those western regions where, in consequence of an imprudent and fatal law, slavery and its iniquities have passed the chain of the Alleghenies and the banks of the Mississippi."

The trip to the interior of Cuba was shortened by a longing for news from the American mainland. Back in Havana, Humboldt found in his mail a most exciting newspaper report: Captain Baudin's expedition had left France and could be expected on the Peruvian coast within a year. Here was a chance to sail around the world with a group of naturalists Humboldt had helped to select in Paris. So tempting was this prospect that it blotted out all other plans. Canada and the United States must wait, the discovery of the Northwest Passage be left to other explorers, like Lewis and Clarke, while Humboldt and Bonpland would sail across the Pacific, perhaps to the South Pole, and on to Africa or India. From Cuba they would return to South America, to take the route from the Isthmus of Panama to the Andes, via Bogotá and Quito to Lima, where Captain Baudin's party was bound to appear.

How did Humboldt know that he and Bonpland would be welcome as members of the French expedition? There was no way of finding out how Baudin might accept this proposal, but in any case Humboldt dispatched a long letter to him, outlining his and Bonpland's past travels and their expected travel route to Lima. If, by chance, Baudin could not accept two additional members, he was implored not to feel embarrassed.

I shall never grumble over events that lie beyond our control [wrote Humboldt]. Such frankness in your decision will be to me the most cherished proof of your friendship. In this event I would simply continue my journey from Lima to Acapulco and Mexico, thence to the Philippines, Persia, and Marseille. I would much prefer, however, to be a member of your party.

One must suspect that this vague hope of joining the Baudin expeditions was not the only reason for Humboldt's change of plan. Indeed, a letter to his brother, written a few weeks later from Colombia, alludes to various reasons without specific mention of what they may have been. Had Alexander come to realize that the Andes of Peru might give him a chance for exploring such geographic principles as climatic influences on plant life and native cultures? Or was it the prospect of visiting in Bogotá the famous botanist José Celestino Mutis, the friend and pupil of Linnaeus? In Bogotá the travelers would be able to compare their plant identifications with Mutis's. Clearly, to return to South America would mean consolidation of the results obtained thus far.

As for North America, John Fraser (1750–1811), the Scottish botanist, had come with his impressive accounts of five exploring expeditions. Fraser and his son had suffered shipwreck off the Cuban coast. Lacking any entry permit for the Spanish colonies, they arrived at Havana destitute, in the company of fishermen who had rescued them from a sandbank. Humboldt received them in his quarters, supplied them with money and clothing, and through the influence of his friends procured for Fraser permission to travel through the island. Humboldt proposed that Fraser's son accompany him later to Mexico, but young Fraser, uneasy over his incapacity to master Spanish, preferred to hasten back to London, there to publish his father's botanical collection from Kentucky. His father agreed to take two cases of Humboldt's plant specimens with him to England, where they would be safe until more peaceful conditions would permit their shipment to Willdenow in Berlin.

It was Palm Sunday, March 30, 1801, when the travelers sailed into the port of Cartagena, Colombia.

We were trying to force our way against the wind into the harbor. The sea was fearfully rough. Our tiny craft (forty tons) could not master the waves, and suddenly was thrown on her beam-ends. A tremendous wave broke over us and threatened to engulf the ship. The man at the helm remained undismayed at his post. All of a sudden he called: "*¡No gobierna el timón!* (The rudder will not work)." We all gave ourselves up for lost. In this, as it seemed to us, our utmost danger, we cut away a sail that had been flapping loosely, when the ship righted herself on top of another wave, enabling us to find refuge behind the promontory of Gigante. But here a new and almost greater danger awaited me. For the better observation of an eclipse of the moon, I put off to shore in a boat. Scarcely had I landed with my assistants when we were startled by the clanking of chains, and a party of powerful

Negroes, freshly escaped from the Cartagena prison, fell upon us from a thicket, brandishing their daggers, apparently ready to seize our boat, as they saw us without arms. We fled at once to the water and boarded ship.

From Cartagena, Humboldt and Bonpland had planned to go first to Panama, and from there to proceed by boat to the Pacific port of Guayaquil in Ecudaor. The Isthmus of Panama presented a special challenge. By navigating the Chagres River and studying its geologic features, Humboldt hoped to solve the problem of a canal. It was a prize he could ill afford to forgo, for world commerce would immensely benefit from it. To see humanity more closely united by an overland passage of the American isthmus was one of his cherished dreams. Yet for a second time Humboldt changed his plans. For one thing, he dreaded the prospect of losing valuable time by attempting to sail from a Panamanian port to Guayaquil in a season of unfavorable winds. He could not risk delaying his arrival in Peru, where Captain Baudin's party was expected. Then also, there was Mutis in Bogotá to be considered. An overland journey to that city would give him and Bonpland a wonderful chance to see the Andean flora from its jungle base in the east to the top of lofty ranges. It was a pity not to visit the Isthmus at this time, but as long as there was a chance of exploring it later from Mexico, he felt the delay to be justified.[1] The travelers dispatched their heavy equipment to Guayaquil and Quito, and in April embarked at the mouth of the Río Magdalena in a native canoe. Hundreds of miles of uncharted jungle

[1] This plan to visit the Isthmus was never realized, but Humboldt obtained sufficient information in Mexico to enable him later to publish his various ideas on a canal project.

country lay ahead. The river would bring them to the eastern foot of the Andes, where they would cross by pack train to Bogotá.

The forest was a green wall of trees and thickets. Now and then they noticed the smoke of Indian campfires. On the sandbanks lay clusters of alligators and water birds. Flocks of parrots rose screaming from under low-hanging clouds. Day by day the pirogue moved against the swift current, the bronzed bodies of Indian paddlers swaying in muscular rhythm. Humboldt charted the stream with his compass while Bonpland gathered plants or fished up tropical fruits drifting on the current. At last, after fifty-five days of river journey, the boat was moored at the jetty of the small town of Honda. The Cordillera Oriental rose before them in a humid, tropically scented haze.

Here was a paradise of exotic growth, with plantations of nutmeg, almond, and cinnamon. Beyond lay the forest, with cinchona trees, whose juice the Indians extracted as a remedy against fevers. To gather cinchona bark, fruit, and flowers was most important, considering how little was known in Europe of this medicinal tree. Humboldt visited mines in the mountains only briefly, for there was no time to lose, their arrival at Bogotá already having been announced to the authorities.

By mule train they proceeded toward Quito. The only way to get there was by a perilous route through narrow clefts of rock, steadily climbing the massive slopes of the eastern Andes. Bonpland complained of headache and nausea. His feverish face was taut and strained; his eyes were barely able to see the changing pattern of plant life, the first mountain laurels and conifers. When they reached a pass, a cooling wind blew from a large elevated plain

dotted with fields and Indian villages. The town of Bogotá could not be far. As they crossed a sun-baked plain,
an Indian messenger was sent ahead to announce their
impending arrival. The following day a cavalcade of color-
fully dressed riders came out to meet the strangers. The
Archbishop had sent his carriage for the last stretch of the
road, and a group of sixty distinguished citizens accompanied the coach to the outskirts of the town as if in
triumphal procession.

It was Mutis the strangers had come to visit, the man
who had spread Bogotá's fame across European lands by
his botanical studies. The honor of this festive reception
was really his, and the Governor was determined to make
the most of this visit. Mutis placed a house next to his at
Humboldt's and Bonpland's disposal. From there it was
only a few steps to their host's library, second only to that
of the celebrated Sir Joseph Banks in London. In another
room they found shelves of plant collections and thousands
of beautifully colored drawings. Humboldt reported to his
brother:

> Thirty artists have been engaged for the last fifteen years in
> painting under Mutis's supervision. He keeps from 2,000 to
> 3,000 drawings, done like miniature paintings, in large port-
> folios. The King pays annually 10,000 piasters toward the ex-
> penses of botanical research. I employed my time in visiting
> the curiosities in the neighborhood and in measuring the
> heights of some of the surrounding mountains, several of which
> rise to 13,000 and 16,000 feet.

On one of these excursions Humboldt came across fossilized mastodon bones, "bones of giants," as the Indians
called them. Nearby he discovered rock salt and coal fields,

which reminded him of geological deposits he had seen on one of his inspection tours in Austria and Poland. Bonpland found time to recover from his illness. When he had regained his health, Humboldt told him of the difficult road to Quito that lay ahead.

On September 8 they left Bogotá for the Magdalena Valley. As the route would lead through uninhabited dense forest, their pack train carried provisions for one month and a minimum number of instruments. The route led via Pandi and Ispinal to Ibaque, where the path began to wind upslope through bamboo thickets and across mountain streams. The forest abounded in majestic wax palms, whose ivory-white trunks rose from a maze of tree ferns, gorgeous passion flowers, fuchsias, and delicately tinted orchids. No sooner had they crossed the wind-bitten Quindio Pass than the Indian porters offered to carry them downhill to the nearest town of Cartago. It was customary for mining officials, Humboldt reported, to saddle the Indians and ride them like horses, the natives walking bent forward supported by walking-sticks. It made his blood boil to witness such cruelty and to "hear the qualities of a human being described in the terms that would be employed in speaking of a horse or a mule." He and Bonpland preferred to walk, difficult as that was, with shoes torn and feet bleeding.

From Cartago they proceeded south along the majestic Cauca Valley to Popayán. There the month of November was spent with botanical and geological excursions, among them an exciting trip to the Puracé volcano, whose gases Humboldt studied for their physical and chemical properties. In order to avoid the torrid and fever-stricken Patía Valley, they proceeded toward Quito over a mountain route via Almaguer to Pasto. The rainy season had begun. "Thick woods interspersed with swamps, where the mules sank up to their girths, and narrow paths winding through such rocky clefts that one could almost fancy one was entering a mine, and the road paved with bones of mules that had perished from cold or fatigue." Sleet and snow greeted them on the Llano de Pasto, a weird landscape where volcanic fumes mingled with low, drifting clouds. At Pasto they rested over Christmas. Shortly afterwards they covered the last stretch to Quito via Tuqueres, Tulcán, and Ibarra, finally on January 6, 1802 arriving in the central plaza of Quito.

Quito was then a town of some 40,000 inhabitants, among them some of the oldest feudal families of Latin America. The Marqués de Aguirre y Montúfar gave the distinguished visitors most comfortable quarters. From Humboldt's luggage appeared a court dress, dark blue with yellow facings, a white waistcoat, and knee breeches. Such a handsome outfit could have deceived nobody as to its owner's actual mission, least of all the hostess. Doña Rosa remembered in her old age how amiable Baron Humboldt had been. Yet "at the table he never remained longer than was absolutely necessary to still his hunger and pay the customary courtesies to the ladies. He seemed always glad to be outdoors again, examining rocks and collecting plants. At night, long after we all had retired, he would observe the stars. To us young women this manner was more difficult to understand than for my father, the Marqués." Indeed, Quito's society had never seen a baron whose principal fancy was to vanish into the mountains hunting for plants and rocks and return late at night with muddy boots. Horses and mules were always at his orders, and young Don Carlos Montúfar was eager to be taken along on hazardous mountain trips.

Soon after their arrival a letter came from Paris reporting that Captain Baudin could not be expected to touch on the Peruvian coast, as his party had taken the eastern route round Africa to the East Indies. This turn of fate would have upset an explorer less resourceful than Humboldt. Of a sudden the prospects of a journey around the world had been reduced to his own plan of visiting the Philippines and India. "Accustomed to such disappointments," Humboldt wrote to Delambre in Paris,

we consoled ourselves in the thought that we had been prompted by a good purpose in all the sacrifices we made. In going over our herbariums, our barometric and trigonometric observations, our drawings, and our experiments on the atmosphere of the Cordilleras, we see no reason for regretting our visit to countries that have remained largely unexplored by scientists. We have come to feel that man ought not to count upon anything which he cannot obtain by his own enterprise.

Quick to respond to unexpected changes of fortune, Humboldt remembered in this moment how supremely promising the Andean world was: it could fulfill the pledge he had made on sailing to the New World, to discover the laws that govern the relationships among land forms, climate, and organisms.

In retrospect the Orinoco exploration could not have fully satisfied such aims. The jungle had afforded only sectional glimpses of what appeared to be a vast incomprehensible wilderness. The Andes, on the other hand, provided a vertical range of vegetations and climates; there it was possible to pass from steaming lowlands to the frozen majesty of tall summits. Here volcanic forces had aided mountain-making on a grand scale, and rivers had cut deep chasms exposing the geologic structures from top to coastal base. The Andes were like a huge ladder leading gradually from floor to floor, each disclosing distinct land forms, climatic conditions, and flora in a state of gradual transformation.

Already in climbing the peak of Tenerife on the Canary Islands, he had noticed how varieties of vegetations follow one another. Here in the Andes such changes of flora were disclosed on a much grander scale. In the lowlands, palms, bananas, sugar, and cacao; higher up, coffee and cotton. In the rain forests grew ferns, and nut and rubber trees. On the *altiplano*, the less eroded uplands, was found Indian cultivation of maize, barley, potatoes, and wheat, interspersed with pastures for cattle and horses. And still higher, on stony slopes whipped by storms and cold winds, llamas and sheep grazed on succulent alpine grasses and herbs. The mountains were a structure with many floors, each furnished by plant associations of its own, and obviously dependent on rainfall, temperature, and soils. This vertical zoning of life gave each plant its special character, its forms and mode of growth, so that you could tell from its shape and flower the kind of conditions required for its existence. Was this not the harmony he had envisioned finding in nature, this orderly balance among weather, earth, and life? If plants and animals were subject to such physical factors, was it not true also of people native to these and other regions?

He began to see what nobody had understood clearly before him: that life's forms and their grouping with one another are conditioned by physical factors in their environment, that atmospheric and geologic conditions need to be known if we are to learn the meaning behind the diversity of organic life. As in his student days he had described rocks and minerals in relation to plants, he now realized more fully that to classify and identify counted for little unless you understood how to relate such information to integrated natural processes.

Quito was admirably located for such explorations. "It seems probable," he wrote to his brother, "that the whole of the more elevated portion of the province is but one huge volcano, of which the peaks of Cotopaxi and Pichincha rise as giant summits whose craters are only vents for the subterranean lava." There the earth was shaken by paroxysms, as by the earthquake of 1797, which had killed forty thousand people. And yet the people of Quito were gay and lively; the town, Humboldt noticed, breathed an air of luxury and easy living "Nowhere perhaps is there a population so entirely given to the pursuit of pleasure. Thus can man get accustomed to sleep in peace on the brink of catastrophe."

In the neighborhood of Quito, Humboldt explored the volcanoes one by one, each demanding a fortnight or even three weeks. Finally, on June 9, 1802, he started for the ascent of Chimborazo, then held to be the tallest summit in the Americas. Bonpland, recovered from his fever, Carlos Montúfar, and an Indian were his companions. He reported:

Fortunately, the attempt to reach the summit of Chimborazo had been reserved for our last enterprise among the mountains of South America, for we had by then gained some experience and knew how far we could rely on our own strength. It is a peculiar characteristic of all such climbing trips in the Andes, that beyond the snow line Europeans are invariably left without guides just at the point . . . where help is most needed. . . .

With extreme exertion and considerable patience, we reached a greater height than we had dared to expect, for we were constantly climbing through clouds. In many places the ridge was not wider than eight or ten inches! To our left was a precipice of snow whose frozen crust glistened like glass. The angle of this icy slope was thirty degrees. On the right lay a fearful abyss, from 800 to 1,000 feet deep, huge masses of rocks projecting from it. . . . At certain places where it was very steep, we had to use both hands and feet, and the edges of the rock were so sharp that we were painfully cut, especially on our hands. To make things worse, I had for some time been suffering from a wound in my foot, caused by the repeated bites of the sandflea. . . .

One after another we began to feel sick from nausea and giddiness, which was far more distressing than our breathing difficulties. Such symptoms were not particularly alarming, for we had grown familiar with them from previous experience. . . . All these symptoms vary greatly in different individuals according to age, constitution, tenderness of skin, and previous training. Yet in the same person they constitute a kind of gauge for the amount of rarefied air and for the absolute height that has been attained.

Suddenly the stratum of mist which had hidden every distant object began to dissipate. Once more we recognized the dome-shaped summit of Chimborazo, now very close. What a grand and solemn spectacle! The very sight of it renewed our strength. The rocky ridge, sprinkled here and there with patches of snow, became somewhat wider. Sure-footed, we hurried on, when all of a sudden our progress was stopped by a ravine some four hundred feet deep and sixty wide. This barrier proved insurmountable, as the softness of the snow prevented all attempts at scaling the walls. It was now an hour after noon. We set up the barometer with great care. Air temperature was three below freezing, but from our long residence in the tropics even this amount of cold was quite benumbing. Our boots were wet with melted snow. According to the barometric formula given by Laplace, we had now reached an elevation of 19,286 feet. We were, at this height, a short way from the summit, a distance equal to three times the height of St. Peter's cathedral at Rome.[2]

We felt isolated as a balloon. A few rock lichens were seen above the snow lines, at a height of 16,920 feet. The last green moss we noticed about 2,600 feet lower down. A butterfly was captured by M. Bonpland at a height of 15,000 feet, and a fly was seen 1,600 feet higher. . . . We did not see any condors, which had been so numerous on the slopes of Pichincha. . . . In descending, we ran into a violent hailstorm, and afterwards into a snowstorm so fearful that the path was soon covered by several inches of snow. . . . At a few minutes past two we reached the spot where we had left the mules.

He had dared and achieved what in his time and age few human beings believed possible and no mortal had previously accomplished. As for the highest of all mountain ranges, the Himalayas, it would be another thirty years before the first surveyors would attempt exploration there. As a feat of endurance, Humboldt's ascent of Chimborazo proved that man was capable of reaching the top of the world. Yet to him, the scientist, climbing for the sake of establishing a world record would have been meaningless. His own description of the ascent gives few clues about the precise motives for this extreme exertion. Mist and snowstorms had concealed the view, preventing a comprehensive picture of land forms and vegetation. He

[2] The actual height of Chimborazo, the tallest summit in the Andes of Ecuador, is 20,577 feet.

had come to know them on preceding climbs of various summits, notably that of the Pichincha crater. On Chimborazo he could not well have hoped for a commanding view, it being the rainy season.

That he attempted the ascent, not once, but twice, indicates how determined he was to scale the highest peak in the Andes near Quito. It was as if Chimborazo exercised an irresistible attraction by the sheer majesty of its remote and shining peak. Remoteness and beauty are powerful magnets for a person bent on penetrating the unknown. To participate, if only for moments, in an earthly beyond may have been felt by Humboldt as a cosmic experience, an attempt to come closer to an image of transcendental proportions. Its appeal, essentially irrational, lay in the supreme heightening of a life experience through a singular effort.

In the annals of mountain exploration the ascent of Chimborazo marks the beginning of a long and exciting history of adventures, which in our time has found its dramatic climax in the conquest of Mount Everest. Much as Humboldt later wished to visit the Himalayas, he was obliged to leave its first exploration to the English and to some of his pupils. When the first news of the Himalayan surveys reached him, he wrote to his friend Heinrich Berghaus, on November 25, 1828:

All my life I prided myself on the fact that of all mortals I had reached the highest point on earth, I mean on the slopes of Chimborazo! It was therefore with a certain feeling of envy that I learned of the accomplishments achieved by Webb and his companions in the mountains of India, whose enormous height was generally conjectured, but had never been verified by instrument readings. I have consoled myself over the achievements in the Himalayas in the justified assumption that my labors in America gave the English a first impulse to pay more attention to these snow mountains than had been accorded them over the last century and a half. . . . I said to myself the Andean ranges of Quito keep their right to be among the highest in the New World, and among them the mighty Chimborazo.

The opening phase of Himalayan exploration was inspired, and actively supported by Humboldt when, in 1854, his pupils, the three brothers Emil, Hermann, and Adolph Schlagintweit, of Munich, started on an expedition to Tibet and central Asia. Humboldt secured substantial backing for them from William IV of Prussia—all the more remarkable because the benefits of this pioneering expedition accrued to the government of India under Queen Victoria's early reign.

The first reports of Chimborazo's conquest reached Paris a few months after the ascent, when excerpts from Humboldt's letters were published in scientific journals. In such moments of supreme achievement he might have wished for the speedier dispatch of news. Mails were lost so frequently that within three years Humboldt had received only six letters from his brother. In the summer of 1801, when Goethe anxiously asked Caroline what sort of news she might have, he was distressed to learn that she had none. A few French and Spanish journals had given scattered accounts, and a magazine in Berlin had managed to gather a few reports from Humboldt's scientific friends.

I never tire [wrote Humboldt to his brother] of writing letters to Europe, though I am convinced that few ever reach their

point of destination. To be sure, mail goes weekly from larger
towns to various ports. However, after my letters have waited
there for six months at a time for the departure of a ship, it
happens that through exaggerated precaution on the part of
a ship's captain they are cast overboard upon the slightest
provocation of danger. Letters from Europe do not fare any
better.

The thought of accidental death caused him anguish
and worry. In such moments he felt like disposing of his
collections and notebooks to his friends. On February 21,
1801 he wrote to Willdenow from Havana:

In this journey around the world when the seas are infested
with pirates, and when passports of neutral nations are as
little respected as ships of non-warring countries, nothing
makes me more anxious than the safety of manuscripts and
herbariums. It is really quite uncertain, almost unlikely, that
both of us, Bonpland and myself, will ever return alive. . . .
How sad if by such misfortune the fruits of all our labors
should be lost forever! . . . In order to forestall this, we have
made copies of plant descriptions (two volumes contain some
1,400 new and rare species). One manuscript we retain; the
copy is being sent in parts through a French Vice-Consul to
Bonpland's brother at La Rochelle, France. We divided the
plant collection into three parts, as we have doublets and
even triplets of all of them. We carry only a small herbarium
with us for comparative studies. A second, belonging to Bonpland (with whom I naturally share everything) has already
gone to France, and the third—two boxes containing crypto-
gams and grasses, some 1,600 different species—I am sending
to London today by way of Mr. John Fraser of Charles-
ton. . . . Should I perish, I would want Delambre to publish
my astronomical, Freiesleben or Leopold von Buch my geo-

logical, Sheerer my physical and chemical, Blumenbach my zoological results, and you, my good friend, I hope, my botanical works under Bonpland's and my name. My brother will forward the manuscripts to each of you. . . . I stick to my promise that all, but all, plants collected by me on this journey are yours. *I never want to own anything.* The only favor I ask is that subsequent to my return I reserve the right of publication and that my herbarium should not be entrusted to you until after publication or after my death.

In the same letter Humboldt sketched an outline of his coming publications. The first volume would render an account of the travels

from a physical and moral point of view, touching only upon such topics of general interest as would be expected to interest the well-educated reader: the characteristics of Indian races, their language and customs, the trade of the colonies, descriptions of towns and aspects of the country, agricultural practices, data on mountain heights, and meteorological results. Then, in separate volumes, 1, *Geology* and earth structure; 2, *Astronomical* observations, determinations of latitude and longitude, observations on the planet Jupiter, experiments in light-refraction; 3, *Physics and Chemistry:* studies in the chemical constitution of the atmosphere, hygrometric and barometric phenomena, pathology, electricity, and the excitability of animal organs; 4, *Zoological description* of new species of apes, crocodiles, birds, insects, anatomy of marine animals; 5, *Botanical researches,* in conjunction with Bonpland, to include not merely the identification of new species and genera, but descriptions, after Linnæus's system, of all those species already known, of which we have seen more specimens than other observers, a type of work which will, I hope, contain between 5,000 and 6,000 varieties. . . .

Such was the first vision of a publication project so huge and ambitious that it would engage Humboldt for more than twenty years. Its scope was staggering. It makes one wonder whether, at that time, he and Bonpland had any clear perception of the great sacrifices such monumental publications would demand.

7

On Inca Trails in Peru

SOUTHEAST OF QUITO rises the dramatic landmark of Cotopaxi volcano, its graceful ice-capped cone an ominous reminder of geologic catastrophe. A devastating eruption in 1769 showered ashes so thickly over the land that people had to use lanterns in broad daylight. But in the autumn of 1802 Cotopaxi seemed to be in a relatively relaxed mood. Humboldt felt tempted to climb to its summit. His party, consisting of Bonpland and Montúfar, came close to the snow line, but was stopped at 14,000 feet by treacherous, soggy ground. Yet Humboldt managed to determine the height of the summit by trigonometric surveying, from which he took time off to make a sketch "of the most majestic and awe-inspiring view I ever beheld in either hemisphere." For him to sketch a landscape was both scientific expediency—a means for synthesizing scattered observations of land forms and flora—and æsthetic pleasure. This sketch was later improved upon by a young German artist in Rome, who, under Humboldt's direction, may have given it more of a romantic touch than Humboldt had originally intended.

From the base of Cotopaxi the party proceeded to the upper Amazon. As it reached the ancient Inca ruins of Lacatunga and Riobamba, Humboldt reported to his brother:

"At Riobamba we spent a few weeks with a brother of Carlos Montúfar who resides there as *corregidor*, a magistrate by royal appointment. There we made a remarkable discovery. We learned that an Indian prince, Leandro Zapla, who resides at Likan, and a man of considerable culture, owns sixteenth-century manuscripts by one of his ancestors. . . . They are written in Purugayan, a language commonly spoken in this province before the Incas came. These manuscripts fortunately have been translated into Spanish by one of his ancestors."

What fascinated him most about these codices was an account of the violent eruption of a volcano, the Nevado de Altár, and the interpretation that the Indian diviners had given to this event. To them the catastrophe was the advent of a new order of gods, heralding an inevitable change in the fate of the Indian nation.

"The discovery of this manuscript," the letter continues, "revived in me the wish to study the early history of the aborigines of these countries, a desire first aroused in me by the traditions I collected at Parime, and by the hieroglyphs [petroglyphs] encountered in the jungle of the Casiquiare River. . . ." The codices spoke of a glamorous past, a world wonderfully rich in cultural achievements. The Spanish conquerors had been utterly blind to such treasures, and consequently Europe had remained ignorant of America's ancient past.

Naturally his brother would understand his enthusiasm over Indian languages.

The Carib language, for instance . . . combines richness with grace, power, and tenderness. It knows how to convey abstract ideas like eternity, future, and existence . . . it is able to express numerical systems in words. I am devoting myself to the Inca language still commonly spoken around Quito and Lima. Young men make use of it when Castilian proves insufficient for expressing their romantic feelings to girls. These languages suffice to give evidence of a higher civilization before the Spanish conquest in 1492. . . . Moreover, the priests of those ages possessed sufficient knowledge of astronomy to draw a meridian line and to observe the actual moment of the solstice. They changed the lunar into the solar year by the intercalation of days, and I have in my possession a stone in the form of a heptagon which was found at Bogotá, and which was employed by them in the calculation of their calendar.

To Humboldt it seemed that the calendric systems of Incas and Aztecs furnished a clue to the origins of the American Indians. That they came from Asia seemed apparent from certain analogies between the Chinese-Tibetan concept of the zodiac and its American counterpart. It was surprising how the animal signs of tiger, snake, dog, hare, and bird corresponded with each other. Not only that, but later Humboldt felt amazed at how similar certain legends were; for instance, the myth of the four disasters of the world and the dispersal of mankind by a deluge. Certain religious symbols used in temple decorations of Yucatán, and Guatemala looked strangely familiar to Humboldt, acquainted as he was with the ancient art of India. In the *Narrative of Travels,* Humbolt wrote:

I regard the existence of a former intercourse between the people of western America and those of eastern Asia as more than probable, though it is impossible at the present time to say by what route and with which of the tribes of Asia this influence was established. A small number of individuals of the cultured hierarchical castes may perhaps have sufficed to effect great changes in the social conditions of western America. . . . We know that adventurers navigated the eastern Chinese seas in search of a remedial agent capable of making man immortal. May not accident have led to similar expeditions to Alaska and California? In the beginning of the sixteenth century it was even believed (by Gómara) that fragments of ships from Cathay had been found on the coast of southern California. . . . We know as yet too little of the languages of America to renounce entirely the hope that amid their many varieties some idiom may be discovered which has been spoken with certain modifications in the interiors of Asia and America.

This concept of an Asiatic origin of American Indian cultures anticipated a theory advanced in our time by scholars like Robert von Heine-Geldern, Gordon Ekholm, and Miguel Covarrubias, all of whom have revealed specific affinities of religious art symbols and ornamental styles between ancient Oriental and American cultures. Humboldt's clear vision of the problem is all the more astounding when we recall that in his time Europe was unaware of the great civilizing achievements of pre-Columbian traditions. By calling attention to their importance, Humboldt contributed to a new orientation toward America, whose natives had been pictured as barbarians devoid of any higher aspirations. Humboldt's writings on the subject inspired men like John Lloyd Stephens to explore the splendors of ancient Maya temples in Yucatán, and prompted William Hickling Prescott to write his *Conquest of Mexico*.

For Humboldt, admiration of the greatness of the Inca and Aztec empires was an effective argument against racial prejudice and a warning to those who perpetrated cruelties in the name of political expedience and of Christ. "A darker shade of skin color is not a badge of inferiority. . . . The barbarism of nations is the direct conse-

quence of oppression by internal despotism or foreign
conquest. It is always accompanied by progressive impov-
erishment and a diminution of public fortune. Free and
powerful institutions remove such dangers." Humboldt's
humanitarian faith held that the iron fist of colonial administration must loosen its grip. The time was near for
mestizos and Indians to take matters into their own hands.
Once they were liberated, the riches of South and Middle
America would help support a new political and social
order in which the Indian element could reassert its rights.
Had it not proved its worth in ancient times, and was the
concern about Inca ruins on this account not of para-
mount interest?

How the Inca palace at Paramo excited his admiration!
With its commanding view it had been laid out as ingeniously and pleasingly as an English country estate.
Nearby he was shown a round stone with intricate designs
which the Indians had venerated as an image of the sun.
It had been inlaid with a mirror of a polished iron mineral
possessing magic qualities so famous that Incas had traveled from as distant a place as Cuzco, the empire's capital,
to visit it.

The Inca roads, Humboldt noted, had not been as
solidly constructed as the highways of Imperial Rome,
yet he found their foundations paved with neatly hewn
volcanic rocks sufficiently hard to have survived the ages.
The travel narrative is full of praise for the vestiges of
roadside shelters, with their servants' quarters and baths.
"The solemn, bleak aspect of these Peruvian highland
deserts contrasts remarkably, and so unexpectedly, with
the wonderful remains of Inca roads." In some places
Humboldt found them cemented by gravel as if built on

"McAdam's plan." The Incas had had no wheeled carriages; these highways had served for marching troops, for the conveyance of loads, and for flocks of lightly burdened llamas.

Consequently, long flights of steps were constructed at intervals, with resting-places, to overcome steep slopes. When Pizarro and Almagro conquered Peru, they availed themselves of these military roads, and the Spanish cavalry found these steps formidable obstacles, especially in the early phase of the conquest, when the Spaniards made use of horses only.

And to think that Spaniards had destroyed these splendid roads by quarrying their pavements! More disastrous still for native economy was the Spaniards' disregard of the masterly irrigation works the Incas had maintained, the terraced fields and aqueducts now falling into disrepair. The very thought of it excited him to visions of ancient Egypt and Mesopotamia, where civilizations had flourished by the harnessing of water-power for irrigation. For most of Europe this was no problem, and yet what could be done to improve upon its old-fashioned farming methods? Had the Incas not given an example by using organic fertilizers? He must look into this possibility when in Lima.

Meanwhile the party descended to the upper Amazon along the Río de Guancabamba, being forced to ford the stream twenty-seven times in one day. So strong was the current that the mules were in constant danger of being swept away with their precious loads of manuscripts, dried plants, and other specimens.

It is delightful [Humboldt wrote in his *Views of Nature*] gradually to descend through the more genial climate of the

Chinchona, or Quina, woods of Loxa [Loja], into the plains of
the upper Amazon. There an unknown world rich in magnificent vegetation unfolds itself. The little town of Loxa has
given its name to the most efficacious of all fever barks, the
quina, or *cascarilla fina de Loxa*. This bark is the precious
produce of the tree. . . . It became known in Europe about
the middle of the seventeenth century. According to some accounts, it was brought to Madrid in 1640, when the Countess
de Chinchón, the wife of the Viceroy of Peru, arrived from
Lima, where she had been cured of an intermittent fever. The
tree is felled in its first flowering season, or from the fourth
to seventh year of its growth, depending on whether it grew
from a shoot or a seed. At the time of my journey in Peru the
quantity gathered of the *Chinchona condaminea* [first described by Humboldt and Bonpland] amounted to only one
hundred weight, or eleven thousand Spanish pounds. To procure this small supply, no less than 800 to 900 trees were
cut every year. The produce is shipped from Pyata on the
Pacific coast via Cape Horn to Cádiz for use by the Spanish
court. . . . This beautiful tree is adorned with leaves five
inches long and two broad . . . and as it spreads its upper
branches, the foliage glistens from a distance with a peculiar
reddish tint when moved by the wind.

The headwaters of the upper Amazon provided channels of communication between the coastal town of Trujillo and the interior. Indian couriers wrapped the mail
in a large cotton cloth, which they wore as a turban when
they let themselves drift downstream. A letter carried in
this fashion reached Humboldt after his return to Paris
and reminded him then of a marvelous scene when an entire party of jungle Indians—men, women, and children—
floated, swimming fashion, to the town of Tomependa.
There the Humboldt party had camped on a sandbank at

the confluence of the Río Chamaya and the Amazon. Downstream lay the celebrated narrows of Pongo de Manseriche, a rocky ravine where his boat was caught in driftwood and tropical foliage.

Surveying and plant-collecting had kept Humboldt and Bonpland seventeen days on the Amazon. Humboldt's magnetic observations had by then been extended sufficiently south of the equator to indicate the line that separates the terrestrial magnetic fields of the Northern and Southern Hemispheres. The route now led via Cajamarca to Trujillo on the Peruvian coast, enabling Humboldt to fix the geographic position of the magnetic equator at 7° 27′ southern latitude, and 81° 8′ western longtitude.[1]

As they were crossing the Andes back to the coast, a weird landscape opened near Gualgayoc, with fantastic rock pinnacles towering above a mountain completely tunneled by silver mines. There Humboldt watched Indians carrying the ore-baskets down steep, slippery paths to the smelters below. There seemed to be no end to the stream of silver which had flowed from here into the coffers of the Spanish Crown. No less than thirty-two million piasters' worth of silver had been mined in thirty-one years, not to mention the uncounted millions of silver and gold forcibly extracted from the Incas by Pizarro and his gang. It was an eerie place, where people spent their lives in reckless gambling and gaudy display of their quickly

---

[1] Humboldt's interest in earth magnetism had been aroused in Paris when H. Borda, of the Bureau of Longitudes, suggested that he take along new instruments for observation of changes in the earth's magnetic field. With Charles A. Coulomb's discovery of magnetic meridians and the subdivisibility of a magnet's force, such studies received a major impetus from Humboldt's American, and subsequent Russian, observations, which led to his discovery of the law of declining magnetic intensity between the earth's magnetic poles.

carned riches. "Here," Humboldt commented, "one is constantly reminded of the anecdote related by one of Pizarro's soldiers, who complained that he had lost in one night's gambling a large piece of the sun, meaning a plate of gold he had obtained in the plunder of the temple at Cuzco."

Going from there to the ancient Inca city of Cajamarca turned out to be a harrowing adventure. A biting wind, with hail and rain, blinded their eyes, the mules finding it hard to proceed. Suddenly they looked down on a wide valley. Amidst cultivated fields and gardens dotted with willow groves and bright flowers lay the ruins of Cajamarca, the palace and fortress of the Inca ruler Atahualpa. In the principal building they were shown the room where, in November 1532, the unfortunate ruler was imprisoned by the Spaniards for nine months. The guide pointed out the wall on which the Inca prince marked the height to which he would fill the room with gold on condition of being set free. A young Spaniard, Garcilaso de la Vega, who left Peru in 1560, had estimated that the treasures brought from the temple of the Sun at Cuzco, and other Inca places, amounted to almost four million gold ducats up to August 29, 1533, the day of the Inca ruler's death. Some of his descendants, Humboldt reported, were said to be still living in the town.

They lived in great poverty, but nevertheless contented and resigned to their hard, unmerited fate. Their descent from Atahualpa in the female line has never been doubted at Cajamarca, but traces of beard would seem to indicate some mixture of Spanish blood. Atahualpa left two children, a son who died young and a daughter who became the mistress of Francisco Pizarro and bore him a son. Besides the family of Astorpilca, with whom I became acquainted in Cajamarca, there were the families of Carguaraicos and Titu Buscamaya, who were regarded as descendants of the Inca dynasty.

The son of the cacique Astorpilca was an amiable youth of seventeen who conducted Humboldt's party through the ruins of the place of his ancestors.

Although he was living in the utmost poverty, his fantasy was filled with thoughts of underground splendor and golden treasures which, he assured us, lay hidden under the rubbish over which we walked. He told us that one of his ancestors once blindfolded the eyes of his wife and then led her through many intricate passages into the underground gardens of the Incas. There she beheld imitations in purest gold of trees laden with leaves and fruits, and birds perched on their branches. Among other things she saw Atahualpa's golden sedan chair. . . . The husband commanded his wife not to touch any of these enchanted treasures, reminding her that the time fixed for the restoration of the Inca empire had not yet arrived, and that whosoever should touch these objects would perish that same night. The youth's golden dreams and fancies were based on recollections and traditions transmitted from remote times. Golden gardens, alluded to by the youth, have been described by various writers who claim to have seen them, such as Cieza de León, Parmento, Garcilaso, and other early historians of the conquest. . . . The son of Astorpilca assured me that underground, a little to the right of the spot on which I then stood, there was a large datura tree, or *guanto*, in full flower, exquisitely made of gold wire and plates of gold, and that its branches overspread the Inca's chair. The morbid faith with which the youth asserted his belief in this fabulous story made a profound and melancholy impression on me.

Humboldt asked him whether he did not want to dig for these treasures.

The young man's answer expressed such quiet resignation, peculiar to the natives in this country, that I wrote it down in Spanish: "Such a desire (*tal antojo*) never comes to me. My father said it would be sinful. If we had the golden branches, with all their golden fruit, our white neighbors would hate and injure us. We have a little field and good wheat!"

In the mind of the Indians the idea of digging for Inca treasures was closely connected with the prospects of restoring their dynasty. Some natives believed that descendants of the last ruler had settled farther east in Guayana, where in their belief existed the golden city of Manoa. To conquer it, Humboldt reported, Sir Walter Raleigh outfitted an expedition there to "establish a garrison of three to four thousand English, and to levy from the Emperor of Guayana, a descendant of the Inca Huayna Capac, an annual tribute of 300,000 pounds sterling, as the price for the promised restoration to the throne at Cuzco and Cajamarca."

There in Peru, Humboldt felt in the grip of history. He recalled his boyhood, when he had read the travel narratives of Captain James Cook and of Vasco Núñez de Balboa, the first white man to behold the Pacific from America. Ever since then Humboldt had yearned for the moment when he too would look out over this ocean like Núñez de Balboa. And now that the moment was near, he could hardly wait, and must hurry to reach a vantage point on the road down the western slopes of the Andes.

The sky, which had so long been obscured, brightened suddenly. A sharp southwest breeze dispersed the mist, revealing a dark-blue heaven between narrow lines of high, feathery clouds. The entire western slope of the cordillera, adjacent to Chorrillos and Cadcas, and the plains of Chala and Molinos as far as the coast near Trujillo, lay extended before our eyes. Now, for the first time, we had our view of the Pacific. We saw it distinctly in the glitter of a vast light, an immeasurable expanse of ocean.

So overwhelming was the view to him and his companions that none remembered to read the barometer! The sparkling sea rolling against the desert sands of Peru evoked the fantasies of unknown shores in China and the Philippines.

From that lookout they descended to the coast at Trujillo, following it southward to Lima, arriving there on October 23, 1802. They stayed for a little over two months, repacking their plant and rock collections for shipment to Mexico and Europe. Lima then the seat of the Viceroy of Peru, was a small and somewhat dilapidated town. In a letter written to the Governor of Jaén in Peru, and dated January 18, 1803, Humboldt gave vent to his unfavorable impressions of the place:

Lima has declined greatly in comparison with Buenos Aires, Santiago de Chile, and Arequipa. Here I never saw well-furnished homes or well-dressed women. If its families are in poor circumstances, the reason must lie in economic conditions and gambling. With the exception of a theater and the bullring, which is beautiful, there are no public amusements. At night it is impossible to travel the streets by carriage, obstructed as they are by mongrel dogs and donkey carcasses. Gambling and separation of the family disrupt all social union. In all of Lima there are no social gatherings of more than eight people at a time. . . . It would seem to be more distant from the rest of Peru than London is. A cold egotism is found here, so that no one cares about anybody else's sufferings. There are no other means to go to Acapulco than the ship *Causino*, which is due to arrive in a few days, returning shortly to that port. We expect to leave in about five or six weeks, and meanwhile we wait patiently, battling against mosquitoes.

Lima's port, Callao, was a regular port of call for small sailing vessels plying between it and the Mexican harbor of Acapulco. The ships carried limited amounts of copper, sugar, oil, Chile wine, and quinine bark, and picked up cacao in the intermediate port of Guayaquil. Such merchandise would find its way to Mexico, Havana, the Philippines and Europe. On the return trip from Acapulco the cargo consisted of woolens from the town of Querétaro and cochineal dye from Oaxaca in Mexico, or contraband goods from the East Indies shipped by galleon to Acapulco from the Philippines. Next to the route round Cape Horn, mariners feared most the run between Callao and Acapulco, for its prolonged calms. The run to Guayaquil would take from six to eight days, depending on whether or not the vessels struck calms and unfavorable currents. Humboldt reported that a boat had been hopelessly becalmed for several weeks so that its crew abandoned it for lack of provisions.

Many visitors in Lima have wished for the skies to clear when ocean fogs shroud the city for weeks on end, and Humboldt was no exception. Ever since his arrival he had cursed the clouds, waiting eagerly for clear nights so that he might check the town's longitude by astronomic observations. More exciting still was the prospect of observing the transit of the planet Mercury. Thank heavens, the skies cleared at last! Humboldt set up his instruments at the port of Callao, and on November 9, 1802 observed the passage of Mercury over the sun's disk. Once more his telescope had enabled him to correct geographic positions, and the transit of Mercury was to add much-needed information as to the planet's speed of revolution around the sun and the shape of its orbit. The significance Humboldt attached to this event is evident from several letters in which he mentioned it along with his botanical studies of the cinchona tree and his survey of the Orinoco. The eminent French astronomer Laplace would be delighted to have Humboldt's observations on Mercury, with which to check his theory of celestial mechanics.

For Humboldt the stars over Lima were lucky in more than one respect, for it was there that his attention was caught by a curious substance known as *guano*. The ancient Peruvians had known its fertilizing capacities for hundreds of years. It was found along the coast, and especially on the islands nearby, where lay the nesting-grounds of innumerable bird colonies, the guano producers. In collecting samples and having them shipped to Paris, Humboldt could have had no other object than to introduce guano fertilizer to European agriculture. Back in Paris, he asked his friends, the chemists Vauquelin and Fourcroy, for analysis of his samples. When they turned out to be richer in nitrogen and phosphate than any other known fertilizer, he felt convinced that guano would help revitalize soils impoverished through agelong exploitation. Here was gold different from what Pizarro had sent to Madrid. Better crops were sorely needed by a world demanding more food for its fast-growing populations. But how was he to persuade farmers to use this new fertilizer? They would certainly not read his scientific monograph on the occurrence and chemical properties of guano. For this idea to become truly effective Humboldt relied ultimately on Justus Liebig, the eminent German chemist, founder of agricultural chemistry. Liebig laid the scientific foundations for the use of organic fertilizers, and English chemists were to follow his lead by experimenting with guano in various types of soil.

When John C. Nesbit made known in 1841 that the fertilizing properties of one ton of guano equaled those of thirty-three tons of farmyard manure, farmers in Europe and America clamored for large quantities of this Peruvian guano. Suddenly Peru, famed for its gold and silver, found itself swamped by guano-buyers, who were barely able to get their orders filled. There did not seem to be sufficient shipping tonnage. In 1844, ten thousand tons of guano arrived in England, and a few years later American farmers began to profit from the first bumper crops. Then the aging Humboldt was to recall his visit to Lima, and he may have sighed a little over the guano boom that he had let pass without earning a penny by it.

At last the small sailing vessel was ready to carry Humboldt's party from Callao to Guayaquil and Acapulco. Young Don Carlos Montúfar had by now been accepted as a permanent companion, and while he was not a scientist, he had somehow managed to impress Humboldt and Bonpland with his gaiety and sense of adventure. The climbing of Chimborazo had made him a member of a team which, on the face of it, could ill afford to be weighted down by a mere travel-companion. That he was more than that, a friend as resourceful as Humboldt might have wished, is evident from the grief that Humboldt experienced when the young Ecuadorian finally returned from Europe to his native land.

The voyage to Guayaquil proved rich in opportunities for Humboldt to survey the coast and offshore islands. This time it was the cold current that flows along the Peruvian coast to which he paid special attention. To measure its flow and temperature was like feeling the geographic pulse of all the lands along the coast of South America. It accounted for their climate and native economies, and had given geographic directions to conquerors and settlers for uncounted generations. But to have measured this important current was not the same as having discovered it, as Humboldt himself would point out later. "I may claim solely the merit of having been the first to measure its temperature and rate of flow," Humboldt wrote to his friend Heinrich Berghaus in 1840. Why call it Humboldt Current when it had been known without a name to sailors for three centuries? But the name had already been put on a map by the geographer Karl Ritter, and thereafter it was accepted geographic nomenclature, a reminder of the man who first recognized the current's geographic properties.

As the ship left Guayaquil in January 1803, the horizon was darkened by thunderous explosions of Cotopaxi. They came at regular intervals like the distant rumble of artillery fire. Long after the boat had lost sight of South America, the volcanic thunder rolled over the ocean, accompanying their ship for several days with awesome salute as if in recognition of the services that the naturalist had rendered to South America.

8

The Challenge of Mexican
Pyramids and Volcanoes

ORDINARILY THE ARRIVAL of a ship from South
America would not have attracted much attention at Acapulco, but when the small frigate *Atlante* cast anchor there
on March 23, 1803, it caused an unusual commotion about
the wharves. Never before had the port officials seen such
strange baggage; nor did it seem likely that its contents
would ever be duplicated, for it included minerals, plants,
mastodon bones, skins of jungle creatures, and specimens
of birds. The owners of this motley collection of scientific
goods, Humboldt and Bonpland, stepped ashore visibly
tanned from thirty-three days of ocean voyage.

The passage had been stormy, the weather foul all the
way; and on top of that, Humboldt had discovered that the
captain's reckoning lay too far to the west. There could be
small doubt but that Acapulco had been incorrectly placed
on the map, which was all the more disconcerting because
Mexico's commerce with the Orient depended on accurate
sailing charts. There was dire need, Humboldt explained
to the port commander, to survey Acapulco Bay and to
obtain accurate astronomical determinations of various
points along the coast.

The baggage had not even been unloaded when the
indefatigable Humboldt was seen setting up his instruments. A few days later it appeared that the port lay many
miles farther west than the maps had indicated. Not that

this would have made any difference to the four thousand mestizos and Negroes of the miserable town, which then enjoyed a dubious reputation as a hide-out for escaped convicts and slaves. But it mattered greatly to Mexican map-makers, whose trigonometric surveys were partly based on such measurements as included the port of Acapulco.

Tropical heat and liquor rendered its people all but insensitive to what was going on, save for two events: the arrival and the departure of the Spanish galleon from Manila. On such days Acapulco awakened from its tropical stupor. No sooner had the galleon unloaded its cargo than suddenly the wharf reflected the glamour of the Orient: bales of Indian muslin and calico prints, Chinese silks, curios, bundles of spices, and strange-smelling perfumes. An express courier was seen galloping on the road toward Mexico City to spread the news of the safe arrival. Within a short time the road to Acapulco was choked with hundreds of carts and riders hurrying over winding trails across mountains and streams, the cartwheels grinding through sands and thickets. The race for the Oriental cargo was on.

On such days Acapulco's population was likely to double. Crowds of buyers, merchants, and speculators would throng around the pier in a wild spree of bargaining. But it often happened, Humboldt reported, that the first-comers were sorely disappointed to hear that the cargo had already been earmarked for a group of speculators in Mexico City. Such transactions were known as the "Chinese fraud," a reckless gamble involving fabulous investments worth a million piasters, some two hundred thousand dollars. Merchants, church corporations, and wealthy aristo-

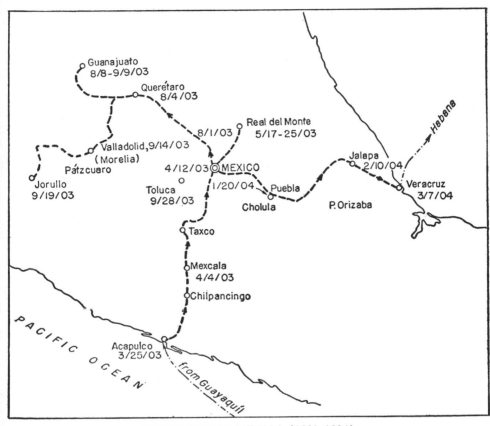

HUMBOLDT IN MEXICO (1803–1804)

crats pooled their resources to corner the market on commodities that would fetch handsome profits in Mexico, the West Indies, and Europe. For months the cargo of the Spanish galleon was the talk of the land, and well it might be, considering that it had once more escaped the hazards of crossing the Pacific. For a vessel of 1,200 or 1,500 tons, the voyage from Manila would take from three to four months. It would leave Manila in the middle of July or at the beginning of August, and would return with a cargo of silver, coined or in bars, cochineal dye, oil, wine, and Spanish wool valued up to four hundred thousand dollars.

The arrival of the Humboldt party provided a welcome change at a time when the port lay deserted amid its reddish hills and palm-studded beaches.

We climbed up naked rocks of strange appearance [Humboldt wrote]. They were scarcely sixty meters [197 feet] above sea-level, and appeared to be torn by the prolonged effects of the earthquakes so frequent on this coast. The earthquakes, which are felt in a southern direction, are attributed to submarine volcanoes, for the people there come to notice, as I often did at Callao, that the sea suddenly becomes agitated to an alarming degree in the most calm and serene weather when not a breath of wind is blowing. . . . On my trip to Acapulco I was constantly engaged in improving the points of reckoning by observations of the sun and moon. Enormous errors in longitude caused by strong currents render navigation in these latitudes equally long and expensive.

The improvement of sailing charts was all the more necessary because English and American vessels had begun to follow the route of sperm whales and of the fur trade along the California coast. From fifteen to twenty vessels had reached the Northwest coast in 1804, forerunners of the proud fleet of China clippers which would proceed to Canton and Macao to exchange their cargoes for tea and raw silk. Thence they would return around Africa to their home ports of Boston and Nantucket.

About April 1 everything was ready for the journey to the capital of Mexico. Marching and riding through the mountains of Guerrero is never comfortable. For Humboldt's party it must have been tough going, what with the temperature at 104 degrees in the shade and the dusty trail leading through an oven of granite rocks. At Chilpancingo they had their first cooling breeze and a refreshing breath of pine-scented air. All this time Humboldt had charted his route, measuring with compass and barometer the exact positions of geologic outcrops, the thickness and composition of rock formations. Nights were given to the careful astronomic observations so essential for reliable calculations of geographic co-ordinates. This surveying resulted in the first geologic cross-section ever based on instrument-readings, a graphic illustration of rock structures as observed over a measured distance indicating their relative thickness and position to each other, and marked by specific symbols for their distinctive features. Such cross-sections, or geologic graphs, had previously been attempted in Europe by a few geologists, but none of them had seen the necessity for rendering a graph of geologic structures based on accurate co-ordinates. There on the hot winding trail between Acapulco and Mexico City, Humboldt had produced a device so practical and essential for geological surveying that no prospector for oil and ores would want to be without it.

From Chilpancingo the travelers proceeded to Taxco, the famous mining town. As its quaint houses appeared, precariously perched on steep slopes, Humboldt's heart must have missed a beat. There lay one of Mexico's greatest silver mines, mountains tunneled in all directions, a subterranean store of fabulous riches. That Mexico, or New Spain, produced two thirds of the world's silver Humboldt had known since his Freiberg days, but Taxco would teach him how fantastically adventurous mining can be.

The story of the Frenchman José de Laborde was still fresh in people's minds. Laborde had come to Mexico a poor young man eager for riches. The shaft of La Cañada at Taxco produced silver in such quantities that Laborde boasted he would pave the road from Veracruz to Mexico City with silver coins if His Catholic Majesty would venture to visit New Spain. Laborde invested some of his money in the building of a church at Taxco so ornate in its splendor as to rival the largest in the land. He was of a reckless disposition, a gambler whose Midas touch could not possibly endure. When the silver veins gave out, their owner asked for the return of the bejeweled tabernacle he had given to the church. The church agreed, and Laborde hastened north to Zacatecas to tempt fortune again. At first his new quest for silver was not successful. He sank one more shaft, gambling with his last cash, and struck it rich all over again. Laborde's only child having entered a convent, he bequeathed his enormous fortune to the Church so that Masses could be celebrated for his soul, which had been so greedily tormented by silver all his life.

Humboldt lost no time in studying mines and mining

methods. His reports on Taxco were later published in his *Political Essay on the Kingdom of New Spain,* and what he had to say about mining has an authoritative ring and an unmistakable concern for human suffering. Indian laborers were treated like dogs, panting day in and day out under the heaviest loads of ore, recklessly blasted by old-fashioned mining methods. Horrified, Humboldt watched men over sixty and boys of twelve crawling through ill-ventilated tunnels—an inferno of powder-smoke and dust, hot as hell. At Taxco mining was as old-fashioned as at the time of the Spanish conquest, and powder was used with such abandon as to make mine operations not only unnecessarily dangerous, but also wasteful in terms of operating costs.

To this day, Taxco has preserved much of the somber tradition of mining. Indian miners can be seen walking over cobbled streets, their lamps swinging gaily as they return from their shifts. They look a bit grimy, as all miners do, but they seem healthy and contented, reminding the visitor how Mexico has progressed since Humboldt's visit, an advancement to be measured in terms of payrolls, social-security laws, and all-around better living. No quainter place may be found in America to remember Humboldt. The *taxqueños* still show the house where he is supposed to have stayed, its stone-flagged patio leading to a terraced garden where flowers grow in profusion to frame one's view of tiled houses and barren hills. Here Humboldt sat with his two companions enjoying a cool evening after a day's work underground, and the nights were brilliant with stars, once more resplendent in their familiar constellations.

From Taxco the road wound its way across limestone

mountains to Cuernavaca, where the great Hernán Cortés had built his first sugar plant. From there it was a day's ride up the forested divide to a lookout above the Valley of Mexico. Before them lay a plain dotted with lakes that had mirrored a cavalcade of civilizations: pyramid-builders, Toltecs, Aztecs, and Spaniards. And there in the blue haze of the afternoon was Mexico City, a cluster of churches, palaces, and houses nestled among gardens that seemed to float on water. It is a sight for every visitor to behold with breathless wonder, and especially Humboldt, who saw it as the unrivaled metropolis of New Spain, which counted California, New Mexico, Arizona, and Texas among its faithful, if sorely neglected, provinces. To the east rose the tall summits of snow-capped volcanoes, glistening like silver above their green mantle of forests. "A fairyland such as cannot be seen in Spain," Cortés had reported to Charles V, a site he would transform by uprooting the might of Moctezuma's empire.

Enchanting as was this historic landscape, "the City of Palaces," as Humboldt was wont to call Mexico's capital, struck him as one of great splendor. Naturally, its churches and ornate private homes did not have the mellowness of patina they have in our time, but a dignity of living was firmly guaranteed by a feudal and ecclesiastical order of things. What fine traditions and what courtly manners! Here was an affable people, endearing by their sense of humor and graced by a deep respect for learning. The Humboldt party could not have failed to feel at home the moment their carriage rumbled over cobblestoned avenues to the center of town. That their host should have been the owner of the frigate that had brought them to Mexico was much in the manner of this hospitable country. Lodgings had been prepared in the Calle de San Agustín,[1] in a simple yet dignified two-story dwelling.

The Viceroy, Don José de Iturrigaray, had sent Humboldt a letter welcoming him as one deserving the esteem and assistance owed to a scholar so nobly devoted to science. The message was accompanied by a special passport and letters of introduction to provincial governors. The Viceroy must have been thoroughly informed about the new guest by various officials, including Don Andrés del Río, Humboldt's former classmate from Freiberg, now director of Mexico's School of Mines. Was Humboldt not the most erudite and learned man ever to have visited Mexico? He was an authority in so many branches of science that one was tempted to forget his expert knowledge of mining. All offices and archives must be opened to him. He should by all means have access to mines and plantations, drainage canals and antiquities. If Mexico was to profit from Humboldt's visit, the Mexicans themselves must do their best to make him happy. How well they succeeded is evident from a passage in Humboldt's work on Mexico in which he pleaded for recognition of the Spaniards' worth:

I have lived with them for years and been associated with all classes of people, Capuchin monks and viceroys, and have come to master Spanish as fluently as my mother tongue. I feel quite convinced that this nation is bound to advance through education, in defiance of the Church and an autocratic government.

---

[1] Now the Calle Uruguay. The house is marked by a commemorative tablet, and is close to the Biblioteca Nacionál, where stands a marble monument to Humboldt.

The city was handsome, with wide, clean avenues, each flanked by iron candelabras, and resplendent with ancient churches, palaces, and shady parks.[2] Nowhere in Latin America had Humboldt met with finer educational institutions or with men more eagerly devoted to learning. If proof was needed, anybody could have found it in the School of Mines, then newly installed in a handsome palace. It was equipped with collections of minerals and rocks all neatly classified by del Río according to Werner's system. The instrument cabinets displayed the finest models, many of which had already been copied with great skill. The chemistry laboratory was amply provided with glassware and expensive scales. Even Lavater's chemistry text had already been translated into Spanish. Del Río was quick to ask Humboldt for a contribution to his geology textbook, whose second volume was scheduled to appear in 1804. When published, it would be the first textbook of geology in the Americas bearing Humboldt's name as co-author, a work destined to aid engineers and miners wherever Spanish was spoken.

Don Antonio Alzate, the famous Mexican astronomer and naturalist, and a publisher of the *Gaceta de Literatura*, had awakened interest in all branches of science. When Humboldt was introduced to the Director of Mines, Don Joaquín Velásquez, he was delighted to know that this experienced surveyor and astronomer would furnish him with the latest calculations of longitude and latitude ranging from California to Acapulco. And Velásquez may have

[2] The Mexican census of 1794 gave the total population as 5,200,000 inhabitants. Humboldt's own estimate for the country was 5,800,000, for Mexico City 137,000, of which 2,500 were Europeans, 65,000 creoles, 33,000 Indians, 26,500 mestizos, and 10,000 mulattoes.

been not a little surprised to learn that Humboldt intended
to issue a new map of Mexico. Naturally, it should incorporate all the latest information, not merely geographical,
but political, economic, and even ethnographic, with the
names of native tribes and indications of roads leading
from the city in all directions, including north to Santa Fe
and the California missions. And for Humboldt to plan a
thing was as good as a guarantee of its execution. The completion of this map would keep him longer in Mexico than
he had planned. When it appeared, with Velásquez's name
on it, it turned out to be of inestimable value for Mexico
and its northern neighbor, the young federation of the
United States.

Humboldt paid visits to the Royal Academy of Arts and
its collection of copies of classical sculptures, to the university, and to a public library—inadequately equipped, he
noted, for so lively a cultural center as Mexico City had
come to be. "The richest and finest collection of this city is
that of Father José Antonio Picardo, attached to the
Church of San Felipe Neri. The home of this enlightened
and studious person was to me the most admirable." Its
owner had sacrificed his small fortune in collecting Aztec
codices and in copying those he could not afford to purchase. Unexpectedly a chance presented itself for Humboldt to purchase a number of these ancient Indian picture
writings, rare even at that time considering how few had
escaped the *autos de fe* of the conquest.

When introduced to the new excavations at the Zócalo,
the central square with its imposing Cathedral, Humboldt
felt inspired to sketch Aztec sculptures, among them the
famous calendar stone. What a thrill it gave him to behold
such evidence of ancient learning! Was it not proof of the

universal ingenuity of mankind? Egypt and China had known their calendars, but here in Mexico was unmistakable evidence of people reaching for the stars without technological aids. Here one could walk for days on end picking up antiquities by the roadside. The very soil under one's feet oozed history as fascinating as anything the Old World had to offer. With Bonpland and Montúfar, Humboldt went by coach to the pyramids at Teotihuacán, marveling at their geometric symmetry, a vast temple city oriented, it appeared, by astronomic observations. He must measure the heights of the Pyramids of the Sun and the Moon. All this time he wondered how they must have looked a thousand years before, their platforms adorned with gilded images of gods. What, he asked, was the meaning of the rubble of sun-baked bricks and pottery found in the core of these monumental structures? Such questions made him long to see Egypt and the Orient. But he must not indulge in such plans now that he had decided to return to Europe.

Back in the capital, he found a letter from his friend Willdenow in Berlin, the first in four years. "It seems as if an unkind star had guided our correspondence," Humboldt answered, "perhaps over the ships that carried them. But I will not complain since I now have the prospect of embracing you so soon again." His impressions in Mexico had been so overwhelming and varied that he had decided to prolong his stay until the spring of 1804, when he would leave for Havana and the United States. What had caused Humboldt suddenly to forsake his ambitious plans to sail around the world? The reasons were carefully outlined in his letter to the secretary of the Institut de France in Paris:

The damaged state of our instruments, the futility of our efforts to replace them, the impossibility of meeting Captain Baudin, the lack of a ship that could bring us to the enchanted islands of the South Pacific, but, above all, the urgent need to keep pace with the rapid advancement of science which must have taken place during our absence, these are the motives for the abandonment of our project of returning via the Philippines and through the Red Sea to Egypt. . . . With an increased store of knowledge, and possessed of better instruments, we may perhaps some day undertake another expedition, a prospect that tempts us with seductive dreams.

A few weeks later Humboldt wrote to the astronomer Delambre:

As for the Philippines, I have given them up temporarily, for I maintain other plans for the East Indies, but I am eager first to publish the results of this expedition. I hope to be with you early next year. It is every man's duty to seek that position in life in which he can best serve his generation. I almost think that to fulfill my destiny I ought to perish in a crater or be drowned on the high seas. This at least is my present opinion . . . though I can readily believe that with advancing age and the enjoyments of European life I may yet live to change my views.

The tenor of these letters clearly indicates that Humboldt and Bonpland could for the moment take no more. There is a limit to the extent that even the most gifted mind can go on enlarging the results of four years of exploration. Humboldt must have clearly foreseen how difficult it would be to catch up with the progress of various natural sciences, a dire necessity for one who planned to publish the results of his travels in co-operation with many scholars. Meanwhile he would get the most out of his stay in Mexico.

The Viceroy had assigned a native guide to the Humboldt party for tours in the vicinity of Mexico City. When this good man was later questioned about his experiences, he said that Humboldt could not possibly be much of a scholar, for the stranger was all the time inquiring about the simplest things, which any child knew, such as the use of the *metate* (milling stone). Every other minute he had asked about the names of villages and streams known to everybody, and because of his weak memory this foreigner had felt obliged to put all such commonplace knowledge in his notebook. Really he had behaved like a little boy, stuffing his pockets full of rocks and plants!

How painstakingly accurate Humboldt's measurements in the city were is obvious from the fact that his astronomical calculations of latitude for the eastern tower of the Cathedral differed by only six hundred feet from subsequent calculations, while his barometric determination of elevation above sea-level for the Convent of San Agustín came within twenty-two feet of the correct estimate.

On August 1, 1803 the party left on an extended tour to the mining district of Guanajuato and the volcanic region in the present state of Michoacán.

On the way they stopped to inspect the enormous canal of Nochistongo, the most ancient engineering project of its kind in North America. Its creator had been none other than Enrico Martínez, the ingenious mathematician and cosmographer of His Spanish Majesty, who had saved the city from inundation by providing this artificial outlet for the flooded valley. In 1607 Martínez had commanded an army of fifteen thousand Indian diggers, and in ten months had accomplished this engineering feat at the cost of uncounted lives. The canal had recently been repaired, and Humboldt was able to talk to engineers and laborers. They brought him fossil mammoth bones dug up in the construction. Surely Cuvier in Paris would be interested in these ancient animal relics, which Humboldt ordered to be brought back to the city.

The silver mines at Guanajuato proved to be so rich in interesting mineral specimens that a special mule train was required for their transport. The memorable visit prompted the owners of hot springs near Comanjilla to name the largest the Humboldt Geyser. Tin and mercury mines were studied, and geographic co-ordinates determined for every important locality. On September 9 the party left Guanajuato for Morelia, or Valladolid as it was then called. Its neat colonial architecture appears to have been wasted on Humboldt, who thought the site ill chosen.[3] The Tarascan Indians, he remarked, had showed more sense in selecting the pleasant shores of Lake Pátzcuaro, where the ruins of pyramids suggested an ancient center of worship. The Tarascans struck him as one of the most gifted races of America, industrious and so clever with their hands that they could make the most wonderful woodcarvings, musical instruments, and colorful textiles.

On September 19 Humboldt and Bonpland reached the crater of Jorullo, near Uruapan. The birth of this volcano had been as sudden and violent as that of its modern neighbor Parícutin was to be in 1943. The Indians told him how

[3] Such adverse opinion did not prevent Humboldt from sending the Bishop of Morelia a copy of his plant-geography studies "in memory of happy hours spent at Valladolid and Zinapecuaro, February 1808, Paris." I saw this volume, with Humboldt's inscription, in a museum exhibition at Morelia.

it had begun in 1759, when their fields erupted with fire and smoke, and how a river evaporated within minutes in a cloud of steam. Now, forty-five years later, the new volcano had spent its fury, but its lava fields were still smoldering from many underground fires, giving Humboldt a chance to measure the temperature of volcanic gases. He descended into the crater and tested the air and hot springs for certain chemical properties, while Bonpland was asked to pick up specimens representative of the curious vegetable life that had sprung up on the black, twisted masses of lava.

What did the Indians think of this subterranean fire? "In their opinion, this volcanic eruption was the work of the monks, the greatest, no doubt, which they have ever produced in this hemisphere!" One Indian reported how, in 1750, the very year of the outburst, some Capuchin missionaries had come to preach at the plantation of San Pedro.

Not having had a favorable reception (perhaps they had not dined to their liking) they poured out the most insulting imprecations against the place, then fertile with corn and wheat. They prophesied that the farm would be consumed by fire, and that soon afterward the air would cool off so that all mountains would be covered with snow and ice. The first of these maledictions having come true, the Indians regard the gradual cooling of the volcano as the sinister foreboding of perpetual winter. It is in this manner that the Church preys on the credulity of the natives so as to render their ignorant minds the more submissive.

This commentary is singular among Humboldt's writings, which were otherwise so carefully worded as to leave few vents for his scorn. As an author, he was often severely

handicapped in expressing views considered anathema by
many authorities, and he avoided insults that could be con-
strued as ungrateful utterances by one who had every reason to be thankful for official assistance. Every so often one
finds in his reports a paragraph or sentence in which his
beliefs erupt with irrepressible force of conviction.

The prosperity of the whites [he wrote] is intimately connected with that of the copper-colored race, and there can be
no durable prosperity for the two Americas until this unfortunate race, humiliated but not degraded by long oppression,
shall participate in all the advantages resulting from the progress of civilization and the improvement of social order.

Such passages have the ring of prophecy and faith in re-
form, a belief that he was wont frequently to refer to the
date of the French Revolution as if he, Alexander von
Humboldt, was at all times proud to acknowledge its
badge. There was need for him to reassert before his reading public his deep-seated faith in the ultimate triumph
of democratic principles, which in his later years seemed
all the more necessary because of the compromising nature of his position at the court of his King.

By September 21 the party had returned to the shores
of Lake Pátzcuaro, whence it proceeded via Morelia to
Toluca. The day after his arrival there, Humboldt climbed
the dormant volcano Nevado de Toluca, the fourth highest
peak in Mexico (14,954 feet), determining the snow line
and highest limit of forest vegetation. This trip into the
alpine world of snow and mosses reawakened his interest
in the vertical distribution of plants previously seen in the
Andes of Peru and Ecuador.

At last they were back in Mexico City packing their

specimens, which were to be shipped from Veracruz directly to Europe. One may wonder at this point about Humboldt's social life in Mexico's capital, if, indeed, he had any, considering his crowded professional schedule. At the time, society was strictly divided according to official rank and personal wealth. At the top stood the Viceroy, who represented the Spanish Crown, with a court of his own as ceremonious as that at the Escorial. His outings were accompanied by a display of pompously uniformed escorts and pages. It would have been impossible for him to invite Humboldt and his friends for dinner. Etiquette forced the Viceroy to dine in solitary splendor with his family except on occasions when he could manage to retreat to one of his country places. His salary was twice that of Thomas Jefferson when he was President of the United States, and that was considered poor pay for a Viceroy when the Conde de Regla enjoyed a private income of half a million piasters (about one hundred thousand dollars) a year.

The higher clergy lived in clover, as Humboldt's statistics indicate. The Archbishopric of Mexico could count on annual revenues of 130,000 piasters, about one fourth of Mexico's total Church income from services, landholdings, and business transactions. The country swarmed with priests, monks, and nuns. For every two hundred inhabitants it counted three priests.

If there was need for Humboldt to feel convinced of Mexico's enormous wealth, the Royal Mint would furnish him with interesting statistics. Between 1726 and 1780 it had coined silver and gold valued at twenty-two million dollars, exceeding the total coinage of the sixteen mints of France by seven million. Humboldt estimated that the silver produced in all the mines of Europe would not suffice to employ Mexico's mint for more than fifteen days a year. Equally impressive is his estimate of the total value of gold and silver minted in Spanish America since the conquest: a little over five billion piasters! The Aztecs had used small copper hatchets and cacao beans for money, a custom that Humboldt observed in some out-of-the-way villages, where one cacao bean, he calculated, was worth about the equivalent of two French sous.

As for Mexican society, Humboldt found time, now and then, to enjoy its company. Madame Calderón de la Barca, American wife of the Spanish Ambassador, related in her amusing autobiography that a friend of hers recalled how Humboldt was struck by the beauty of a young mother of two children. "From that moment on, he [Humboldt] was always at her side, more captivated it is said by the graces of her mind than by her beauty. He came to regard her as an American version of Madame de Staël." This anecdote was to mislead some biographers of Humboldt into assuming that he had fallen in love with a Mexican lady and that in consequence he had yearned forever after to return to Mexico for the sake of this attractive woman. Nothing seems less likely. That Humboldt could have been fascinated by the intellectual graces of this young woman is probable, but he was hardly a man to be swept off his feet by feminine allure and to stake his future on a romance that could not have been very' rewarding in view of the lady's married status. If Humboldt ever entertained plans for returning to Mexico, it was for a very different reason.

But this was not the only instance when Humboldt was credited with love affairs in Latin America. How else is one to account for rumors, all ensuing from Latin America, that the famous naturalist had left offspring behind? The German geographer Baron von Richthofen reported in his memoirs that he learned of a man in Havana who claimed to be Humboldt's natural son. When the aging Humboldt was told of such rumors, he replied that he had heard of five such cases in which a rogue had found the courage to claim him for a father!

Time in Mexico City passed much more quickly than was good for Humboldt's crowded schedule. Copyists were kept busy for him, extracting from government archives statistics on commerce, mine production, population censuses, and farm commodities. The large map of Mexico had been started, and a smaller one dealing with the Valley of Mexico was almost ready. Every day Humboldt was seen working in the School of Mines, directing the draftsmen, studying reports, and attending classes.

Del Río had asked him to deliver lectures. The subject was one Humboldt had pondered over for some time: criteria useful for systematizing and illustrating geologic observations. In these lectures he presented his own system of correlating rock formations on a regional scale, and he may be credited with an original contribution to a branch of geology known as stratigraphy. In this field his ideas clearly rivaled the system presented by William Smith in England, though Humboldt's pioneering views did not find such ready acceptance as Smith's. The reason is to be found in Humboldt's emphasis on mineralogic criteria rather than on fossilized remains, which later were to give Smith his ingenious claim that geologic strata of equal age contained the same types of fossils. To these Humboldt had paid but little attention on his travels, engrossed as he then was with the Wernerian concepts of rock classification.

Vulcanism was on his mind in Mexico, as in South America, and in this field he made a major contribution to the young science of geology. He had been impressed with the regional alignment of volcanic centers on a belt extending from the Pacific coast to the Gulf of Mexico. This arrangement, Humboldt claimed, could only mean that the liquid magma had risen on a line of weakness of the earth's crust, the solid structure of which had been rent by fissures forcing the magma to the surface. Much as the Andes had indicated intimate geologic relationships between earth structures and vulcanism, it was in Mexico that Humboldt claimed to have found conclusive evidence.

But posterity would remember him as the encyclopedic interpreter of Mexico more than of any other country. It is as if circumstances had there favored Humboldt's scientific genius: geographic variety of scenery, mineral wealth, vulcanism, and the impressive records of pre-Columbian traditions. From each of his subjects his mind had struck new sparks, all of which would interest another generation, helping to inspire the leaders of Mexican independence and the founders of the United States. The great Mexican patriot and statesman Benito Juárez was to confer on Humboldt the title "Benefactor of the Nation" (*Benemérito de la Patria*) years after President Comonfort had invested the naturalist with the Grand Cross of the Order of Guadalupe, and Mexico might have honored Humboldt's work more lastingly by naming a town in the Isthmus of Tehuantepec after him if Comonfort's decree of 1859 had been allowed to stand. But less ephemeral than all these honors, more satisfying to a mind like Humboldt's, would have been the knowledge that his interests in Mexican archæology challenged men like William Hickling Prescott, John Lloyd Stephens, and Eduard Seler to interpret afresh what for so long had remained hidden in ruins and graves.

Equipped with codices and Aztec sculptures, minerals and plants, the Humboldt party said farewell to Mexico City. On January 20, 1804 its members were on their way to Puebla and Veracruz. Ahead the snow peaks rose dazzling against the dark-blue winter sky, and beyond lay the city of tiles, Puebla de los Angeles, and the Pyramid of Cholula. As Humboldt surveyed its height, he noticed that its internal structure had been bared by a new road cut. There in the rubble of a thousand years he could ponder problems of age and correlations with other civilizations long extinct. The pyramid-builders of Mexico must have been preceded by much more ancient people, Humboldt thought, possibly early agriculturists who possessed a knowledge all their own and artists capable of portraying their deities in clay. In his *Researches Concerning the Institutions and Monuments of the Ancient Inhabitants of America* Humboldt suggested that the great temples of Cholula´ and Teotihuacán had been constructed earlier than the Toltec civilization, before A.D. 648, an idea recently confirmed by archæologists. Whereas the Egyptian pyramids had served as sepulchral shrines, the Mexican temples seemed to have been massive foundations for elevated sacrificial platforms that the worshippers reached by outer staircases. The Cholula Pyramid inspired him to ponder certain analogies between Mexican and Oriental traditions: the concept of an earth goddess rejected from paradise, a flood legend depicting people who escaped on rafts, idols made of flour and distributed to worshippers in the temple, monastic institutions, and a belief in a savior, a fair-skinned hero known as Quetzalcoatl, the Plumed Serpent, who came from across the sea. The early Spaniards, recognizing such analogies with Eastern traditions, had been prompted quite mistakenly to believe in early Christian influences in Mexico. Had the New World partaken in the most ancient heritage of Mesopotamia and India?

Fascinating as such problems were, he would have to leave their solution to others. En route from Puebla to Jalapa, he collected plants and rocks on the slopes of tall mountains like the Cofre de Perote and Orizaba. He made another geologic graph of rock structures, this time to illustrate the great descent from the Mexican plateau to the Gulf of Mexico. From Jalapa the party followed the Camino Real to Veracruz, Humboldt noting with considerable amusement the Indian ice-carriers who came from the snow fields of Orizaba bringing their ware to the sherbet-makers in Veracruz. There ice sherbets had sold at a premium during the last yellow-fever epidemic. It had worried Humboldt and his companions to think that this epidemic might delay their departure from Mexico and their visit to the United States. His mind was made up to visit Thomas Jefferson. He must know Jefferson in person, must report to him and his circle of naturalists in Philadelphia about Mexico and South America. What a grand prospect to talk to the man who combined so admirably the faculties of statesman, philosopher, and naturalist! More than that, a visit to the United States would be the chance of his life to see the new republic at work, the American nation that had managed to throw off the yoke of colonialism.

The party reached Veracruz on February 19, 1804, and was delighted to hear that a packet for Havana was scheduled to leave on March 7. Three whole weeks in which to survey the harbor, redetermine its geographic position, and improve sailing charts. Veracruz was, and still is, Mexico's gateway to the West Indies and Europe. Here Cortés had landed with his fleet, burning it so as to give cowards no chance to return to Spain. Not even Humboldt foresaw that from this port the Spanish rulers would soon depart, leaving Mexico to take its fate into its own hands.

9

The Visitor at Monticello

THE HAVANA PACKET had been buffeted by terrible seas, and while it had delayed Humboldt's arrival in Philadelphia, tormenting him with the prospect of losing his collections, he felt supremely confident. Impossible to imagine that he should lose them now that he had shepherded them safely across the Andes and Mexico! He and Bonpland had staked their fortune on the safe arrival of thirty cases of botanical and geological specimens. There had been anxious moments, and God knows there would doubtless be others on the return journey to France. The British Navy was reported on the seas again, watching for contraband. But now the spires of Philadelphia were in sight, the waters of the Delaware River splashing gingerly around the ship. The stopover in Havana had been profitable in all respects except for the usual delays with the officials. They had warned him about yellow fever, saying that his party would require health certificates for landing at Philadelphia.

This was the end of May 1804, and Philadelphia still recalled the dreadful fever epidemic of two years before, imported, it was said, from Mexico or Cuba. If any of the port officials had read the latest French papers, which had reported Humboldt dead from the yellow scourge, they would not have believed their eyes. As early as the summer of 1803 Humboldt's death had been announced, and now, while he was stepping off the ship, another newspaper in Hamburg was saying that the celebrated traveler had succumbed at Acapulco. Bursting with energy, his full face luscious with the joy of life, his blue eyes smiling at the customs officials with roguish mockery, Humboldt seemed more alive than ever.

The inn on Market Street was not far from the harbor, and there they registered: Alexander von Humboldt, Aimé Bonpland, the French botanist, and Don Carlos Montúfar, of Quito, Ecuador. Alexander sat down to announce his arrivel in a letter to Thomas Jefferson.

May 24, 1804

Mr. President,

Arrived from Mexico on the blessed ground of this republic, whose executive powers were placed in your hands, I feel it my pleasant duty to present my respects and express my high admiration for your writings, your actions, and the liberalism of your ideas, which have inspired me from my earliest youth. I flatter myself in the expectation of expressing my sentiments orally to you, remitting at the same time the attached parcel, which my friend the Consul of the United States in Havana asked me to send to you. . . .

For moral reasons I could not resist seeing the United States and enjoying the consoling aspects of a people who understand the precious gift of Liberty. I hope to be able to present my personal respects and admiration to one who contemplates philosophically the troubles of two continents. . . . I am quite unaware whether you know of me already through my work on galvanism and my publications in the memoirs of the Institut National in Paris. As a friend of science, you will excuse the indulgence of my admiration. I would love to talk to you about a subject that you have treated so ingeniously in your work on Virginia, the teeth of mammoth which we too discovered in the Andes. . . .

Even if Jefferson had more pressing matters on his mind than mammoth teeth, he was bound to receive a visitor who had so cleverly played up to his scientific interests. Before the day was over, Humboldt's message was on its way to the Executive Mansion in Washington. Meanwhile he could look around and see what sort of place Philadelphia was.

At first sight it could hardly compare in size and architecture with Mexico City. Yet the City of Brotherly Love was fair enough to look at, with its stately brick buildings and cobbled streets. It reminded him a bit of Europe, and that alone was refreshing after five years of travels in Spanish America. The touch of Old World culture was everywhere. Ladies wore the same fashions, and men sported round hats with high crowns, a habit not favored by the patriotic Dr. Rush, who suspected that it affected the brain adversely. Around the State House and Philosophical Hall the streets were tolerably clean, but other parts of the city were sorely in need of gutter-cleaning. The pump water tasted a bit salty, and the wharves were littered with smelly refuse attracting all sorts of vermin. No wonder so many citizens had succumbed to the last epidemic.

Philadelphia might not boast of palaces like those Humboldt had admired in Mexico, but it had cradled American independence, a fact sufficient to make it important. Here Jefferson had drafted the Declaration of Independence, and what he had proclaimed then concerned people everywhere. He was a sovereign human being who had a way of making others feel sovereign as well. In life it was a question of choosing one's allegiance, and as Humboldt's was to science, he could not help believing in freedom of the mind. It was grand for him to move above this town and

Landscape near Quito, with Chimborazo in left background, after a sketch by Humboldt

A South-east view from Market Street, Philadelphia, showing Christ Church. An engraving dated 1799

feel reassured by the memory of the American Revolution. The French had sold their birthright of freedom to the tyrant Napoleon, dimming the hopes that Washington and Jefferson had proclaimed for all mankind. Who among Philadelphians would value Humboldt for his allegiance to a free mind if not the naturalists? He must call on them at once.

Humboldt may have announced his visit from Havana or Mexico to John Vaughn, secretary of the American Philosophical Society, America's celebrated center of learning. Here Benjamin Franklin had lectured on electricity, Joseph Priestley on the discovery of oxygen. Quite a few members recalled having heard or read about Humboldt. Had he not attempted to explore the secret of live nerves and muscles by subjecting his body to painful experiments with the electrical current? He must be the same Humboldt who had invented a new safety device for miners, and on top of that had described subterranean flora from the mines of Germany. French scientific journals had lately reported his exploits in South America, and if any of the Philadelphia naturalists had overlooked them, the librarian could easily have taken Humboldt's reports from the bookshelves in Philosophical Hall.

Five years of constant travel in the wilds had made Humboldt thirsty for intellectual company, which Philadelphia could offer to his heart's content. There was Dr. Caspar Wistar, noted for his efforts to make vaccination compulsory, a chemist and brilliant anatomist. With Benjamin Smith Barton, Humboldt could discuss botany and the traditions of American Indians. And there was Dr. Benjamin Rush, a signer of the Declaration of Independence, eager to hear Humboldt speak of Indians who cured a certain kind of fever with the bark of the cinchona tree. For Rush it was exciting news that the Baron would submit his samples of the Peruvian quinine bark to French chemists for analysis.

Charles Willson Peale, the painter and friend of Jefferson, immediately insisted on showing the Baron his museum. This was a show no visitor would want to miss. It was, Peale assured the distinguished foreigner, a museum unique in the New World. A sign above its entrance read: "School of Wisdom," and one beneath read: "The Book of Nature Open—Explore the Wondrous Work and Institute of Laws Eternal." Its spacious halls were cramped with exhibits of thousands of birds and insects, stuffed alligators, mountain lions with glass eyes as fiercely real "as though they were alive, even the eyelashes being complete." And there were the five-legged cow with two tails giving milk to a two-headed calf, pantaloons made of the intestines of a whale, and the shoes and stockings of the Irish Giant Obrian, who stood eight feet seven and one-half inches tall. His bulky figure was surpassed only by the mammoth, the first fossil skeleton ever mounted in America. Peale, the creator of this wondrous show, beamed with pride. Well he might, for his museum was the largest of its kind, and was admired even by the great Mr. Jefferson.

A special place was reserved for Peale's portraits of famous Americans, and other paintings to which the unsuspecting visitors were lured by the other exhibits. Attracted by the mammoth, they might feel inclined to take a kind interest in art. Peale had turned showman, but not solely for profit's sake. His museum was to spread knowledge and religion. Humboldt was told, if he did not know it already, that Peale had dared to challenge the French naturalist Buffon, who had belittled the size and variety of America's fauna. Could France perhaps boast of a mounted mammoth skeleton, of fossil bones of the giant sloth, of mountain lions and leopards? The Baron might have contributed an electric eel from the Amazon to the museum if it had not already been shipped to France. Surely the Baron would agree that the museum was worthy of being purchased by the government? If anyone as learned as he could put in a good word with the President, a deal might yet be made. Peale offered to introduce the travelers to Mr. Jefferson. In fact, he would be delighted to arrange for entertaining traveling companions for the trip to Washington.

On May 26 they left by coach for Baltimore and the nation's new capital. With Peale and Humboldt were Bonpland, the young dashing Don Carlos Montúfar, Dr. Antony Fothergill, and the Reverend Nicholas Collin of the American Philosophical Society. In Humboldt's pocket was Jefferson's cordial reply to his letter:

A lively desire will be felt generally [the President had written] to receive the information you will be able to give. No one will feel it more strongly than myself, because no one perhaps views this New World with more partial hopes of its exhibiting an ameliorated state of the human condition. In the new position in which the seat of our government is fixed, we have nothing curious to attract the observations of a traveller, and can only substitute in its place the welcome with which we should receive your visit, should you find it convenient to add so much to your journey.

Humboldt would be welcome with his statistics and maps of New Spain, the Mexican possessions that extended far north to San Francisco and Santa Fe. His visit could not have been better timed. The Louisiana Purchase treaty had been signed in Paris. For fifteen million dollars Napoleon had sold one million square miles, from which thirteen states would be carved. Without firing a shot, the new republic had doubled its size. It had gained a frontier with New Spain which extended along the Red River to the upper reaches of the Missouri drainage, where Lewis and Clark would explore the passage to the Pacific coast. The empire-building days were at hand, and so was Humboldt, with his expert knowledge of mines and roads, of commerce and settlements south and west of the new border.

Peale's diary of the trip recorded how the nearsighted Reverend Mr. Collin, misjudging his distance at the first ferry crossing, stepped into the river. At the next inn he hung up his money-sock to dry. Several miles farther on, he suddenly remembered that he had forgotten it, with all the cash he was accustomed to hide in it. Having retrieved the purse, the company proceeded on its way, reaching Baltimore the following morning. Peale's son-in-law, Alexander Robinson, sent his coach to fetch the visitors for a sightseeing tour of the town, a dinner party, and a theater performance. Then they continued on their way to Washington.

"The Baron," Peale reported, "entertained us generously with travel stories." If they were anything like the accounts in Humboldt's *Narrative of Travels*, he must have amused his company tremendously. He probably told them of his encounter with an Indian in Peru whose life span could be traced back one hundred and forty-seven years, with a marriage record of ninety years. The Baron had climbed the highest mountain ever scaled by man and had camped with Indian cannibals. Near Lima he had collected the dung of sea birds which might help farmers raise two green blades where one had grown before.

The coach rolled into Washington, bumping and pitching over half-finished streets, past miserable small houses lacking the basic necessities of urban living. Gouveneur Morris of Philadelphia had described it as "the best city in the world for *future* residence." Peale managed to introduce the foreigners to the President, who invited the whole company for dinner at the Executive Mansion, a dinner in Jeffersonian style, without formal toasts and speeches, with plenty of good food, choice French wines, and animated conversation.

Politics had no place on this occasion. They talked of the manners of different nations, of Indian relics, and of scientific subjects. Jefferson's interest in meteorology, paleontology, and astronomy and his broad knowledge of these subjects must have impressed his guests as uniquely stimulating. While Ambassador in France, Jefferson had recorded his meteorologic observations. In Italy he had studied the cultivation of upland rice, which he meant to introduce as a food crop in America. As for French wines, he hoped to cultivate certain varieties of grapes on his own plantation. To hear Humboldt talk of his geological studies may have reminded Jefferson of Cuvier, Buffon, and Blumenbach, whose works he had read with great interest. It occurred to him that geology might be introduced with good profit into the University of Virginia.

Peale retired early as was his custom, but before going to sleep he entered Humboldt's room to tell him how well he had succeeded in interesting the President in the future of his museum. The following day the party visited Mount Vernon. This time it was Peale's turn to entertain the company with stories about George Washington. Their return ride to the capital ended in a furious race between the two coaches, whose drivers were slightly tipsy on corn liquor. The evening was spent with Dr. Thornton, the naturalist, James Madison, the Secretary of State, and Gilbert Stuart, the painter. Later they visited Stuart's studio to look at the portrait of the celebrated Dr. Priestley, the discoverer of oxygen, which had been commissioned by the American Philosophical Society. The following night they had dinner with Madison. Suddenly Peale appeared uncomfortable and begged to be excused. His dental bridge having broken, he rushed out to look for a gunsmith to borrow his tools to repair it. For one who had mounted the skeleton of a mammoth, this was a fast and easy job. Luckily he carried a few pieces of gold in his pocket, and so managed to mend his artificial teeth in time to rejoin the company for the rest of the evening.

The following day Humboldt spent with Albert Gallatin, Secretary of the Treasury. The Swiss-born wizard of finance was not a man easily taken in by fast talk and foreign manners, but when the day was over he had to admit to his wife:

We all consider him [Humboldt] as a very extraordinary man, and his travels, which he intends publishing on his return to Europe will, I think, rank above any other productions of the kind. I am not easily pleased, and he was not particularly prepossessing to my taste . . . for he speaks twice as fast as anybody I know, German, French, Spanish and English altogether. But I was really delighted, and swallowed more information of various kinds in less than two hours than I had for two years past in all I had read or heard. He does not seem much above thirty, gives you no trouble in talking yourself, for he catches with perfect precision the idea you mean to convey before you have uttered the extent of your sentence. . . . The extent of his reading and scientific knowledge is astonishing. I must acknowledge, in order to account for my enthusiasm, that he was surrounded with maps, statements, etc., all new to me, and several of which he literally permitted us to transcribe.

Gallatin's office desk was littered with Humboldt's maps and notes on mine production, commerce, census reports, and the Indian settlements of New Spain. What the traveler had to report on America's wealth of precious metals was welcome news. Since the Spanish conquest the mines of Spanish America had produced gold and silver worth 5,600,000,000 dollars. If the Mexican mountains contained as many riches as Humboldt claimed, there was hope for locating mining prospects in the western cordilleras. Gallatin later checked Humboldt's figures and found them correct, which would hardly have surprised anybody who knew of Humboldt's successful career as a Superintendent of Mines in Germany.

On June 9 the President had written to Humboldt concerning the boundary region between Louisiana and New Spain. Spain claimed as a frontier the Sabine River and a line northward to the headwaters of the Red River. "We claim to the North River from mouth to source either of its eastern or western branch, thence to the head of the Red River. Can the Baron inform me what population may be between these lines, of white, red or black people? And whether any and what mines are within them? The information will be thankfully received."

Every scrap of information on Mexico's northern provinces would be helpful for the President's report to Congress on the Louisiana Purchase. To weld an empire, Americans needed to be informed of how incredibly rich the continent was in precious ores, forests, soils, and rivers. A symphony of promises was awaiting orchestration. In Spanish America, Humboldt had heard its rhythms and the discords occasioned by colonial mismanagement. For North America, Jefferson had his own plans, and Humboldt's information could contribute to their realization at that preparatory stage. But the man behind this expert information interested the President as much as all of Humboldt's encyclopedic data. He must come to know him better and invite him to his country home at Monticello.

The Virginia countryside was in full bloom, and Jefferson's home provided its most precious ornament. Its gardens and tasteful interiors invited the friendship of these two men to unfold with graceful ease. They were delighted to discover how much they had in common: interests in science and history, a great respect for French culture, and an almost religious devotion to Nature. But they differed in their emotional make-up. Jefferson was hesitant in expressing feelings that his guest could display with little reserve. The host loved music, which Humboldt found so irritating that he spoke of it as a social calamity. Monticello had been created by a man deeply rooted in family and country. The visitor, on the other hand, was the cosmopolitan scholar more likely to live in a bachelor's apartment in Paris, close to scientific institutes and libraries, than on the family estate near Berlin. He was of a restless disposition, always searching for a harmony that Jefferson appeared to possess in a remarkable degree. Humboldt would have agreed with Jefferson's view that only the active mind can feel truly happy. While Humboldt's mind was circling the globe, soaring into cosmic space, Jefferson's pondered scientific principles for practical ends. If they discussed the future of Latin America, Humboldt most likely expressed his deep concern over the oppression of Indians and Negroes, whose liberation he advocated vigorously on all occasions.

The New World, the two men agreed, was destined for democracy, and Humboldt's reports on New Spain and Cuba were to furnish the new republics with a proper knowledge of their resources. He had been singularly fortunate, his host wrote to him in December 1813, that his travels

were so timed as to make their results known to the world in the moment the American lands were about to become actors on its stage. . . . That they will throw off their European dependence I have no doubt. History, I believe, furnishes no example of a priest-ridden people maintaining a free civil government. . . . But of all this you can judge best, for in truth we have but little knowledge of them to be depended on but through you. . . .

In the same letter Jefferson assured Humboldt that he would gladly join him in Paris were it not for the cords of love to his family and country.

The guest of Monticello became vehement and even eloquent when he spoke of geographic maps and the corrections he had been able to make by his own astronomic observations. Places like Santa Fe and points along the Pacific coast had been placed too far to the north and east, as Lewis and Clark were soon to find out by hard experience. And what could be the origin of the name America?

The learned guest might not have been able to enlighten his host then and there, but he would find out in time. "I believe to have earned a modest merit," Humboldt wrote many years later, "by having proved that Amerigo Vespucci had no part in the naming of the New Continent, but that the name America originated in a hidden spot of the Vosges Mountains." There a certain map-maker by the name of Martin Waldseemüller had boldly put it on the map that illustrated Vespucci's wonderful voyages. Almost three hundred years had passed since then, and so much remained to be discovered in America!

Jefferson's newly appointed secretary, William A. Burwell, found Humboldt looking younger than his thirty-five years, "of small figure, well made, agreeable looks, simple unaffected manners, remarkably sprightly, vehement in conversation and sometimes eloquent. Jefferson welcomed him with greatest cordiality and listened eagerly to the treasure of information."

One morning, while the guest had breakfast with the President's secretary, Jefferson came down the staircase waving a newspaper clipping in his hand. It was, he remarked, filled with the grossest personal abuse of himself. He was presenting it, he said, to Humboldt with the request that he exhibit it in a European museum as "evidence how little mischief flowed from the freedom of the press. That notwithstanding innumerable pieces of similar nature issued daily from the press, his administration had never been more popular."

The days at Monticello passed all too quickly. In Washington there was a round of farewell calls to make and a last dinner with the President. Stephen Decatur was present, and Peale had brought the Oriental hookah that he had just repaired for Jefferson, who used it as a peace pipe when receiving Indian chiefs. Much as Humboldt would have liked to stay, he must leave and prepare for his return to Europe. Nobody in this company at table could blame him. They would understand that he must go to Paris to work on the results of his travels.[1]

If Jefferson regretted Humboldt's leaving, he must have consoled himself, philosopher that he was, with the thought that true friendship knows no geographic obstacles. Humboldt would leave and yet stay with him, would nourish their friendship with letters and gifts of his books long after Jefferson retired to Monticello. How greatly they had enjoyed each other's company is evident from Humboldt's farewell letter to Jefferson, of June 27. He wrote it, like the others, in flamboyant French:

My departure is scheduled for tomorrow, and it shows me quite clearly that I achieved the purpose of my visit. I have had the honor to see the First Magistrate of this great republic living with the simplicity of a philosopher, receiving me with such great kindness as I shall always remember. . . . I take leave in the consolation that the people of this continent march with great strides toward the perfection of a social state, while Europe presents an immoral and melancholy spectacle. I flatter myself in the expectation of enjoying this consoling experience again, and I sympathize with you in the hope . . . that humanity can achieve great benefit from the new order of things to be found here. . . .

[1] That the Philadelphia naturalists desired Humboldt to stay with them is evident from the following passage in a letter that William Thornton wrote on July 6, 1804 to John Vaughn, the secretary of the American Philosophical Society: "But I am sorry the interesting Baron has pocketed all South America. I wish he could have rested his limbs awhile and published his works here. . . . The treasures of knowledge he has amassed are worth more than the richest gold mine."

There would be long intervals between letters, and brief confessions to Jefferson of how unhappy Humboldt felt in Paris in the summer of 1809, but how consoling was the memory of his visit at Monticello.

I should repair the injustice that I committed in regard to the Southern States in a special note and an appendix of my work . . . I call your attention to what I wrote about slavery. . . . My work was dedicated to King Charles IV of Spain, thereby to pacify the ill humor that the Madrid government maintains toward certain people in Mexico. . . .

On September 23, 1810, Humboldt wrote to Jefferson:

Tears come to my eyes when I recall that the most virtuous of men is also the happiest.

And Jefferson, in acknowledging Humboldt's work on Mexico, replied:

It gives us a knowledge of that country more accurate than I believe we possess of Europe—the seat of science for a thousand years. It comes at a moment when those countries like Mexico are beginning to get interesting to the whole world. They are now becoming the scenes of political evolution to take their stations as integral members of the great family of nations. . . . I fear from some expressions in your letter that your personal interests have not been duly protected while you were devoting your time, talents, and labor for the information of mankind. I should sincerely regret it for the honor of the governing powers, as well as from affectionate attachment to yourself and the sincerest wishes for your felicity, fortunes and fame.

Such generous expressions of friendship made up for Humboldt's lack of the felicity that Jefferson enjoyed in full measure. And it would be good to remember that he had other friends in the United States, men like Madison, Gallatin, and the enterprising Peale.

Back in Philadelphia, Humboldt sat for his portrait in Peale's studio. There the painter of Washington and Jefferson depicted him as a man in his prime, with inquiring eyes and a round face, luscious red lips, and a strong chin. It was the first portrait that the artist had painted in six years, and for this reason might have turned out less well than it did. When it was exhibited later in New York, a journalist was so struck by its fine likeness and coloring that he thought it better than many of Peale's other portraits.[2]

For Humboldt and Bonpland, Philosophical Hall remained the center of attraction. Its members were invited to a special showing of Humboldt's landscape sketches from Mexico, and Dr. Rush entertained the party on several occasions in his home. The departure scheduled for June 28 having been delayed, Dr. Rush invited the naturalist on June 29 to sup with him and John Francis Mifflin, youngest half-brother of General Thomas Mifflin. The host noted in his diary that the Baron ascribed great importance to the moral influence exerted on European manners by the coined gold and silver shipped from Spanish America to the Old World. Whatever these morals were, they must certainly have been at a low ebb, judging by the latest newspaper reports. Every new ship brought alarming stories. Napoleon's armies were on the march again, had passed into the Lowlands and crossed the Rhine into Germany. Admiral Nelson was reported bracing himself for a decisive naval engagement with the

---

[2] This portrait is preserved in the library of the College of Surgeons in Philadelphia.

French. British men-of-war had been seen off the mouth of the Delaware searching for ships suspected of carrying contraband to France and Spain.

Press reporting in those days was not the high-pressure type of business it is nowadays. The *General Advertiser*, Philadelphia's daily paper, published a notice of Humboldt's visit on June 1, and informed its readers that "these gentlemen [Humboldt and Bonpland] have discovered during their researches more than three thousand species of plants not before described." A Washington paper had published an interview with the travelers, and on June 14 the Philadelphia *Aurora* devoted half a column to a brief account of their travels and explorations, noting with obvious satisfaction "that the citizens of Washington, and more especially the President, impressed with the great and disinterested service of the Baron, have, by their attentions, paid his talents the respect to which they are so eminently entitled." In the same paper Humboldt could have read, on June 29, 1804, that an "English gentleman has lately been making experiments in order to ascertain whether it might be practical to erect telegraphs."

In the local newspaper records available from the time of Humboldt's visit, there is no indication that his privacy had ever been invaded by interviews. Bonpland and Montúfar were mentioned but once, as if they had been unable to converse in English, as Humboldt could. One suspects that the attention accorded him was the result not solely of respect, but also of his being the most talkative and lively member of the party. Neither Rush nor Peale mentioned in their diaries that Bonpland and Montúfar had anything to contribute. They must have seemed like shadows of the man who dominated by his rich and generous nature.

Inconspicuous as these travel companions seemed, we must picture them standing next to Humboldt on July 9, 1804, when the ship was ready to carry the trio of friends to Europe. They would remember this farewell each in his own way. The Ecuadorian, Montúfar, might dream about a freedom that it would be worth fighting for in his own land. Bonpland had accepted this American interlude of civilized life like one eager to return to Paris, but tormented by nostalgic memories of tropical jungles and plant-collecting. And Humboldt, seeing America's firmament bright with hopeful stars, had perhaps been unaware of how they would come to be reflected in him.

10

Famous in Paris

UNDER THE HOT sun of an August noon the grapes were ripening in the vineyards around Bordeaux. Soon they would be gathered, and delicious wine would fill the ancient vats for the vintage of 1804. Friend and foe might relish it each to his own taste, toasting the new Emperor of the French or wishing him in hell, depending on which side of the British Channel, or Rhine, or Danube the glass would be raised. For Napoleon had overthrown the Revolutionary Directorate in Paris, had proclaimed himself First Consul of the Empire, and was about to summon the Pope from Rome for his coronation. The days of *gloire* and *victoire* were at hand, and soon Parisians were to shout themselves hoarse with *"Vive l'Empereur!"* How vastly different this new Paris would be from the one Humboldt had seen in 1798, when he and Bonpland had left for Marseille with their uncertain plans.

Could Humboldt pretend that politics was nothing in a scholar's world? He had gathered his own brand of grapes, and felt eager to let his scientific vintage ripen where the mental climate was hottest. Only in Paris could he hope to be received and acclaimed as he wished, as was his due for his glorious explorations. Only the French scientific genius would be able to appreciate the results of five years of studies; only French scholars could aid him in the preparation of his scientific publications. Paris was Europe's greatest book-publishing center. In Humboldt's own estimate the achievement of his American travels justified his decision to live in Paris. Again it was a question of allegiance. His devotion to natural science could not be allowed to conflict with feelings like patriotism or family traditions, not at least for the present.

His ship had escaped the watchful eyes of the British Navy by making what was then considered a record crossing from Philadelphia to Bordeaux in twenty-seven days. On August 1, 1804 the Humboldt party looked out on the vine-clad hills of France. A few days later Bonpland rushed home to visit his brother at La Rochelle; Humboldt and Montúfar prepared for a coach ride to Paris. While still on board, Humboldt had written letters to his brother Wilhelm, to Freiesleben at Freiberg, and to Kunth, his former tutor, now manager of his estate. An urgent note went off to the Institut National in Paris to say that he had returned at last, soon to shake hands with his colleagues. In these letters Humboldt's pride in his accomplishments is mixed with a warmhearted feeling for all his friends, as if he needed them more than ever. "I confess," he wrote to Freiesleben, "that it was with a heavy heart that I parted from the bright glories of tropical lands. I quite dread this first winter. Everything will be so strange, and it will take me some time to settle down again." Such anxiety was unnecessary in view of the pleasant surprise that was awaiting him in Paris.

His sister-in-law Caroline, had arrived in the French capital six weeks earlier. She had been visiting relatives in Germany to recuperate from the tragic loss of her oldest son in Rome, where her husband was Minister Plenipotentiary to the Papal court. What prompted her to prolong a separation from her husband by going to Paris? Was it the prospect of welcoming Alexander in all the glory of his fame, or was it a temporary romantic attachment to her old friend Burgsdorff, a German diplomat and traveler? Whatever the reason, Caroline was elated over Alexander's arrival, and we may presume that her brother-in-law was deeply moved to be welcomed back to Europe by a member of his family. How greatly impressed Caroline was is evident from letters she wrote to her husband.

Alexander continues to make the greatest impression. His collections are immense, and to work them over, to compare and develop his ideas, will require from five to six years. . . . He is not in the least aged . . . his face is decidedly fuller and his liveliness of speech and manner has increased—as far as that is possible. . . . He was awfully busy in the first eight days. He is with Kohlrausch [the Prussian Minister] a lot, meets him as early as six in the morning, works and talks all the time. At nine he comes over to my apartment for breakfast. If not engaged otherwise, he takes lunch with me. He really treats me with great affection.

Alexander wrote to his brother: "I live extremely close with Li [Caroline]. While I am much engaged in society, we see each other daily. It is you alone we miss."

Six years earlier, Caroline had planned to make a more permanent home for him, and what had become of that plan? Here was Alexander in her hotel apartment, as excited and talkative as ever, full of projects, overflowing with stories of jungles, jaguars, and Indians, and apparently none the worse for all his appalling adventures. And, most interesting of all, Alexander was still on friendly terms with Aimé Bonpland, and had even acquired a new friend on the way through America, a young Ecuadorian nobleman named Montúfar. She thought it a bit shocking for Alexander to bask in the fame of his accomplishments.

"Alexander lets himself be carried away by French charm," she wrote to Rome. He was feted all over town, acting like a Frenchman, and so neglectful of his German heritage! Reading this, Wilhelm became alarmed. Alexander must at all costs be brought back to Berlin, he wrote to his wife, no matter how much his brother despised the idea. Had Wilhelm forgotten that Alexander had written him from America "to do everything in your power to prevent me from ever seeing Berlin again"? "After all," Wilhelm wrote to his wife, "one must respect one's country even if it is a sand desert [Alexander's own term for Prussia]. He will soon come to realize that he will not find recognition except in Germany." But for Alexander the hour of fame had struck, and he seemed determined to make the most of it.

Six weeks after his return to Paris, Humboldt read his first travel report to a festive gathering at the Institut National. After the lecture, everybody flocked around him to see his exhibition of drawings, fossil specimens, and minerals. How many craved to touch a bit of rock from Chimborazo or the piece of quinine bark from the Amazon! The Emperor, busy with preparations for the coronation, had been prevented from attending this memorable meeting. All Paris had been talking about it for weeks. Even Wilhelm had urged his wife to stay in Paris for the occasion. As for Alexander, she should not take her brother-in-law's social ambitions too seriously. They might please him for a while, but as long as Alexander remained receptive to criticism he was really in no danger of letting himself be ruined by vanity.

He cannot praise you enough in his letters, and mentions specifically that he did not find you much changed. That *he* did not change I can fully understand. Neither he nor I will ever alter fundamentally, considering that both of us were subjected in our youths to an austere and lonesome upbringing, so that the influence of later years can count for nothing. . . . From his boyhood on, Alexander strove toward outer activities, whereas I chose a life dedicated to the development of the inner man. Believe me, dearest, in this lies the true value of life.

In October, Alexander prepared the first exhibition of his collections and drawings at the Jardin des Plantes. Caroline reported that she did not feel greatly impressed with Alexander's artistic accomplishments. His sketches were nice enough for illustrations of adventure stories or, at best, geographic reports. On October 16 she confided in Wilhelm that her attempts to bring Alexander into contact with the Berlin court had been successful, for the King and his Minister, Hardenberg, had answered Alexander's letter most cordially. But what fuss her brother-in-law made over his dress coat for the coronation! All velvet and embroidered at a cost of eight hundred francs! He had already spent twelve hundred francs for new suits and shirts.

On the reverse side of the same letter Alexander added a note saying how frightfully busy he was, and how happy. The members of the Institut who came to see his drawings and collections were unanimous in praise of the care with which each portion had been prepared. Even Berthollet and Laplace, who had previously criticized him on occasion, acted enthusiastic over it all. The same Berthollet would say of Humboldt: *"Cet homme réunit toute une académie en lui."* As for his tailor bills, Alexander added good-humoredly: "After such a journey as mine one cannot afford to look as though one has gone to the dogs."

Meanwhile Humboldt had managed to enlist the co-operation of various French institutes. The Bureau of Longitude Studies had already started on his astronomic observations; the Observatoire was working over his baro-metric measurements; the etcher Mafford had begun the illustrations of Mexican monuments, another artist the plant drawings. Bonpland had returned to Paris and was busy with his American plants at the Jardin des Plantes, where Humboldt was seen almost every day sorting out specimens and discussing the first botanical report. Such were the first revolutions of a wheel that was destined to grind its way through the most colossal of all scientific publications. Unhappily for Humboldt, one record of his travels, the climbing of Chimborazo, had been dimmed by the balloon ascent of Jean-Baptiste Biot and Joseph-Louis Gay-Lussac. The two physicists had launched their first attempt to reach the upper atmosphere on September 16, 1804, attaining an altitude of only 13,000 feet. The second ascent had brought the balloon to 22,000 feet, an altitude higher than Humboldt could claim to have reached near Quito. But to Humboldt it seemed more important to learn that his colleagues had made a new contribution to atmospheric physics, a subject in which he himself was greatly interested.

How Humboldt's friendship with Gay-Lussac began was related later by François Arago, the physicist and statesman. "Among the person's assembled in the draw-ing-room of the country house at Arcueil, Humboldt ob-served a young man of tall stature and of a modest but self-possessed demeanor. In answer to his inquiries he was informed that it was Gay-Lussac, the physicist, who had made some of the most daring balloon ascents at that time on record. 'It is he, then,' exclaimed Humboldt, 'who wrote the severe criticism of my work on eudiometry!' " Soon repressing the feelings of animosity which such a reminiscence could hardly fail to arouse, Humboldt approached Gay-Lussac and, after a few complimentary remarks about his aeronautic exploits, offered him his hand and begged to be allowed the favor of his friendship. From then on, Humboldt pursued Gay-Lussac in characteristic fashion, inviting him for a tour through Italy and sharing a studio apartment with him for several years.

The great coronation festival approached. On November 25, 1804 Napoleon rode to one of the city gates to welcome Pius VII. A week later, on December 2, Bonaparte received the ancient crown of Charlemagne in solemn ceremony at Notre-Dame. Paris was beside itself with the joy of celebrations. Their Majesties Napoleon and the Empress Josephine held a grand reception at the Tuileries. On this occasion Humboldt was introduced to the Emperor. "I understand you collect plants, monsieur?" Napoleon was heard to ask. When Humboldt confirmed it, the Emperor, shrugging his shoulders, said: "So does my wife," and turned his back. In that moment a genius of political action had showed in his characteristic abrupt manner how utterly distasteful Humboldt was to him, a foreigner, from an enemy country at that! Napoleon must have been aware that Humboldt was more than a plant-collector, for he received the reports of the Institut de France, of which he was a member.

How Humboldt took this deliberate insult from the

most powerful man in Europe, surrounded as he was by watchful eyes and gossiping courtiers, is not difficult to imagine. Always courteous, he may have spoken a few polite phrases to the Emperor's adjutant and then turned to mingle with the crowd and perhaps tell his sister-in-law about it. Obviously the disdain felt by these two men was mutual. As far as Humboldt was concerned, he would avoid the weekly levees of Napoleon's court, where it would soon be known how greatly this foreigner preferred the company of writers, scientists, and artists. But Alexander would not allow himself to leave this festive occasion without having done a service for his friend Bonpland. In talking to one of the Emperor's ministers, he had at least succeeded in obtaining the prospect of an annual pension of three thousand francs, which Napoleon confirmed in recognition of Bonpland's services to French science.

For some time it had been planned for Alexander to accompany Caroline on her return to Rome, but at the last minute he decided to stay in Paris. It was impossible for him to leave just then, when he and Biot were to present an important address on terrestrial magnetism at the Institut de France. But on the morning of Caroline's departure he saw her off, with best wishes to his brother and a firm promise to join them in Rome. Until March, Humboldt, was busy writing the first volume of his Mexican book, and it was then that he announced to the Director of the Mineral Cabinet in Berlin that he was preparing to leave Paris and travel with Gay-Lussac to Italy. They would make some observations on atmospheric physics in Switzerland, and then would proceed to Rome.

"I am working with greater effort than ever, and trust

that my publications will turn out to be less immature
than my last. My health is better than it has ever been."
He had packed seven large boxes of rock and mineral
specimens for shipment to Berlin, and had added some
ancient Mexican sculptures, gold coins, and a "feather
picture"—presumably a sample of Aztec feather mosaic.
The letter is curiously apologetic in its repeated assurances
that the shipment was only a small gift to the Berlin Museum, but that the director should understand that half
of the collection had gone to Bonpland, and that much
material had had to be discarded in America for lack of
transportation. He had traveled, the letter stated, for five
years, carrying the collections around with him, and while
all this time he had been showered with praise, nobody
had bothered to give him financial support.[1] Was this a
hint to his friends in Berlin that the Prussian government
did not deserve a larger share, or was he asking for financial compensation? In any case, Humboldt did not fail to
point out how much time and effort he had spent on
labeling the specimens, giving detailed descriptions of
each piece.

Before leaving Paris, he had drawn up a preliminary
prospectus for his and Bonpland's publications. In February 1805 Humboldt wrote to his friend Pictet in Geneva
that the prospectus would be issued in French, German,
English, Dutch, Spanish, and Danish, "for I am informed
that preparations are being made for publishing my works
in these six languages. . . . Meanwhile, we must publish
a travel narrative in a manner to interest people of taste,

[1] According to Humboldt's own estimate, the total cost of his American travels was 33,500 thalers, a little over one third of his inheritance.
This sum includes 5,000 thalers given to Don Carlos Montúfar for travel
expenses.

but to amuse the public we should also publish something more comprehensive. . . . People like to see. . . . I therefore think that the charlatanry of mere literature will thus be combined with utility." Pictet was to use his connections with English publishers, and was requested to advise Humboldt on an American edition as well.

I do not hesitate to say that among the anti-Federal party [in America] the success of my travels has produced quite an enthusiasm, as anyone can judge by the newspapers that find their way here. The sale in the United States will be very large, and should it be requisite to find subscribers—a method that always seems to me wanting in delicacy—I am sure that my friends Messrs. Jefferson, Madison, Gallatin, Wistar, Barton, and others will be able to obtain a large number. An English edition, therefore, ought to consist of at least 4,000 copies.

In the light of subsequent publication procedures, such plans were nothing short of fantastic. After six months of living in Paris, acclaimed as the most successful traveler of all time, Humboldt could not have failed to feel intoxicated with illusions of grandeur. And yet, strangely enough, Paris must have seemed not quite so ideal a place as Humboldt had hoped at the time of his return. The letter to Pictet concludes with a sentence that could only have meant that the writer would find it rather agreeable to live in Geneva: "May fortune ever preserve the enviable place of your happy shores, where I hope to find a home one day, and a place so necessary to the active exercise of genius and the development of social virtues." What could Geneva have offered him apart from a closer co-operation with Pictet or Augustin de Candolle, the botanist? Had Napoleon's insulting behavior left a sting?

Within seven months Humboldt had launched his first reports. Among the staggering wealth of scientific subjects two permitted ready presentation: the data on earth magnetism and those on plant geography. The former needed only to be tabulated in relation to their geographic positions to show the declining of magnetic intensity with growing distance from the north magnetic pole, whose position was roughly known at the time. Biot's collaboration helped greatly in the speedy presentation of these results.

As for Humboldt's ideas on the geographic control of plant distribution, he had formulated an outline in Quito and Mexico. This is the theory by which Humboldt's scientific work is best remembered. It concerned the distribution of vegetation as conditioned by the annual temperature range at different elevations above sea-level. The Andean mountain slopes and the peaks of Tenerife and Mexico had given Humboldt ample opportunity to study the gradual transformations of flora, which he classified in six zones, assigning to each its most characteristic plants. From sea-level to about 3,000 feet grow palms and pisang plants, then upward to 4,900 feet ferns, and from there to 9,200 feet oak trees. Then came the evergreen shrubs (*Wintera, Escallonicex*, etc.), and at the highest elevation, in two alpine zones, the herbs (between 10,150 and 12,600 feet) and alpine grasses and lichens (between 12,600 and 14,200 feet). Obviously these categories corresponded to the vegetation zones known to follow one another between the equator and the polar region, so that the latitudinal range of floras repeated itself, in telescoped fashion, on mountain slopes rising from the sea to snowy summits. Their respective altitude range was for the first time seen in its dependence on temperature, exposure to winds and solar radiation, topography, and soils.

This geographic concept of vegetation opened new fields for botanical studies and atmospheric physics, some of which, like the geography of cultivated plants, turned into an economic tool of prime importance to agriculture and plantation economy. What is nowadays known to almost every owner of nurseries, fruit orchards, and forests—the importance of seasonal frosts, maximum rainfall, dew point, and exposure to wind and sun—was contained in this first geographic theory of vegetation.

The progress and specialization of plant physiology since Humboldt's first publication has derived varied concepts from his studies. In his two principal botanical publications (see Appendix), Humboldt speculated on how to account for the great variety of plant forms and their possible origin. The laws of selective evolution and heredity not having been discovered at that time, Humboldt felt inclined to accept Goethe's concept of "archetypes" (*Urformen*), from which most plant families and orders were derived. He argued for the relative stability of plant and animal life in the last few thousand years, but admitted that in the course of geologic time it had undergone considerable changes, which he was wont to relate to fluctuations of solar heat at various latitudes. Most interesting is Humboldt's concept of social and antisocial, co-operative and competetive plant societies, an idea that permitted him to compare grassland floras with insect communities that exclude other organisms. The tropical forest, on the other hand, appeared to him as a "balance of life," with its highly competitive plant associations, almost comparable to urbanization on a human level. Plants were subject to organizational tendencies, like animals and people, whose final grouping resulted everywhere from physical agencies in their environment. It is easy to understand how such concepts led Humboldt in later years to his philosophy of a cosmic unity in which atmospheric, geologic, and organic forces act upon each other in complete harmony.

A report on physical and chemical studies of the atmosphere had been prepared with the aid of Gay-Lussac. The first volume of the *Plantæ æquinoctiales* was waiting for the last illustrations. The observations on zoology and comparative anatomy, and a report on *Astronomic Observations and Measurements Obtained on a Journey to the Tropics* were completed. In Humboldt's absence, proofreading and editorial work were to be entrusted to Bonpland. A diagrammatic chart on the geographic distribution of plants in various latitudes was soon to be issued. The journey to Italy and Germany would interrupt the steady flow of manuscripts, but the trip was bound to aid Humboldt considerably in his comparative studies of vulcanism and botany. More pressing still, the reunion with his brother's family could no longer be delayed. On March 12, 1805, Humboldt and Gay-Lussac left Paris for Switzerland and Rome, where they arrived at the end of April.

Seven years had passed since Alexander had said farewell to Wilhelm in Paris. The Palazzo Tomati had never seen such rejoicing and gaiety. The brothers admitted with glee that they had changed little over the last seven years. If anything, they had both grown more serious. To be sure, Wilhelm's face looked a bit drawn, but his large eyes, with their searching inward look, seemed as brilliant as ever. His was the face of a poet and thinker. How happy Alexander was to see Wilhelm's youngsters frolicing about the garden! Caroline had put up her guests on the upper floor. The kitchen, she assured Alexander, was ample to accommodate his chemical equipment if he felt like doing laboratory work there.

Wilhelm's position as Prussian Minister to the Vatican was one for which he was eminently suited by taste and inclination, for he enjoyed almost equal distinction as a diplomat, a man of letters, and a lover of the arts. His home was a center of the most distinguished society, frequented by writers, statesmen, scholars, and artists. Among the frequent guests was August Wilhelm von Schlegel (1767–1845), the eminent philosopher and translator of Shakespeare and Calderón, who was traveling in Italy with Madame de Staël. She had come from Germany, and she brought the latest news about Goethe. There was Karl Friedrich Schinkel, the young architect and painter, who was destined to embellish the Prussian capital with palaces and museums. With him came the sculptors Christian Daniel Rauch and Thorvaldsen, the Italian sculptor Antonio Canova, and Jörgen Zoëga, the Danish archæologist.

The Italian archæologists would benefit from Alexander's mineralogical knowledge when it came to identifying the stones of Greek and Egyptian sculptures. But it was at the library and museum of the Vatican that Humboldt benefited in his American research from a wealth of ancient Mexican manuscripts. Quite unexpectedly, his brother was able to procure the assistance of draftsmen for certain maps and illustrations of Alexander's manu-

scripts, so that his visit to Rome turned out to be produc-
tive in many respects.

The climax of this happy period came with the arrival
of Leopold von Buch, Humboldt's former classmate at the
Mining Academy at Freiberg, known already as a brilliant
pioneer of geologic science. As if nature herself was intent on favoring them with exciting spectacles, Vesuvius
was about to have another eruption. Humboldt and Gay-
Lussac left for Naples on July 15, and in the company of
von Buch proceeded to witness and study the spectacle
from a vantage point close by. By a miracle, the party
escaped the dreadful earthquake that made a shambles of
much of Naples. A few days later they visited several private art collections and museums, among them that of
Dr. Thompson, who acceded to their requests for a visit
on the condition that they divide the party, as four visitors were too many to watch among his treasures!

On their return to Rome, Wilhelm may have reminded
his brother of the necessity of visiting Germany. Alexander had had such a glorious time that the prospects of returning to the gloomy north were anything but pleasing.
The thought of it was made bearable by Gay-Lussac's
consent to accompany him to the Prussian capital. On
their way north they called briefly on the physicist Volta,
and in wintry weather crossed the St. Gotthard Pass into
Switzerland and Germany. In the middle of November
they reached Berlin. Now it was Berlin's turn to shower
her native son with distinctions of all kinds. By royal order
he was elected a member of the Academy of Sciences and
awarded a pension of 2,500 thalers (a little over two thousand dollars). Friedrich Wilhelm III, appointed him
Court Chamberlain, a distinction that Alexander found

irksome. To his friend Pictet he wrote: "Pray do not mention that upon my return to my country I was made a Chamberlain! Say something complimentary, however, at the end [of the introduction to the English edition of his prospectus] about the King, for he has really treated me with great distinction." It was obvious that the sovereign and his Minister, Hardenberg were trying their utmost to tempt him to stay. Their chances of succeeding were small, for Humboldt felt unhappy in his home town. "A desert devoid of humans," he called it in a letter to one of Goethe's friends, and continued in a desperate vein: "I am brooding over my position here. There is really nobody with whom I feel congenial, and this is a frightful experience."

What kept him in Berlin and delayed his departure, was a number of professional contacts, notably those with the botanist Willdenow, the astronomer Oltmanns, and a talented young architect, Friessen, who did the maps for his work on Mexico. He drowned himself in work, shutting himself up in a garden house equipped with instruments for magnetic studies. His correspondence with friends, publishers, and scientific academies occupied several hours a day, though most of the time he was chained to his magnetic observations.[2] Nathan Mendelssohn, the

---

[2] From May 1806 to June 1807 Humboldt and Oltmanns made six thousand observations on the daily variations of the magnetic needle, chiefly to ascertain the progressive changes of the earth's magnetic behavior in that latitude. At that time Humboldt's nocturnal habits enabled him to observe that the magnetic needle advanced a little more to the east at midnight as compared with the morning hours. The display of northern lights (aurora borealis) on December 19–20, 1806 led to the first uninterrupted recording by Humboldt and Oltmanns of a "magnetic storm," a phenomena which in our time has engaged the attention of nuclear physicists.

youngest son of Moses Mendelssohn, had constructed some novel physical instruments that Humboldt promptly demonstrated at the Academy of Science. To his old friend Henriette Herz he wrote a letter in Hebrew, telling her how sorry he was not to have seen more of her. He felt exhausted from lack of sleep, having spent his nights watching his magnetic instruments, which he dared not leave out of sight for any length of time. For a whole week he had been able to snatch only brief intervals of sleep between half-hourly observations. He lectured at the Academy on major scientific results of his American explorations: temperature variations at high altitudes, plant physiology, American Indians, and the significance of species variations of the cinchona tree.

The winter of 1806–7 was as grim for Berlin as any since the Russian invasion during the Seven Years' War. Napoleon had defeated the Prussian Army at the Battle of Jena. His troops occupied Berlin, and the royal court fled in panic before the victorious colors of the French guards. Humboldt would not allow himself to be swept away by the general misery. Stoically he tried to negotiate with the French commander on behalf of the University of Halle, which Napoleon was determined to eliminate because of the patriotism of its students. Of a sudden, city officials had discovered in Humboldt an ideal negotiator with the occupation authorities, for he knew Maret, the future Duke of Bassano, Napoleon's Secretary of State, and Marshal Daru, the Comptroller of the Imperial Household. Such useful acquaintances were not sufficient to prevent the plundering of Tegel, the Humboldt estate, by French troops.

In the midst of such suffering and confusion, Humboldt

decided to write his *Views of Nature*. An inner voice challenged him to give the public what he had experienced so many times in hours of hardship: the solace that springs from nature's harmony. He dedicated this collection of essays on nature to

minds oppressed with care. He who needs escape from the storms of life will follow me joyfully into the depth of forests, over vast steppes and prairies, and to the lofty summits of the Andes. . . . Let those who are wearied with the clash of warring nations . . . turn their attention to the silent life of vegetation, therein to contemplate the mysterious workings of nature. Let us yield to those impulses which have been felt by mankind from earliest times; let us gaze with wondering awe upon celestial orbs that pursue their ancient and unchanging course in unfettered harmony. . . . When, under the relentless bludgeonings of our time, the charms of intellectual life fade and the productions of creative art begin to perish, let us remember that the earth continues to teem with new life.

He must fling his gospel of nature at the tragic follies of war, must challenge despair with a philosophic orientation. "Although a thousand wondrous forms of life have passed before my mind . . . I have been constrained to admit while ranging the Amazon forest or scaling the heights of the Andes that there is but One Spirit animating the whole of nature from pole to pole—but One Life infused into stones, plants, animals, and even into man himself." If mankind's lot was tragic, if at times it appeared hopeless, it could at least be borne with greater fortitude in the larger perspective of man's participation in a universal and lawful natural order. Had not the great artists of the past expressed such visions, and was it not

true that eminent French and Dutch landscape-painters
had felt inspired to portray moods in which people, animals, and plants appeared not in competing violence, but
linked to one another in companiable association?

In these essays Humboldt's style became poetic in the
sense that it was inspired by æsthetic feelings. Yet they
carried an authoritative and pleading ring like the consoling echo of a man's desperate cry for the company of
an entire universe. To write well, Humboldt needed the
agony of loneliness, despair over a mankind blind to its
proper station and capacities. The *Views of Nature* came
to be his favorite book, as it was the one which, next to
Cosmos, found the widest distribution of all his writings.
Translated into half a dozen languages and republished
several times, it was read by tens of thousands.

In curious contrast to Humboldt's self-assurance of
style was his anxiety over his writing ability in the case
of his *Physiognomy of Plants,* which preceded the essays
by almost a year. In dedicating the first copy to Goethe,
he wrote:

I would not have wanted to present myself to you after so
many years of absence without a small token of my esteem
and sincere gratitude. While in the lonely forests of the Amazon, I often relished the thought that I might dedicate the first
fruits of my travels to you. It is a crude attempt to treat physical and botanical subjects æsthetically. *If I only knew how to
describe adequately how and what I felt,* I might, after this
long journey of mine, really be able to give happiness to
people. *The disjointed life I lead makes me feel hardly certain
of my way of writing.* Nevertheless, one of my cherished
wishes would come true if you, most admired Sir, who so often
inspired and encouraged me, would read my humble publica-

tion. Surely it will take you no longer than half an hour. After all, it may be pleasant on raw winter evenings to saunter in a leafy tropical forest.

Goethe was so moved by Humboldt's botanical study that he made a drawing of an ideal landscape

in which the heights of European and American mountains are indicated on opposite margins, with their respective snow lines and limits of vegetation. I am sending a copy to you [he wrote on April 3, 1807], a sketch I quickly made half in jest and half in earnest, and must ask you to correct it with pen and colors, and return it with your marginal notes as quickly as possible. Interrupted by the war, my Wednesday meetings have begun again, and I find nothing more interesting and convenient than to rely on your works on these occasions. . . .

Humboldt's productiveness under stress was all the more remarkable for the unhappy circumstances in Berlin. His native city had failed him woefully, or was it that he deliberately had turned a cold shoulder to all the honors by which his countrymen tried to entice him to reconsider his decision to return to France? Kunth must have sent some candid reports to Wilhelm in Rome, whence he received an equally candid criticism of Alexander's life in Berlin.

As precious as he is [wrote Wilhelm], he depends greatly on the opinions of people who are frequently of smaller caliber than he, so that by his own standards he cannot find contentment in those he approaches. Very often he does not judge the degree of other people's receptivity correctly, which gets him into trouble. But much more should have been done for him in Berlin, though unfortunately he has a tendency to freeze people. If he had gone to Berlin right away as you

[Kunth] and I suggested to him so urgently on his arrival at Bordeaux, advice that he declined by chiding me for not practicing it myself, all would most likely have been different.

Alexander was determined to return to Paris. All he needed was the chance for a graceful exit. Prussia had capitulated to Napoleon by signing the humiliating Treaty of Tilsit on July 18, 1807. The royal family had returned to Berlin. Soon after, Humboldt was summoned to present himself at court. What he learned there was as surprising to him as it was unexpected: Friedrich Wilhelm III needed his help with a diplomatic mission to Paris, with which his younger brother, Prince Wilhelm, would be entrusted. The Prince would be expected to negotiate for more favorable conditions of peace than Napoleon had been willing to grant to his arch foe. It would be Humboldt's lot to introduce the Prince to French society, thereby making his delicate mission more congenial and possibly more fruitful. Fortune smiled on Humboldt again—for what could have been luckier for him than to escape Berlin under the august protection of his sovereign? At first he may have concealed his joy over this fortunate turn of events, for he answered the King a few days later by acknowledging the sovereign's interest with expressions of grateful devotion. "I consider myself very fortunate in accompanying the brother of my sovereign, as it affords some proof of my zeal and reverence, so that I may not be found unworthy of Your Majesty's high protection."

The King had acted cleverly in letting Humboldt go to Paris on an easy and ample leash. How soon that leash would snap only time could tell.

11

A Scientific Harvest
from America

WHEN HUMBOLDT RETURNED to Paris in January 1808, after an absence of two and one-half years, the metropolis had found its new style as the hub of Napoleon's empire. The Emperor proceeded to make Paris the dazzling center of his power. No such building and embellishing had been seen since the days of Louis XIV: new palaces and government buildings, a triumphal arch at the Tuileries, and new space for an ever swelling tide of art treasures and scientific collections. Here was gathered the loot of past civilizations: Greek marbles and Egyptian statuary, Roman jewelry, Italian paintings, and Babylonian antiquities. At the Jardin des Plantes and the Institut National, at the Observatoire and the Muséum d' Histoire Naturelle, scholars competed in staking out new frontiers of science. They discussed new theories of earth magnetism and chemical valences, zoological systems and celestial mechanics. Nothing like it had happened in Europe since the days of the Renaissance. Professors had begun to invent scientific terminologies that foreshadowed an age when scientists would barely be able to understand the lingo of specialties other than their own. From Egypt had come the Rosetta stone. Thomas Jefferson had sent giant fossil bones. From Africa and Syria new minerals and plant collections arrived. All the world seemed to be paying tribute to Paris.

Such cultural opulence was carried on the wave of a new prosperity. Napoleon's court was in a spending mood, catching the fancy of fun-loving Parisians. Twenty years after the Revolution, nobody seemed to object to the Empress Josephine's giving presents worth hundreds of thousands of francs. Entertainment had become a lucrative career. Angelica Catalani, the Italian coloratura, earned twenty thousand francs for two performances at the Opéra. To listen to her, or see the famous Talma act his celebrated roles at the Comédie Française, was for many as good a treat as to attend a learned lecture at the Athenæum. There one could listen to Cuvier's zoological discourses or Laplace's fascinating astronomic theories.

Sometimes, when the Athenæum held a *bal soirée,* one could catch a glimpse of the famous Humboldt. By now Parisians had accepted him as one of their stars. He moved in the discriminating circles that gathered in the salons of a Chateaubriand, a Madame de Staël. Prince Wilhelm had found the sympathetic ear of Talleyrand, Napoleon's Foreign Minister, so that by the end of spring a secret convention was concluded between France and Prussia. Napoleon would exempt his enemy from a war tax of forty million francs in consideration of Prussia's cancellation of all private claims against Poland, which, under the Treaty of Tilsit, had become a principality bestowed upon one of Napoleon's ambitious allies, the King of Saxony. By this treaty certain private properties held by Prussian subjects in Poland were sequestrated, among them a large mortgage held by the Humboldt brothers in the Grand Duchy of Warsaw. Since 1806 they had received no profits from their Polish property—their only source of regular income.

Much as Alexander had hoped that his participation in the diplomatic mission of the Prince would help him recover his Polish revenues, he did not succeed at first. In March 1808 he wrote a letter to Pictet which leaves little doubt that he was forced to reduce his living standards:

I work and sleep at the École [Polytechnique], where I consequently spend my nights and mornings. I share the same room with Gay-Lussac. He is my best friend, and I find his company most consoling and stimulating, and the stimulus seems to be mutual. Although I have lost everything, I fancy that I shall be able to enjoy independence on forty sous a day.

He was placed in the embarrassing position of having to pay for publications and for an upkeep fitting his social rank. At the time, Humboldt drew an annual pension of ten thousand francs from the King of Prussia, a sum wholly inadequate for his varied and often very pressing financial needs. In Paris it was impossible for him to be without a coach and a servant. Bills from printers and illustrators began to swamp him in an ever rising tide. What was he to do?

In this hour of dire need Alexander remembered his old friend Baron Forell, who had helped him in 1799 to secure a passport at the court of Madrid. He implored Forell to intervene with the King of Saxony. "I am not without hopes," he wrote to Forell on November 16, 1809, "that through the influence of the King's envoy some alleviation may be procured of the dreadful financial embarrassment in which my brother and myself are at present involved." For three years he had received no interest from his mortgage. He enclosed a petition to the King asking for com-

plete exemption of the entire fortune held in his brother's
and his own name. In concluding the urgent appeal, he
stated: "This unfortunate sequestration of my property
is the greatest hindrance to the publication of my works."

To be handicapped at a time when he had embarked on
the most costly publication project was grievous, and
could be fatal in every respect. It might nullify ten years
of hazardous work and perhaps force him to leave Paris.
The calamitous situation had induced his brother Wilhelm to resign his diplomatic post in Rome. He had returned to Berlin to find Tegel pillaged by French occupation troops and his manuscripts scattered. To Caroline he
reported that the china and mirrors had been saved, as
had his Greek and Roman antiquities. They had been
buried in haste and had miraculously escaped a band of
marauding soldiers who had smashed furniture and fer-
reted out the winter supply of potatoes. From what remained Wilhelm could just about manage to furnish two
rented rooms in Berlin. Caroline was to join him with the
children in the spring. Alexander had written her a very
strange letter, she said. "He lives solely by the work of his
hands, from writing, I suppose, and from this he sent a
draft of five hundred francs to poor Rauch [the sculptor],
who will be glad to have it."

Wilhelm replied in March 1809:

Our family is really very badly off. The captain [half-brother
of the Humboldts] is mired in debts. Alexander owes his
banker in Berlin 16,000 thalers at twelve per cent interest. My
entire fortune is blocked in Poland; the confiscation continues. . . . But a new ray of hope came today in regard to the
Polish money. Alexander has been exempted by intervention
of the King of Saxony, and as my investments are so closely

linked with Alexander's, we may indirectly derive some profit from this.

Caroline felt certain that he would manage, but as for Alexander! "Where are the great treasures to come from which he expects from his publications? I am afraid his so-called friends in Paris cost him an awful lot. We know all about his generosity. He eats dry bread so that they can feast on roast."

For the first time in his life Alexander wrote for a living. Had he been able to write travel adventures, lurid tales of Amazons and exotic Indian rites, he might have done well. The French edition of his *Views of Nature* helped somewhat, but what could he expect from the sale of his scientific reports, from descriptions of tropical plants and fishes? Another man in his situation might have reefed his sails and made for a safe port, a position with a foreign government or perhaps one in his native city. But as long as there were friends to give him credit, Humboldt saw no reason for quitting. Had fate not been kind to him all those years? Had he not escaped drowning in the Amazon?

The task of floating his publications was staggering. At first he had planned on something like seventeen volumes to be published in six years, but he soon found that his project would have to be extended until it would finally reach thirty volumes, requiring a total of thirty years to complete. They were issued in folio and quarto size and provided with 1,425 illustrations and maps, many hand-colored. The general title of this colossal work was *Voyages aux régions équinoctiales du Nouveau Continent, fait dans les années 1799 à 1804* by "A. de Humboldt and A. Bonpland." It was divided into six parts, published without references to the order in which they were numbered.

The first part consisted of three volumes in quarto size containing the travel narrative up to the spring of 1801 (*Relation historique;* Paris, 1814–19), the period when Humboldt and Bonpland had reached Peru. A fourth volume was to complete the narrative up to the year 1804, but it was never published, leaving Humboldt's own description of the journey fragmentary. A pictorial atlas with 60 plates and text gave illustrations of landscapes, archæological monuments, and Indian types (*Vue des cordillères et monuments des peuples indigênes de l'Amérique;* Paris, 1810, in folio). This was supplemented by a geographical atlas with 39 maps in folio (*Atlas géographique et physique du Nouveau Continent*), waterways, portions of the Amazon and the Río Magdalena, and many detailed surveys of volcanoes and regions in Peru and Mexico. The last subdivision of the first part consisted of five volumes (*Examen critique de l'histoire de la géographie du Nouveau Continent et des progrès de l'astronomie nautique aux XVᵉ et XIᵉ siècles;* Paris, 1814–34 in folio). They constituted a critical study of all the source materials of the discovery of the Americas and early exploratory voyages and expeditions there. Humboldt was the sole author of these nine volumes of text, sufficient to guarantee his fame as the foremost authority on the Americas. His actual explorations and surveys presented a physical frame of reference for the zoological and botanical results. Organic life was to be seen in conjunction with the geographical environment in all its variety as he had explored it in South and Middle America.

The second part dealt with the descriptions of animals,

crocodiles, monkeys, birds, fish, and insects (*Receuil d'observations de zoologie et d'anatomie comparée, faites dans l'océan Atlantique, dans l'intérieur du Nouveau Continent et dans la Mer du Sud pendant les années 1799–1804;* Paris, 1805–32). Its two volumes were richly illustrated with engravings, many of them artistically colored by hand and reminiscent of the Audubon pictures. In this work he had the co-operation of men like Cuvier, Pierre-André Latreille, the insect specialist, and Achille Valenciennes, who described fishes and shells.

The third part was again entirely written by Humboldt, his *Essai politique sur le royaume de la Nouveau Espagne* (Paris, 1811). This was the geography and political economy of Mexico, including the American Southwest and California. It was the first authentic geographic treatment of an American country. In it he supplemented his own studies and surveys with a wealth of statistical data gathered from government archives. It appeared in two volumes, with an atlas in quarto, and simultaneously in an edition of five volumes in octavo size. It was provided with a map of the region between Guatemala and the headwaters of the Rio Grande and extending westward into the present states of Utah and Arizona. The map incorporated his own as well as Mexican surveys, and came to be of inestimable value for such subsequent American explorations of the western territories as those carried out much later by John Charles Frémont. This work on Mexico has been an unrivaled source of information, and has remained the most comprehensive reference work, unique for its consummate treatment of geographic, economic, and political features.

A fourth part dealt with astronomic, barometric, and

trigonometric observations (*Receuil d'observations astronomiques, d'opérations trigonométriques et de mésures barométriques;* Paris, 1808–10). As its main author appeared Jabbo Oltmanns, the German astronomer and mathematician who had been a classmate of Humboldt's at Göttingen University. Its two volumes were issued in a German edition dedicated to the famous mathematical genius Friedrich Gauss, and to Franz von Zach, director of the Gotha Observatory. The German edition was the most ill-fated of all of Humboldt's publications, as is evident from an autograph note dated 1850 which was found in his own copy of its volumes:

> This German edition of my astronomical observations was cast into the sea by order of the book trade so as to avoid payment of duties on books occasioned by a speculative transaction in Napoleon's time whereby English goods were to be brought into France in exchange for an equal value of French books.

The note was meant to be "a momento of the barbarism of booksellers."

The fifth part was again Humboldt's own work (*Physique générale et géologie, essai sur la géographie des plantes;* Paris, 1807), in one quarto volume. This monograph established the science of plant geography. It was illustrated with an ingenious schematic diagram of plant distribution at various latitudes and elevations, and included atmospheric, geologic, and magnetic data as well. An advance copy was sent to Goethe with a dedication. The diagram introduced a graphic method subsequently adopted and refined by makers of geographical and botanical atlases all over the world.

The sixth and final part contained the botanical studies. It came to be the most voluminous of all, consisting of eleven volumes, of which the *Nova genera et species plantarum* was the principal publication (in seven volumes, with 700 engravings; Paris, 1819–24). As main authors appeared A. Bonpland, A. Humboldt, and C. S. Kunth, a nephew of Humboldt's former tutor.

This mammoth publication in twenty folio and ten quarto volumes was offered unbound at a minimum price of 9,574 francs, or about $2,000. The seven volumes of the *Nova genera* alone were worth half that much, while single volumes sold for between 400 and 700 francs. At such prices, few scholars could be expected to purchase them, so sales came to be made chiefly to libraries, governments, and wealthy private collectors.

Humboldt had overestimated the demand for his works, and it is a mystery how he was able to find publishers willing to undertake such risks. Over the years, several Paris publishers were willing to share this unprecedented venture: E. Schœll, Gide, Dufour et Maze, or Gide *fils;* Gide and Baundry; Fuchs, Levrault and Smith. In Germany the firm of J. G. Cotta at Tübingen and Stuttgart, Goethe's and Schiller's publishers, stuck to the author to the end of his days. According to one estimate, the cost for the copperplate illustrations of 1,300 folio sheets amounted to 840,000 francs. The total cost for about 12,000 pages printed in antiqua type on handmade paper may well have amounted to half a million francs. Only one publication in France rivaled the production costs of Humboldt's works: the *Déscription de l'Égypte,* for which the French government advanced the sum of three million francs.

The order in which these works appeared did not conform to the consecutive numbering of the various parts. Delays were occasioned by unscheduled interruptions, like Bonpland's departure for America in 1816, which forced Humboldt to engage the substitute co-operation of Karl Willdenow and C. S. Kunth. Humboldt's occasional absences from Paris would not allow him to supervise the editing job throughout, so a number of volumes were allowed to appear without the main title. No sooner had the first volume been published than Humboldt handed to the printer several incomplete manuscripts of such other parts as the half-finished fourth volume of his travel narrative, most of which had been written by 1810. Its printing was suddenly stopped by Humboldt's order, and the sheets were impounded. The bewildered publisher was paid the sum of 9,500 francs as indemnity for a volume that never saw the light of day. The third volume of the travel narrative might have suffered the same fate if Humboldt, after a delay of some fifteen years, had not finally decided to incorporate certain up-to-date statistics. When he felt dissatisfied with the quality of illustrations, Humboldt ordered them destroyed, together with the copperplates; a new set was made at enormous expense. Under such conditions, the publishers had to be pacified by extra payments to make up for the delayed sales. Humboldt was known to pay handsome honoraria to co-authors and artists, often advancing substantial sums that he later forgot in the final accounting. It is doubtful that any other author of equal industry ever struggled so dismally in the meshes of his literary work. Of him it could be said that the cross he had to bear was in his books—and in his inability to cope with their editing. He was a St. Michael in mortal combat with a dragon that spewed bills and debts.

Small wonder that the money from his Polish mortgage was consumed almost as soon as he got hold of it. Bills from printers, artists, and publishers kept coming, with no end in sight. All this time he sustained his collaborators with enthusiasm and exemplary industry, though there were moments when he despaired over unwarranted delays. On one occasion, in September 1810, Humboldt wrote Bonpland:

You do not send me a line on your botany. I beg and beseech you to hold out until the work is completed, for since the departure of Madame Gauvin I have received only half a page of manuscript. I am quite determined that the results of our expedition shall not be lost. Please persevere to the end. It is an objective of the highest importance, not only in the interests of science, but for the sake of your own reputation and the fulfillment of those agreements into which you entered with me in 1798. Do pray send us some manuscript. . . . The public is under the impression that you have lost all interest in science over the last two years. They will not be eager for a new work on botany before the first is completed. I embrace you affectionately, and in the course of a month I shall know whether you still love me sufficiently to gratify my wishes.

For a scholar, Humboldt seems to have been uncommonly sensitive to the public's interest in and devotion to his work, but he had good reasons for constantly promoting his publications through magazines and newspapers. Who else could have done it? He labored alone, unaided by government or institutional support. Too, he was at all times the fervent protagonist of a philosophic creed meant to give solace and perspective to a public suffering from war and uncertainties. If only people could be made to understand the kind of orientation and æsthetic pleasure

he had experienced in his nature studies! His emotional
and romantic style betrays a mind deeply concerned with
man's place in nature and convinced that man was meant
to partake of a harmonious universe. His manner of writing
was much criticized, even by his own countrymen, and especially in England, where more matter-of-fact phraseology was generally preferred as the sign of true scholarship.
The French idiom permitted him to weld the crispness of
logic and speculative ideas. Many of his Paris friends
judged him to be a Frenchman rather than a German because of his fluent French style.

Most unfortunately, neither the English nor the German
translation of his works was able to do justice to his manner of writing. Still, it would be a mistake to rank Humboldt among the outstanding writers of his age, as he
assuredly was not. His friend Arago remarked one day:
"Humboldt, you really don't know how to write a book.
You write endlessly, but what comes out of it is not a book,
but a portrait without a frame." Except for certain chapters and magnificent passages in his *Views of Nature* and
Cosmos, his writing was labored and ponderous, and in
later years repetitious to an irritating degree. But as long
as his reading public could participate in the glamour of
his subject matter, exciting for its exotic character, and
could experience this intangible sense of living with Humboldt's experience and thoughts, it accepted and relished
his more popular books. These contributed to Humboldt's
legendary fame, which came to be unrivaled by that of any
of the other naturalists of his time.

In Paris, to be gifted and titled was almost synonymous
with fame, especially for a man who was social-minded
and equipped with a Gallic sort of wit. At one of the in-

numerable soirées a lady was overheard to say that she would hardly dare to leave before Humboldt for fear of missing a *bon mot*, which all too often was pointed at guests who begged to be excused at an unseemly early hour. Entering a salon, he would find himself surrounded by a group of eager listeners, whom he entertained with anecdotes, travel adventures, and brilliant ideas that came like a fresh breeze of spring. His store of knowledge was inexhaustible, and could at any time be delivered in French, Spanish, English, or German. Some thought him vain. Others were struck by his kindness and warm humanity, but few escaped in his presence a sense of awesome wonder. Hostesses, except those closely connected with the Imperial court, vied with each other for the privilege of his company. He spurned Napoleon's weekly levees in the Tuileries. He had been snubbed by the Emperor, and anyhow would have felt out of place in Napoleon's circle of marshals and parvenu courtiers, with their customary disdain for intellectuals. Soon enough the court learned of Humboldt's preference for Chateaubriand, François Gérard, the painter, and Arago, the physicist. With them he felt more at home than in the society of the *ancien régime*, like the Orléans, d'Angoulême, and Broglie families. His disdain for the tinseled upstarts of Napoleon's court was shared by most of them except for his friend Gérard, who kept on painting portraits for the Bonaparte family and large canvases of the Emperor's battles.

Most salons had their appointed days on which Humboldt could drop in without previous formal invitation. A liveried servant would usher the newcomer into the salon by calling his name, and it would have been strange for Humboldt not to discover a familiar face among the assembled guests. With Chateaubriand he argued the respective merits of life in America and in England, which the famous writer had visited as a refugee after the Revolution. On one such occasion Humboldt read from Columbus's diary. In the winter of 1813 he dined quite regularly with Chateaubriand, usually in the company of artists and writers. With Madame de Staël he could talk about his brother Wilhelm, who corresponded regularly with the gifted woman. Her courageous book on Germany earned Humboldt's admiration despite the embarrassment occasioned by her temporary banishment from France. At that time he denied having been one of her circle, because he hated to be implicated in political quarrels.

With few exceptions Humboldt's most satisfactory and enduring friendships developed through his professional contacts with scientists. His first intimate friend in Paris was Gay-Lussac (1778–1850). Nine years younger than Humboldt, and unattached, the young French physicist shared his friend's adventurous approach to science. Gay-Lussac gladly interrupted his laboratory research in Paris to accompany his friend to Italy and Berlin, where Humboldt deplored his quick return to Paris in the most outspoken terms of grief. In the difficult years of Alexander's financial worries, the friends shared the same room at the École Polytechnique, and for several years afterward lived together in an apartment in the rue de l'Estrapade, east of the Luxembourg. From there they would walk together to a laboratory or scientific meetings, discussing their joint researches on atmospheric physics and chemistry.

That Humboldt should have nicknamed him "Potash" was not so much a tribute to Gay-Lussac's temporary interest in that substance as an example of a habit practiced on many other friends. He was wont to refer to Chateaubriand as the "Pilgrim from the Holy Land." Nicknames were coined as a spontaneous response to a specific trait or event that seemed slightly incongruous or even a bit ridiculous, like Chateaubriand's trip to Jerusalem. It was good-natured irony, with no intent to slight except where Humboldt's ire was roused by an objectionable trait encountered among official careerists and busybodies. Titled visitors from England, for whom Paris was finally to be made safe under the restoration of the Bourbon monarchy, came in for sarcastic blasts of Humboldt's wit, as when he spoke of Lady Randall and the Duchess of Devonshire as "the leopards from Albion who stalked their prey among the social set," in which he himself was an exotic specimen.

His other friendships with scholars were dictated by a deep respect for their scientific achievements and humanism, especially if they shared his universal interests in art or history. On them he would confer the honor of naming new genera and species after them, as he named the giant Brazil-nut tree *Bertholettia excelsa* for the chemist Claude-Louis Berthollet. To La Métherie, the founder and editor of the *Journal de Physique,* Humboldt felt especially obliged for having printed several scientific articles and excerpts from his American exploration reports. As between the zoologists Georges Cuvier and Étienne Geoffroy Saint-Hilaire, Humboldt preferred the latter for his original and courageous stand against Cuvier's theory of cataclysmic changes in the development of earth and organic life. The co-operation of the able zoologist Achille Valenciennes led to a close friendship, marked by Humboldt's fatherly at-

titude toward a young man who had "the imprudence to
burden his life with a family." In later years Humboldt
brought his powerful influence to bear, through his friend
Guizot, the statesman, to lighten the burden of his collaborator and friend. Through Guizot's help, Valenciennes received a professorship of anatomy and was made a member of the Academy of Sciences in Paris. This was only one
instance of many in which Humboldt exercised the kind
of loyalty and helpfulness for which he became famous in
his old age.

Of all his Paris relationships, none proved to be more
exciting and enduring than his friendship with François
Arago (1783–1853). A prodigy in mathematics at the age
of fourteen, and at twenty distinguished by his researches
in astronomy and physics, Arago possessed a range of intellectual facilities which struck Humboldt as a supreme
manifestation of genius. What impressed him about Arago
was his upright courage in defense of his liberal views,
often bordering on radicalism, his forceful style of writing,
and a compassionate nature. At a time when reactionary
politics dimmed the brightness of French intellectual life,
Arago carried the torch aloft by writings and political
speeches in which he pleaded for liberty of thought and
correction of national prejudice. In him Humboldt recognized a force akin to his own, though more outspoken and
less given to compromise. Arago was a fearless man, supremely comforting to his friend in Berlin, who was wont
to growl over reactionary politics and then seek refuge
in scholarly studies. They maintained their friendship
through many years of separation.

When at the age of seventy-two Humboldt visited Paris,
Arago was the first of his friends he wanted to see. Hum-

boldt had written him a note asking whether his visit
would be inconvenient for Arago's family. Arago replied:

Can it be that you doubt my inalienable affection? Let me
assure you that I should regard such hesitation as a cruel in-
jury. Outside of my family circle, there is none to whom I am
more deeply attached than to you. . . . You are the only
friend upon whom I could count in difficult circumstances. I
am delighted at the prospect of spending a few evenings in
the company of one to whom I owe my taste for meteorology
and physical geography. I shall have a bed prepared for you at
the Observatory.

The friendship lasted half a century and found a touching expression when Humboldt was asked, at the age of
eighty-five, to write the preface for the collected works of
Arago, who had died in 1853.

In the winter of 1810 Humboldt made the acquaintance,
at Chateaubriand's, of a young writer named Guillaume
Guizot (1787–1876). Shortly after, Guizot sent Humboldt
reprints of his early pamplets, which so impressed the
naturalist that he read them aloud to a group of friends.
On May 4, 1811 Humboldt wrote him:

I feel that I have been very remiss in not thanking you
earlier for your kind present. . . . I read your admirable introduction among some friends, who fully appreciated the
generosity of feeling and the soundness of judgment that characterize your writings. I should like to discuss these views with
you, for *I feel more than ever the necessity for* awakening *an
understanding of all that is truly lovable.* I am wholly without
pecuniary means, and though pleased with your work from
the ideal manner in which you have developed the principles
of education, I still feel I ought to see you and talk with you

about your project. . . . We must arrange some day to go together to Saint-Germain.

A few days later, acknowledging a second pamphlet of
Guizot's, he wrote:

In a country where metaphysics are as much shunned as the
yellow fever or liberal sentiments, the tone of thought must
often be lowered to suit the reader, and maxims be expressed
with greater definitions of form. I was glad to see that you
have revised Campe's method. You may perhaps not be aware
that Campe was tutor to my elder brother. . . .

The system referred to was based on active practice of
Christian ethics, and stressed their importance as a charac-
ter-building force.

Guizot's betrothal in 1812 elicited from Humboldt generous praise unusual from one inclined to regard a new
bond of matrimony as a threat to friendship.

You are about to enter upon a new existence, and everything
around you will be changed. The world will dress itself in
smiles, and life itself will assume a new charm. . . . In the
midst of your preoccupation there will doubtless be moments
that you can still devote to friendship. I shall then be happy
to hear when I may have the honor of being presented to
Mademoiselle de M—. I shall be eager to win her favorable
regard.

Eighteen years later, when Guizot became the leading
statesman under Louis-Philippe, Humboldt used his influence on behalf of Bonpland and Valenciennes. In doing so,
he may have deliberately overlooked Guizot's resistance to
political reforms in France, which eventually led to the
July Revolution of 1848. Genius was to be accepted as an
elementary manifestation of methodical creativeness. It

gave Humboldt license to overlook in his friends certain character strains or beliefs with which his own were at variance. He accepted them with patient indulgence like an oddly shaped part of an otherwise perfect plant. It remains to be seen how far, at a greater age, this indulgence could be stressed to suit Humboldt's needs for friendship.

At the end of the summer of 1811 Humboldt suddenly decided to visit his brother in Berlin. The news of the founding of the University of Berlin, which was largely Wilhelm's doing, may have excited his imagination. All of a sudden he appeared at the end of October in the company of a librarian from Paris. "Alexander," Caroline reported, "is always the same. Impossible to describe him. He is such an incredible mixture of charm, vanity, soft feelings, cold, and warmth as I have never seen in anyone else."

After a separation of six years, Wilhelm was overjoyed at seeing Alexander. He wrote to a friend of Schiller:

My brother's visit was remarkably pleasant and deeply stirring. Even for me, who keep natural science at arm's length . . . his company was so attractive because he always moves in the orbit of his knowledge, but never on its peripheries. He really attempts to embrace all in order to explore one thing, which can be done only by approaching it from all sides. He maintains a horror for the single fact—hence his disdain for botanical nomenclature. . . .

Wilhelm's new position as Minister of Education gave him little time to work on the American Indian linguistics which Alexander planned to incorporate in one of his volumes. Yet if Wilhelm had hoped to lure his brother back to Berlin he was greatly disappointed.

Humboldt was mysteriously hasty about his visit. What

was he up to now? He was to meet the Emperor and Empress of Russia at Pressburg, in the Czechoslovakian part of Austria. Alexander I had heard about Humboldt's interest in central Asia from his envoy in Paris. Now that he was preparing his alliance with Austria and Prussia, a friendly diplomatic visit at Pressburg offered a chance to invite the eminent explorer Humboldt to present himself. Count Romanzov, the Russian Minister of Trade, had called on Humboldt in Paris with certain definite proposals. Was the Baron perhaps interested in exploring the Ural Mountains or the snow-capped ranges of Mongolia? His Majesty's government would be too happy to defray his travel expenses and to prepare for such an eventuality with all the powers at its disposal. It sounded exceedingly attractive to one cooped up in endless writing on America. Why, it might give him the chance of his life to see the towering ranges north of India! No doubt the Tsar of Russia encouraged him to think it over. An expedition to Asia! Humboldt was forty-two years old, young enough for another expedition. He would stay seven or eight years, but before he could agree to sacrifice a visit to the equatorial regions of Asia—meaning India and Java—the Russians would have to draft a plan sufficiently big and comprehensive.

On January 7, 1812 Humboldt wrote to his Russian friend Rennenkampf in St. Petersburg:

> The Caucasus is less attractive than Lake Baikal or the volcanoes of the Kamchatka Peninsula. Can one penetrate to Samarkand, Kabul, and Kashmir? Is it hopeless to survey the Gobi Desert and Mustagh [the Pamir]? Is there in the Russian Empire a man who has been to Tibet or Lhasa without having used the usual roads to Teheran, Kashan, and Herat, or those

from Calcutta? My principal aim is the high mountain range that extends from the sources of the Indus to those of the Ganges [the Himalaya]. I should love to explore Tibet, though this is not my chief object. I should like to spend a year in Benares. If it should prove impossible to reach Bokhara and Tibet, I could proceed across the Indian peninsula to Ceylon, the Malacca coast, and visit Java and the Philippines. . . . The political situation in Europe will fix my date of departure —when the road to Istanbul, Basra, and Bombay is clear. Such, my dear friend, are my intentions and plans. At this moment I can flatter myself in the expectation of sufficient funds for the realization of this project. I am extremely happy over the interest constantly evidenced by inquiries from St. Petersburg.

On the following pages of this letter his thoughts rambled widely over specific scientific aims and his promises of collecting scientific data for the Russian government from little-known regions of Asia. All this could be done, provided that the project was sufficiently ambitious and "worthy of a sovereign who rules over half of the Old World. I shall refuse nothing that might come in handy for the realization of this useful and glorious aim." Only one thought cast a dreadful foreboding on all these bright hopes: war between France and Russia. Napoleon also was planning an expedition to Asia. Already his agents were busy recruiting an army for his greatest gamble. Which of the two would reach Moscow first, the Emperor or Humboldt?

12

The Ominous Shadow
of Politics

THE WINTER OF 1811–12 found Paris in an anxious mood. Ominous signs suggested that Napoleon would soon be on the march again. New conscripts poured into the city for army training, and foreign visitors spread rumors that the Emperor was massing contingents from all over Germany and Austria for a major campaign. On the surface everything seemed normal. Around the Palais Royal wintry weather may have accounted for fewer street-singers, beggars, and flimsily attired girls, and in the rue d'Enfer, near the Observatory, a drafty studio-apartment made Humboldt suffer from rheumatic pains. His friend Bonpland had been seen less regularly at the Jardin des Plantes, the Empress having asked him to attend to her gardens at Malmaison. People said that Bonpland saw a good deal of a certain lady who appeared determined to marry him; Humboldt had every reason to rely on Gay-Lussac's company more than ever. Montúfar, the young Ecuadorian, had left Paris the preceding year, determined, it seemed, to serve his country in the struggle for independence. He would enlist in the rebel army under his father's command, finally to be captured and executed by the Spaniards. Humboldt would never recall the young hero without thinking of Simón Bolívar and his meteoric career as general and liberator in South America. In 1804 Humboldt had met the young Bolívar in Paris, and Bolívar had also joined him for a while in Rome. Then suddenly he had returned to South America to lead the insurrection against Spain, fulfilling in the grandest manner the vows he had made for the liberty and independence of the new continent. At the height of his career the Liberator told Gaspar Rodríguez de Francia, then dictator of Paraguay, that from the early days of his youth he had had "the honor of cultivating the friendship of M. Bonpland and Baron de Humboldt, whose learning has done America more good than all the conquerors." Some have credited Humboldt with having inspired Bolívar to liberate South America, but the records of their correspondence are too incomplete to sustain such claims. Nevertheless, enough is known to document Bolívar's admiration for Humboldt and thankfulness to him for the inspiration to gain a deeper knowledge of those countries—including Bolivia, which bears his name—which Bolívar rid of colonial rule.

For Humboldt, life in Paris had settled into grooves. He rose early, took a light breakfast, French fashion—coffee and heated brioches—and with Gay-Lussac left home around eight, going first to visit Arago or some other friend for an hour or so. Then he went straight to the library at the Institut National on the bank of the Seine. For two years he had enjoyed the privileges of an associate foreign member, having been nominated to fill the vacancy occasioned by the death of Lord Henry Cavendish, the eminent English discoverer of the gaseous nature of hydrogen and carbon dioxide.[1] In the library of the Institut, Humboldt usually worked till seven in the evening, with a brief inter-

---

[1] When letting Humboldt succeed to this honor, the members of the Institut de France must have remembered that it was he who had refuted Cavendish's idea that magnetic intensity increased in southern latitudes.

ruption for a quick lunch in one of the smaller restaurants nearby. Now and then the afternoon might be interrupted by an urgent conference with a publisher or illustrator. He customarily took dinner with friends. Afterwards the coach would carry him to a soirée, or to several, but rarely, if ever, to a theatrical entertainment. To be part of an audience was never to Humboldt's liking, for if anybody was meant to provide entertainment, it was he. The soirées were a sort of special stage to satisfy his craving for intellectual company and conversation. If, as happened on occasions, the company was not to his liking, he could always feign some urgent work and flatter his hostess with the comforting thought that the departing guest had been inspired by a new idea that demanded immediate attention. At midnight he returned to his studio, to write or read till two in the morning. A four-hour sleep was all that he needed in order to rise the following morning as fresh as ever, except on days when a rheumatic pain or a toothache made him uncomfortable. He ascribed the pains in his right arm to rheumatism contracted in the damp climate of the Amazon.

Painful as they may have been, and downright annoying for one engaged in writing, it is doubtful that this affliction entitled him on all occasions to excuse himself for his illegible handwriting.[2] In Humboldt's time a per-

---

[2] The most recent biographical sketch of Humboldt, by Ewald Banse, contains a brief attempt by Rolf Hübner at graphologic analysis of the naturalist's handwriting. Among other character traits mentioned are a mixture of sobriety and fantasy, an unusual openness and sensitivity, the latter to be held accountable for Humboldt's scattering of interests. According to the same source, Humboldt's handwriting shows a strong sense of self-esteem and of longing for a central position. Great capacity for adjustment and social life would seem to be verified by Humboldt's final position at the court of Berlin. His handwriting in old age, according

son's script occasioned much more comment than it does now: people were more conscious of it, more likely to judge a writer's character from the way he handled his pen. Humboldt's script was tightly spaced; its fine lines had a sort of galloping motion, "like dusty particles carried by the wind," as he himself said on one occasion. It was a scholarly script with an imaginative and optimistic touch: the lines were carried upward with complete disregard of margins, and often with letters so tiny as to defy the most earnest attempts at deciphering. For Humboldt to acknowledge his "hieroglyphs," as he called his script, as his own normal handwriting would never do. Time and again he must call his friend's attention to his failing, and self-consciously add the excuse of his rheumatic pains, conjuring up his former sufferings in the jungles. Yet it is evident from the passport application of 1798 that the illegible nature of his writing was established before he ever set foot on American soil.

His self-consciousness would seem to indicate that he desired to cover up with good-humored excuses what he regarded as an imperfection that might possibly detract from his stature. That he could write well on special occasions is clear from a manuscript page of a second edition of his *Political Essay on the Kingdom of New Spain,* in which his writing is artful and handsome. But such examples of perfect composure are rare, as if a special effort or perhaps a truly creative mood was required for Humboldt to produce a pleasing script. There is plenty of humor in

to Hübner, reveals a conflict between the writer's will to act and his remaining strength, which led to artificial acceleration (almost "neurotic") in his use of his remaining energy and a state of self-delusion that deprived him of philosophic serenity.

the way he excused himself, as for instance in certain letters to Friedrich Wilhelm III of Prussia, in which he signed
himself "Your devoted servant, forever acting straight but
writing crookedly," or "With profoundest respects in my
most legible writing without the customary oblique battle
lines." An ink spot would be surrounded by a thin line and
marginally referred to as the "Black Sea."

He was likely to toss off little notes on odd sheets of
paper, sitting down in a boulevard café, asking the waiter
for pen and ink, and on the spur of the moment hurriedly
writing a note to Arago or Gérard. Few men have lived by
pen and ink as devotedly as he, and fewer still have sustained a world-wide correspondence with such zest. His
letters and notes ran into many thousands; unfortunately,
many of them have been lost or destroyed.

Some time in 1812 Humboldt's routine of living under-
went considerable changes. First he moved to the Hôtel
d'Anjou in the rue des Francs-Bourgeois. Later he moved
again, this time to a studio on the Quai Malaquais. Was it
that he had tired of the company of Gay-Lussac, or did he
perhaps find the neighborhood of the Observatory less
convenient? Whatever the reason, his change of domicile
coincided with his interest in a young painter whom he
had met in Gérard's studio. This was a countryman of his,
Carl von Steuben, a good-looking man of twenty-three
who had surprised the Paris art circles by his canvas *Peter
the Great on Lake Ladoga*. This subject was most timely,
for everybody was talking about Napoleon's campaign in
Russia and the fact that the Emperor had purchased the
painting. The artist was the son of a German painter who
had secured for his offspring the position of a page at the
court of Weimar before he took him to St. Petersburg,

where the lad became a student at the Academy of Fine Arts. Thence Carl von Steuben had gone to Paris with letters of introduction from Schiller and Madame de Staël to Gérard. Gérard appears to have taken the poor art student into his family, as Humboldt mentioned in a letter he wrote in March 1812 to a friend in Weimar.

He [Steuben] lives in closest company with Gérard, who relishes his manners and talents greatly. But I fear that his position is not comfortable. The shy, delicate nature of this excellent young man forbids me to make the necessary inquiries, for which reason I should be glad to receive some information about him through you.

The following year Humboldt disclosed to his sister-in-law Caroline that he had seen his new friend Steuben daily for one and one-half years.

He is twenty-three, and of a quiet, noble disposition. Retired as I am from all other social life, this company is my only joy. Steuben supports his mother by his work. . . . The enclosed letter contains money, a draft that the son sends to his mother. I implore you most earnestly to forward this to St. Petersburg soon. I am preparing a present for you and Wilhelm, a family memento. It is my portrait, life-size, nine to ten feet high, by Steuben. He already has sketched it with incredible faithfulness and likeness in head and posture. . . . This is a present for you, my dearest Li. But should such a painting not turn out to be useful in other ways?

Ten days later another note followed, with a similar mention of Humboldt's daily sessions with Steuben, who had suddenly become his favorite companion. The letter contained another draft for Steuben's mother and a brief description of the young man's poor circumstances. It al-

most seems that Humboldt was supporting Steuben's
mother. If so, he could not very well have admitted it to
his sister-in-law, always quick to draw her own conclusions from Alexander's fervent friendships. He was so preoccupied with his new interest that he was rarely seen in
society. One of his countrymen, an aristocrat of the Weimar circle living in Paris, complained to Caroline that he
had not seen Alexander in ages. When his brother Wilhelm went to visit Steuben's studio in April 1814, he reported to Caroline:

> He [Steuben] is really a very pretty and charming man,
> though he hardly speaks any German. . . . Alexander's pic-
> ture is surely of some merit. I cannot claim to have been
> impressed by the likeness. It really does not exist when you
> look at it closely. . . . Honestly, judging by Alexander's por-
> trait, I cannot say that Steuben's manner of painting has much
> of the French school. Posture and treatment are ever so much
> more natural than in Gérard's pictures, and the colors are
> much more vivid and pleasing.

Actually, Steuben's work came to be recognized as sufficiently important for the Louvre and the Luxembourg to
acquire a few of his pictures. Moreover, he was commissioned to paint some ceilings at Versailles and in the
Louvre. Humboldt felt obliged to boost Steuben's art.
First, he commissioned Steuben to illustrate one of his
botanical works, which he promptly dedicated to the
artist—an honor usually reserved either for his most distinguished collaborators or for royalty. Then Steuben was
asked to paint Humboldt's portrait at a time when Alexander could ill afford to add to his financial commitments.
He went out of his way to praise Steuben's work, soliciting
commissions for an artist of whom few people had ever

Caroline von Humboldt, *ca.* 1804,
after a painting by Gottlieb Schick

Wilhelm von Humboldt, 1825,
after a sketch by Joseph Schmeller

ALEXANDER VON HUMBOLDT in later years,
after a painting by J. R. Lambdin
(*courtesy of the American Philosophical Society*)

heard. The biggest chance for Humboldt to repay Steuben's friendship and help him out of his pecuniary difficulties came with the arrival in Paris of Friedrich Wilhelm III in April 1814, a week after the ceremonious entry of his Austrian and Russian allies. Humboldt took the King to Steuben's studio for a sitting, procured commissions from the Crown Prince and other members of the King's suite, only to remember later that as between Steuben and Gérard, the latter enjoyed greater fame.

Humboldt arranged for the King and the Tsar Alexander I to have their pictures painted by Gérard. These were lucrative days for the artist, with prices for a portrait ranging from twelve to fifteen thousand francs. At the same time Humboldt improved upon his own artistic abilities; in the year 1814 he made a crayon self-portrait that shows him with tousled hair and a full, healthy face, a sensuous mouth, and large, serious eyes.

The friendship with Steuben came at a distressing time, marked by turbulent political events. Napoleon's defeat in Russia sent the battered remnants of his army reeling back to Paris. Suddenly its streets were full of invalided veterans. From beyond the Rhine came news of an impending uprising of the German people. The Russians were advancing steadily westward to join German and Austrian contingents. In February 1813 the foreign colony of Paris was so fearful of an invasion that thirteen hundred foreigners applied for passports. On April 1 the French government declared war on Prussia, and a week later Napoleon left Paris to join his army in Germany. He must brace himself for the onslaught of the allies—England, the German states, Russia, and Austria, marching in unison to crush his power.

Millions in Germany rose up in arms, poets like Karl
Theodor Körner and Ernst Moritz Arndt joining the ranks
the better to inflame uniformed youth with patriotic songs.
Napoleon's famous regiments would take their stand at
Leipzig in the most colorful battle ever to have been
fought on Europe's blood-soaked soil. Russian Cossacks
and bowmen from Mongolia fought in line with German
student corps and Austrian Imperial troops. Napoleon's
crack guards soon yielded the battlefield. Then they re-
treated, their glory broken, and the Emperor in flight to
Paris.

Humboldt was safe in his library in Paris, comforted
by the loyal sympathy of his French friends, who would
not permit their high regard for him to be swept away by
nationalist feelings. The physicist Biot reminded his colleagues that there was only one Humboldt in Europe, "a
universal genius the like of which has not been seen since
the days of Aristotle." With friends like Biot, Humboldt
could feel assured that he had chosen well to stay in Paris.
What could the patriotic clamor from beyond the border
have meant to him? "German patriotism is a high-sound-
ing phrase" he wrote to his friend Berghaus in 1825. "In
1813 it served to fire the hearts of German youth on the
other side of the Elbe! And what has resulted from that
infinite waste of blood and treasure? The probable outcome was already evident in 1814, when the crowned
heads congregated in Paris." The crowned heads, leaders
of the Holy Alliance, stood for resurrection of the Bourbon
dynasty in France and the reinstituting of a feudal order
in Europe as a way to delay democratic reforms.

But Wilhelm saw his brother's position in Paris in an
altogether different light.

I must confess quite candidly [he wrote to his wife in 1814 from allied headquarters] what otherwise I won't admit—that I cannot endorse Alexander's stay in Paris. It is true that he could not do anything for the war comparable in importance to what he did in Paris. It would have been an irreparable calamity if he had been killed in action. But the honorable thing is not to weigh profits. To value one's own personality so highly and spare oneself is beyond all my estimation of a good character. Æschylus would have considered it very strange indeed if anyone had prevented his fighting at Marathon just so that he might do a few more rhymes.

Wilhelm had joined the patriots. He had asked to be released from his diplomatic post in Vienna in order to be of better service in allied headquarters. His son Theodor was fighting in the volunteer army. Alexander's sympathies went to him.

My dearest Li, we are indeed living in a stirring period of history when everything is rapidly hastening to its consummation. Scarcely a week has passed since I wrote to you through a business firm, and now we hear that the mails have probably been stopped, and that my letter cannot have reached you . . . thus every avenue is closed, and I shall live here as isolated as I was on the Orinoco. I don't want to grumble, but shall joyfully endure if God in His overruling providence should bring succor to oppressed humanity. . . . Every battle fills me with anxiety about Theodor. For the first time I am experiencing what it means to be personally connected with the bloodshed of war. A feeling of dread mingles with all one's plans, hopes and wishes. . . . I am very well except for frequent fits of melancholy and annoying stomach pains, and am working hard without feeling it to be an effort. My works ought to provide a support for both myself and my immediate dependants, and this I think I can accomplish.

He worried over the payment of his pension, and was appalled at the thought that Theodor should ever need his intervention (as a prisoner of war?).

Should Providence, however, so ordain it, you may depend, dear Li, upon my tenderest love and affection. There is nothing that I would not then sacrifice to alleviate his position. . . . Farewell, my dear sister, these are wonderful times. I feel convinced that providential gifts are bestowed so that we can be useful to others in times of distress.

When had he ever used such words as *God* and *Providence*, and when had he addressed his sister-in-law with greater affection? War seemed beyond his comprehension. It made his own efforts at creating a new human perspective of nature seem transitory and ephemeral. The world he had known was tottering around him with the violence of an earthquake.

The crowned heads were gathering in Paris. They filed past the Tuileries in a glittering cavalcade, posing as the harbingers of a new world order. And the Parisians loved the spectacle and shouted themselves hoarse with praise for the victorious allies who were to rid them for all time of tyrants like Napoleon. The Parisians were in no position to bargain for a new freedom: they would have to submit to a restoration of the old monarchy, and meanwhile to suffer the billeting of foreign troops. Wilhelm von Humboldt had been decorated for his wartime services with the Order of the Iron Cross, First Class, which prompted Alexander to remark: "I would have preferred the Southern Cross." If the military appeared to have a monopoly on heroism, Alexander could at least claim to have saved the Muséum d'Histoire Naturelle from ransacking by foreign troops.

On the day following the entry of the victorious allies, Humboldt was asked to present himself to the King. It was almost as if Friedrich Wilhelm III could not wait to see the man who had dared to disregard the war of liberation by staying in the enemy's capital. Was it Minister Hardenberg or perhaps Wilhelm von Humboldt who urged the King to call for his renegade subject? Whoever it was must have known how useful Alexander could be. Nobody could seem more suited to entertain the monarch, show him Paris, and provide amusing diversions. Now that the tables were turned, with Friedrich Wilhelm III made into a Nestor among European monarchs, and Humboldt into an impoverished scholar with an unpatriotic record, the outcome of their meeting was anybody's guess. But those who knew the King as Hardenberg did were certain that he could profit greatly by forgiving the lost son and offering him friendship.

The truth is that His Majesty was a badly educated and rather complicated human being. Son of a debauched father and an unhappy mother, he occupied a throne that had barely escaped Napoleon's fury. Hardenberg had said of him that "he was great in suffering, but not in acting." The King's face, with its narrow forehead and long nose, had none of the marks of genius of his great-uncle, Frederick the Great. If it expressed anything, it was a complacent expectation of misfortune, a reflection of uncertainty and inferiority. His manner of speech was hesitant to the point of stuttering. A few days after his marriage, Queen Louise discovered to her dismay that she had married an insufferable bore whose main interest was winding clocks and designing new uniforms. That she had been frivolous in her youth and for a time had looked for love elsewhere had dismayed nobody but her weak spouse, who tearfully acknowledged her disloyalty by saying that as King he was obviously in no better position than any ordinary husband! But the Queen's courage had sustained him on the throne. She had borne all privations admirably. "The man should have been a tailor," Napoleon was heard to say of him, "he always knows how many yards of cloth are needed for a soldier's uniform."

For Humboldt to meet the King could at first sight have been but an act of grateful acknowledgment: the sovereign had graciously allowed him to stay in Paris by remitting the pension without which Humboldt could hardly have managed. On second sight, the King quite obviously represented a potential patron capable of dispelling financial gloom. Humboldt was faced with mounting obligations. Several of his manuscripts were ready for the printer; his collaborators were waiting anxiously for publications necessary to a successful pursuit of their careers. Paris had momentarily lost its prosperous status, and many of Humboldt's friends felt anxious about a possible restoration of the Bourbon monarchy. The outlook was not reassuring. In this perspective, the King's arrival promised delivery from a most uncomfortable situation.

The meeting was very cordial: the King obviously prepared to forgive Humboldt's unpatriotic record. During the following week, in April 1814, the sovereign enjoyed his new guide, who showed him art collections and historic sights. All he had to do was to listen to his new mentor, play audience to this lecturer, and be seen in the company of a famous scholar whom he could always introduce as his Court Chamberlain. To do so was flattering to a crowned head steeped in ignorance and inferiority. It made him appear significant in the eyes of his entourage, and pleased his ministers, Hardenberg and Wilhelm von Humboldt. How comforting this new friendship may have looked to the Comptroller of the Royal Purse is another matter. Humboldt was in debt and needed support for his publications. For reasons of prestige, Humboldt must be encouraged in his scientific publications regardless of his obstinate insistence on living like a Frenchman in Paris: the King ordered his newly discovered chamberlain compensated by a gratuity of five thousand francs for personal services. Wilhelm von Humboldt had reminded the sovereign of his brother's need for financial help. A year later came the munificent grant of twenty-four thousand francs as a contribution to Alexander's American works. The recipient of this gift would later reciprocate the royal gesture by presenting the King with four copies of his publications.

In June, the King invited Humboldt to accompany him to London, where the allied monarchs and diplomatic personnel were to gather for another round of celebrations. Nothing could have been more attractive to Humboldt than a visit to England: he could discuss his exploration project for Asia with the officials of the East India Company, renew acquaintance with English savants, and study botanical collections. The Russians had evidently shelved his plan for an expedition to central Asia, preoccupied as they must have been with recuperating from Napoleon's invasion. Friedrich Wilhelm III might put in a good word for him with the Prince Regent and ask for official approval of Humboldt's intentions regarding India and Tibet. It turned out to be an extremely busy month. Whenever Humboldt could sneak away from bothersome social obligations, banquets, and receptions, he was seen in the library and offices of the East India Company, studying maps and travel reports. If it was Field Marshal Blücher's turn to be honored at Oxford University as the somewhat illiterate man of the hour who had beaten the "antichrist" Napoleon on the field of battle, Humboldt could look the other way and discuss the geography of India with his English colleagues.

His plan was to go to Persia, then to the Pamir and the Kunlun Mountains, whose snowy ranges skirt the great Takla Makan Desert of inner Asia. He meant to cross the giant Karakoram and Himalaya highlands to the plain of the Ganges. He would traverse the Indian peninsula from Benares to Ceylon, sail on to the Malay Peninsula, Java, and the Philippines, and return via America to Europe. His main objects were to explore the mountains between northern India and inner Asia to ascertain their heights and geologic structure, to study the adaptation of plant and animal life to the rarefied atmospheric and desert conditions, and to find out to what extent the native races were capable of making a living in the world's most elevated and challenging environment.

The project was ambitious and dangerous. The highlands north of India were practically unknown save for travel reports of Catholic missionaries and native traders. No scientist had ever scaled those fabulous mountains. Not even Marco Polo had penetrated the mysterious uplands of Tibet. They were almost as blank on the map of the world as the Polar Regions. The possibility of filling such blank spaces by his own surveys, perhaps of discovering the sources of the Ganges and the Indus, must have inspired Humboldt's mind with brilliant visions. Where could he hope to round out his picture of earth and life but in Asia? There mountains and plains had cradled the first civilizations; the Himalayas beckoned with the glitter of unconquered summits. How irksome for him to be caught in a web of scheming monarchs and diplomats when his head was full of travel plans, of scenes along the Ganges! The King had spoken about his plans to the English sovereign; he had almost promised Humboldt financial support. But the English government had shown only very mild and polite interest. If the officials needed further proof of Humboldt's scientific intentions, he would, on his return to Paris, complete the American publications and prepare a geographic paper on the Himalayas. Impossible for him to leave Europe before finishing the American studies and his popular travel book.

At long last his *Narrative of Travels* was to appear. Everybody had been waiting for this popular account of his American explorations, expecting to be fascinated by descriptions of jungle life, shipwrecks, and other adventures. Did they not know that Humboldt had more weighty subjects on his mind, and that he found time only at intervals for the writing of a travelogue? When the first two volumes appeared in Paris (1815), many were disappointed to learn that the author intended to deliver the entire report at some future time. Could he never write except in installments? This series would be continued until 1826, when the twelfth volume had not even covered half of his American travels! This was the year when he decided to turn toward Asia with his projects, when he knew for certain that he would not return to the Americas. Coming, as it did, eleven years after his return to Europe, and being a scholar's attempt at popular writing, with its rambling manner of describing Indians, mission life, scenery, and scientific studies, it is remarkable how the public craved this fragmentary report. Its four English editions inspired several eminent men like the young Charles Darwin and prompted Louis Agassiz to make his expedition to the Amazon, whence William James, the philosopher, wrote to his father in 1867 how enlightening he found the reading of Humboldt's travels.[3]

Back in Paris, Humboldt found himself so short of cash for his personal living expenses that he reminded his brother of his urgent need for payment of the expenses incurred by his duties as a member of the King's suite. "In 1814," Wilhelm wrote to Caroline, "the King gave Alexander three thousand thalers for his companionship, and now that he has done much longer service [in London and after the Battle of Waterloo], he has received nothing at all. You know how much Alexander needs it, and that he lives by his time. I wrote twice to the Chancellor [Hardenberg], and nothing happened." At last, in May 1816, the money was paid—barely enough for Humboldt to repay his debt to a Paris banker.

How much of a consolation it may have been for Humboldt to learn of Napoleon's banishment to St. Helena is difficult to estimate. The very absence of any reference to the Emperor's fate in Humboldt's letters suggests his disdain of the man who had treated him with ill-mannered scorn. Much as Humboldt disliked the prospects of po-

---

[3] From his journey on H.M.S. *Beagle*, Darwin wrote to his teacher, Professor Henslow: "I used to admire Humboldt, now I almost worship him." Upon his return to England he asked the botanist Hooker to let Humboldt know that Darwin's entire career was a consequence of his reading the *Narrative of Travels*.

litical reaction which the Congress of Vienna (1815) produced, it is obvious from his cordial relationship with the succeeding French monarchs, especially Louis-Philippe, that he preferred a peace-loving dynastic tradition to the military tyranny of a Napoleon. It is reported, though not verified, that Napoleon was seen reading one of Humboldt's works on South America on the day of his abdication at Malmaison. Was the Emperor in his darkest hour dreaming of escaping to South America, there to found a new empire and draw some sort of sustenance from Humboldt's studies? History, which would not allow this to happen, was to permit Humboldt, the "plant-collector," to match his fame with the Emperor's and to survive him for many years.

After the Battle of Waterloo, Wellington was in charge of an allied commission in Paris whose meeting Humboldt attended on occasions in a purely advisory capacity. In the spring of 1816 his final work on the geographic distribution of plants was ready to be sent and dedicated to Goethe, then mourning the death of his wife. "I owe to your brother," wrote the poet in May to Wilhelm von Humboldt, "a sweet consolation, as his pamphlet reached me in one of the saddest moments. I liked it so much that it came to be the daily text of my contemplations. Please forward the grateful note to him." The poem read:

To Alexander von Humboldt

In sorrow's darkest hour
Your book arrived to cheer me in my grief.
It urged with power:
You labor gladly then for quick relief.

The world still thrives and blossoms wide and fair
By Nature's vast eternal force,
This you had come to know, do not despair,
Oh, let such tidings banish your remorse!
Weimar, June 12, 1816

At this juncture Humboldt's publication plans received an untimely blow: Bonpland left for South America. Whether, as some have asserted, Bonpland left to escape from his unhappy marriage, or whether he was impelled by a yearning for a freer life in the tropics, there to continue his botanical studies, it is difficult to say.[4] In 1814 Bonpland had lost an influential protector by the death of the Empress Josephine, whom he had assisted in laying out the gardens at Malmaison, which came to be a much-admired showplace. In Buenos Aires, where Bonpland became professor of natural history, all would have gone well with him if he had not ventured into the disputed border country between Paraguay and Argentina. On this plant-collecting tour he was attacked by Paraguayan soldiers, his servants were slain, and he himself was wounded and carried off in chains, ultimately to be pressed into medical service at an inaccessible place in the interior. His desperate fate prompted Humboldt to move heaven and earth to get his friend released from involuntary banishment, but nobody, not even the English Prime Minister, Canning, succeeded. For nine years Bonpland was forced to suffer a miserable existence. When, in 1830, he was finally released, his spirit was so broken that he chose a

---

[4] At forty Bonpland married a twenty-four-year-old French girl. Because of her doubtful reputation, Bonpland's parents chose to ignore the marriage. Madame Bonpland accompanied her husband to South America, but left him when his fate took an unfortunate turn.

primitive life in the wilderness. He never returned to Europe.

With Bonpland gone, Humboldt must look around for a substitute collaborator to complete the botanical volumes. He succeeded in persuading his old teacher Willdenow to come to Paris, but Willdenow was too old to adjust himself to a new domicile in the French capital. He was soon replaced by the botanist Karl Sigismund Kunth, the nephew of Humboldt's early tutor.

Life in Paris was not what it had been. Its mental climate had been severely affected by the reactionary trend symbolized by the Congress of Vienna, at which Metternich's policies had won the upper hand in reinstituting Europe's feudal order. It shocked Humboldt violently to hear that the Academy of Sciences had sunk so low as to form a secret committee to purge the library of all books which, like Voltaire's and Rousseau's, were held to insult the monarchical order. Germany fared even worse. Metternich's agents were busily suppressing free speech everywhere. To be branded a liberal meant removal from the pulpit, from academic teaching—even banishment. This worried Humboldt so much that he longed to get away, to sail for India. If only the British government and the East India Company could be made to understand how valuable his explorations in Asia might be! Perhaps his brother Wilhelm might help in his new position as Ambassador to the Court of St. James's.

In October 1814 Arago accompanied Humboldt to London, where the matter of his passport for India was to be discussed again. "Alexander," Wilhelm reported to Caroline in November 1814, "is much the same, though more portly and greatly aged. You know his passion always to

cling to one person who strikes his fancy temporarily.
Right now it is the astronomer Arago, from whom he cannot be separated." Obviously angered over Alexander's re-
fusal to stay with him, Wilhelm continues in a critical
vein:

You know him and his ideas well enough. They cannot be
ours, much as I love him. Our companionship is truly comical
at times. I let him talk as much as he likes. What use is it to
quarrel when we do not share the same set of principles?
Alexander is not only unique in his great knowledge, but of
truly good disposition, warm, helpful, and capable of sacrifice.
But he lacks the quiet satisfaction of his inner self and of his
ideas. . . . Because of that, he does not understand people,
though he craves their company. . . . He really does not know
art, much as he comprehends its technique, painting as he does
with tolerable talent. . . . Religion he has none, and does not
even miss it. . . .

Had Wilhelm perhaps overlooked the fact that his
brother felt tormented by the delays in his negotiations,
and did he not understand how desperately Alexander
wanted to get away from Europe—that his fate was in the
balance? Under such strain, Alexander may well have
looked older, nervous as he was over the uncertainty of
his future. When he returned to Paris, he had not obtained his travel permit for India. Now the obvious thing
for him to do was to wait for his next meeting with Friedrich Wilhelm III at the gathering of diplomats scheduled
for 1818 at Aix-la-Chapelle. Meanwhile he would work
out his travel plans in great detail and submit them to a
sovereign who had given him hopes of financial support.

In the fall of 1818 the crowned heads and their ministers
gathered at Aix-la-Chapelle to renew the Holy Alliance,

thereby to guarantee the frontiers of all European nations and prevent the threat of a new aggression by France. It was a lively Congress, interesting for the fact that Humboldt's advice was sought about the Spanish colonies in America and the slave traffic. What he had to tell the diplomats may not have been altogether to their liking, for he pleaded for effective legislation on behalf of slaves, and may have warned the delegates about any such military intervention in Spain as Tsar Alexander I had suggested. Spanish America was in open revolt, and in Humboldt's opinion would be able to take care of its destiny, considering its natural riches. He talked to Castlereagh, the British Prime Minister, and to Friedrich Wilhelm III about his travel plans.

On October 19, 1818 the sovereign wrote him the long hoped-for letter in which Humboldt was granted the munificent annual subsidy of twelve thousand gold thalers for a period of from four to five years, and the best of instruments for his coming explorations. It was a magnificent gesture. Now all that Humboldt needed was permission from the English government, and this would depend on the new Prime Minister, Canning, who was to succeed Castlereagh very shortly. Canning, dependent as he then was on the advice of the East India Company officials, may have had his own opinions about Humboldt's plans. In their eyes Humboldt may not have seemed the pure scholar others had judged him to be. Was he not a partisan of the movement against slavery, from which the British still derived profit, and had he not evinced a more than ordinary interest in certain Russian proposals for explorations in central Asia? Why should a foreigner like him be permitted to travel in the border regions of India when it was known that the Tsar's government showed a political interest in central Asia? Canning and his advisers may have judged Humboldt's plans with suspicion. Unfounded as they were, these suspicions would continue to stall him. There was always a chance that a man as restless as Humboldt would change his mind and direct his interests elsewhere.

How long Humboldt may have entertained hopes of setting out on his Asiatic travels is unrecorded, but in about 1821 he suddenly decided on a radical change of plans. In that winter he was approached by a group of French financiers to act as their consultant for a large mining enterprise in Mexico. "I would take no responsibility," he wrote to his brother the following year from Italy,

in this large financial adventure, which, however, should prove to be useful for the best naturalists who, like myself, want to leave Europe. They would be employed by those who put up the money, and they could rely on my advice as often as I am able to give it. . . . I have a big plan for a large Central Institute of Natural Science that would serve all of the liberated portion of America in Mexico. The viceroy will be replaced there by a republican government, and I have got it in my head to end my life in the most agreeable and, for science, most useful manner. I could live in a part of the world where I enjoy great prestige, and where everything is so conducive to my leading a happy existence. *This is my wish, not to die without fame,* to gather a number of scholarly men around me, and *to enjoy the liberty of thought and feeling so indispensable to my happiness.* This plan for a Mexican Institute does not exclude the possibility of a journey to the Philippines and Bengal. . . . For this Mexican Institute I am counting on Kunth [the botanist] and Valenciennes [the zoologist]. By doing this I could greatly enrich the King's [Friedrich Wil-

helm III's] collections. The zoology of Mexico is largely unknown, and one could introduce the cultivation of many Mexican plants into our forests. You may laugh at my Mexican
project, but owning neither family nor children, one should
plan ahead on how to make one's old age as pleasant as possible. . . . All letters from Germany are censored.

The reference to censorship appears to underscore Humboldt's resentment against the poisonous tide of reactionary thought, with its dimming effect on his life. It threatened the very core of his beliefs, made him live the
nightmare of intellectual persecution. Among the thousands who felt its heavy grip, few were granted the choice
of seeking refuge in Mexico and become useful to science
under the protection of a republican government. To understand the significance of this letter one must picture
Humboldt in the company of Friedrich Wilhelm III, who
had asked him to attend the Congress of Verona (1822),
thence to accompany the royal party to Venice, Florence,
and Naples. To the painter Gérard, Humboldt wrote that
the retinue of the King, diplomats, and courtiers plagued
him more than the mosquito stings on the Amazon, but
the thought of returning to Mexico made everything more
bearable for the moment.

At fifty-four, Humboldt was ready to do something decisive about his life. Eighteen years before, he had returned to Europe hoping to see the New World again. He
had promised Jefferson and Madison that he would return.
But was he truly prepared to fulfill his pledge?

13

Compromise with Royalty

AT NO EARLIER time had Humboldt been exposed to so
many uncertainties and conflicting currents. He was eager
to flee Europe: to seek his fortune in Mexico or to go on
a prolonged expedition to Asia. True enough, the British
government had cloaked itself in silence since his London
visit, and the Mexican prospects had not advanced beyond
some preliminary negotiations. So there he was, caught by
the friendly overtures of a King who did everything to
draw him closer, befriending him by such tokens of sympathy as inviting him for a tour through Italy. On one
occasion during this tour it had become quite plain how
concerned the monarch was about his companion. Humboldt had visited Vesuvius, and on returning had found
himself cornered in a canyon where a torrent threatened
to cut him off in a terrific storm. He had escaped sure
death by braving the current, and had arrived at Naples
with his boots muddy, drenched to the skin. Hearing about
this adventure, the King had rushed to Humboldt's quarters to congratulate him on his safe return, obviously terri-
fied by the thought of losing his precious companion. A
person who has been given a new lease of life is likely to
cherish a sudden sign of friendship, especially if he feels
uncertain about the directions the new lease may take—
as did Humboldt. In the King's company he had been
equal to all occasions, had spoken about a painting by
Leonardo da Vinci with as much fervor as about vulcanism

or Mexican codices. In Venice, Florence, and Rome the King had listened to him like a devout pupil in Sunday school.

The education of the King had progressed with such rapid strides that he desired nothing better than to entice Humboldt to return to his native city for good. The teacher, on the other hand, had showed a certain measure of willingness by joining the sovereign on his return to Berlin. He was not ready to commit himself by any loose promises, but he could at least take another look at a place he had not seen in fifteen years.

Curiously enough, Berlin did not seem to be so much of a desert as Humboldt had thought. He had celebrated Christmas and New Year's with his brother's family at Tegel, and in January he presented a most important, and for him most exciting, address on vulcanism before the Academy of Sciences. This lecture flung the gauntlet into old Werner's special reserve. To have related vulcanism to mountain-making forces was an unheard-of challenge to Werner's ideas and a downright outrage to a man like Goethe, who would never accept revolutionary concepts in geology. "This Humboldt," Goethe told a friend at Weimar, "never had any higher method than just good ordinary sense, much energy, and perseverance. In the field of æsthetics anybody may believe and feel as he pleases, but in the natural sciences absurdity and falsity are truly insufferable." Yet in the same year Goethe paid a singular tribute to Humboldt's stature as a scientist by stating that "the extraordinary men of the sixteenth and seventeenth centuries were academies in themselves, as Humboldt is in our time." What had roused Goethe's ire was Humboldt's bold concepts of geological dynamics, of the birth of mountains from volcanic upheavals.[1] The violence of the controversy was sure proof of the value of the lecture, which Humboldt delivered with much force of conviction.

The family circle at Tegel was entertaining in many respects. There Humboldt would sit watching the wintry sun cast blue shadows around ancient oaks, a sight familiar from his boyhood days. And Caroline's youngster Hermann was just at the right age to listen to his uncle's stories about Indians and jaguars, pyramids and buried Inca treasure. Out there in the park, young Alexander had collected rocks and minerals, and suddenly he recalled how he had felt like owning them through the very magic of their Latin names. Now, at fifty-four, he knew better: you could not possibly own the smallest particles of nature by just naming them; they were more like temporary aggregates of a vast universe, a cosmic substance related to the stars. In that respect minerals and flowers were quite different from sculptures such as his brother Wilhelm had collected. But his brother would never understand that he had found the companionship of natural things much more attractive than works of art because they seemed more dynamic in the infinite range of their transformations.

What had his life been but a search for the organization of matter? It had started with the primordial structures, rocks and minerals. How odd to think that their economic uses had not sidetracked his larger visions into a mining career! And more odd still how plant life around the mines

---

[1] Goethe's controversy with Humboldt and the English geologist James Hutton is reflected in the dialogue between Seismos and the Sphinxes in *Faust*, Second Part, Act II, and again in Act IV, where Mephistopheles presents the Huttonian and Faust presents Werner's concepts of earth origins.

at Freiberg had led him to the secretive chemical and physical factors of plant growth. There the adventure with
plant life had started, and then he had taken the world as
laboratory to explore, the incredible range of nature's energies: vulcanism, magnetic forces, the atmosphere, and
ocean currents, shaping life and grouping it in zones that
one could outline on a map. Now that he had done with
these plant-geographic studies, he must devote more time
to astronomy and magnetism. His friend Arago had shown
him how the spectrum of starlight could disclose the properties of matter in outer space. Was this ingenious device
not a bridge to the universe? And Ampère, at the École
Polytechnique in Paris, had told him that magnetism may
well be derived from small circular electric currents in
iron molecules. Was light a manifestation of electromagnetic energy, a primary and unifying force of matter? Spectrum and magnet might provide the key to an understanding of nature as one organic whole.

When he came to think of it all, it was cosmic companionship he enjoyed, a sort of possession that might well
make him feel dispossessed in the cozy comfort of his
brother's home. A close look at his brother's home sufficed
to convince him of this fact: books stacked to the ceiling,
classical antiques in study and living-rooms. And his
brother was full of building-plans, always eager to discuss
architectural details with the architect Schinkel, who was
to rebuild the old house and make it a fitting home for a
lover of classic art. The vestibule would have Doric col-
umns and an ancient Greek marble basin, the one that
Pius VII had given Wilhelm as a farewell present. Alexander listened distractedly when the architect suggested
placing the sculpture of Medusa and the statue of Psyche

in the large room facing the park so that the sun might enliven the marbles with as much light as the dreary northern skies would permit. In Wilhelm's mind was a plan to spend the rest of his life with beautiful things, to enjoy them with period furnishings in Biedermeier style, couches and chairs of birch and cherry wood, sharing his retirement with Caroline, so lovely to look at and an exemplary mother to her five children.

How quickly the years had passed! It made Alexander feel old to recall how he had picked flowers for his niece Gabriele in Rome, she who now was to be married to a young diplomat. At fifty-four he found that life had a curious way of letting time gallop, urging him to plan for the remaining years. But what was there to plan when he did not know where to turn? Would it be Mexico or Asia, Paris or Berlin? There was always a chance that the Russians would renew their offer. The Tsar was said to entertain plans for exploring the border regions of Persia and China and might need Alexander's aid. If so, the Tsar would have to defray Humboldt's expenses, for his financial situation was anything but reassuring. Having cleared up some debts, Humboldt did not have more than twelve or thirteen thousand thalers—barely enough to pay for the last publications. All considered, his brother may have been right in urging Alexander to return to Berlin. The King could hardly be expected to pay a pension to a Court Chamberlain who insisted on spending the rest of his life in Paris, and had, in fact, indicated that much to one of Wilhelm's friends. But though Berlin may have looked better to Humboldt than ever before, it was still not a place he would accept readily in exchange for Paris. To complete his publications on America he must return to France and ascertain the Mexican prospects.

"How can I express to you and dear Li my gratefulness for the infinite kindness you showed me on my last visit in Berlin?" Alexander wrote from a stagecoach stop at Strasbourg, "The memory of this happy time will never fade. Where can one find a family so wonderfully united by happiness, activity, and energy?" And in the following letter, from Paris: "The time we spent together seems like a year crowded with so many impressions and memories. What luck when love binds all family members!" He seemed overwhelmed by the sudden infusion of family feeling. "Writing to you, dear brother, touches me to tears when I think of you and dear Li, and the wonderful expressions of love while I stayed with you. I say I am touched to tears because there is no really deep feeling in man which is not painful. Such is our lot. . . . The reputation of your house in Berlin is so impressive in my imagination as to make that oasis [Berlin] less terrifying than I thought it was." The letter was followed by presents: Champollion's study on hieroglyphs and a Chinese grammar for his brother, a pendant for Caroline, and a drawing set for Hermann. "Why am I not among you?" he asked in another letter complaining of the despotic government and the hatred of foreigners in Paris.

In that summer of 1824 Humboldt received a visitor he had hardly expected: the Archbishop of Mexico. His Eminence brought greetings from the new republican government, assuring Humboldt of Mexico's esteem and admiration. President Lucas Alamán had written Humboldt a special letter to say how grateful the Mexican people were for all he had done, but failed to mention the project that might bring him back to Mexico. Had the financiers in Paris dropped their plans or, what would seem more likely, turned them over to friends in England? Humboldt wrote to his brother: "Without my work it would have been impossible for English financiers to put up three million pounds sterling for investments in Mexico. It is grotesque that one should be unable to profit from fame. Virtue is of little use in life." While English businessmen would proceed to gain from his optimistic reports on Mexico's mineral wealth, Humboldt must await another chance for explorations. Now he knew that he would not return to the Americas and that he must bide his time for the trip to central Asia.

As early as 1816 Humboldt had presented an address to the French Academy of Sciences on Himalayan geography, a subject to which he now returned. He continued his former studies of Persian and Sanskrit, discussing with Heinrich Julius Klaproth the Chinese sources of historical knowledge of the mountain systems of central Asia. In Paris none equaled Klaproth as Sinologist and historical geographer, and it was Klaproth's new map of central Asia that served Humboldt admirably in developing his new plans for exploration. That would occupy him in his spare time when he was not busy finishing his geological studies of Europe and America.

This work had been in Humboldt's mind since he had resigned from his position as Superintendent of Mines. Time and again he had delayed writing it, expecting his explorations in other lands to yield more substantial information on rock structures. Now that the Latin-American nations were ready to embark on a new political and economic life, a geologic treatise might be useful for further explorations. This *Geognostic Essay on the Rock Formations of the Two Hemispheres* was to sum up his consummate knowledge of geology. It was meant to provide a useful text on rock formations, their relationship to one another and their transatlantic affinities. While Humboldt still held to Werner's system and its concept of fluids holding all mineral substances in solution, as in the forming of granite, porphyry, and gypsum, it is nevertheless evident that his observations in America and his studies of Vesuvius had induced him to change camp. The lavas came from the "interior of the globe, in which, to all appearances, a very elevated temperature prevails." All volcanic formations had been produced by fire, and "formations of igneous origin must be of very ancient date." For him "the existence of volcanic products from different epochs" was firmly established.[2] This veering away from Werner's ideas brought Humboldt's concepts closer to those of James Hutton, who represented the "plutonist" school.

As for the diagnostic value of fossils, it is interesting that Humboldt referred to Brogniart's studies in the Paris basin, where the formations were so clearly marked by a distinct and changing sequence of fossil remains. But Humboldt questioned their widespread usefulness, and failed thereby to acknowledge their importance as William Smith had done in England. Yet in posing the question: "In what proportion does the number of identical genera and species augment as the rocks or earthy deposits are newer?" he may have given the great English geologist Sir Charles

---

[2] How advanced Humboldt's geological views were may be appreciated from the contemporary work of the English geologist William Buckland: *The Relics of the Flood* (1823), a final attempt to combine geology and theology.

Lyell, the germ for the idea that subsequently established
the subdivision of the Tertiary epoch on such evidence.[3]

Shortly after the appearance of this work the young
Lyell paid Humboldt a visit in Paris. From there the
twenty-six-year-old student reported on July 3, 1823 to his
father: "He [Humboldt] was not a little interested in hearing me detail the critiques which our geologists have made
on his last geologic work, a work which would give him
a rank in science if he had never published aught besides."
Humboldt presented Lyell with a copy and took him to see
the observatory. "He appears to work hard at astronomy,
and lives in a garret for the sake of that study. . . . He
speaks English well." On August 28 young Lyell wrote to
his father: "There are few heroes who lose so little by being approached as Humboldt. Of Cuvier this cannot be
said." Nine years later Lyell commented in his *Journal*
about Schlegel, the philosopher, and Humboldt, saying:
"He [Schlegel] is full of conceit, talks incessantly and of
everything, not like Humboldt, whose loquacity bored
some people, but never me, because un-mixed with self-
conceit like Schlegel's."

In the fall of 1823 Humboldt felt the need for a brief
vacation. Madame Béranger, the former Duchess of Chatil-
lon, had invited him to her country place in Brittany, but
if she had hoped to see much of her distinguished guest,
Humboldt was bound to disappoint her. He visited a few
mines in the neighborhood. He was restless and full of

---

[3] I consider myself fortunate in having been able to discuss Humboldt's geologic book with Dr. E. De Golyer, the eminent consulting
petroleum geologist and student of the history of science. Dr. De Golyer
agreed that Humboldt's significance as a geologist lay in the results of
his far-flung explorations and their fertilizing capacities rather than in
systematic enlightenment such as the work that Werner and Hutton had
produced.

forebodings of a change in his life. Returned to Paris, he shunned social life, simulating illness. This prompted his favorite newspaper, the *Journal des Débats,* to spread reports of his ill health.

The same winter he dropped in at a meeting of the Academy and was agreeably surprised to hear a young man lecture on research in organic chemistry. At the close of the meeting Humboldt walked up to him and, without introducing himself, inquired about his studies and plans for the future. "This conversation laid the foundation of my future career," wrote the celebrated chemist Justus Liebig of his first meeting with Humboldt, "for I thus acquired a kind friend and a powerful patron for my scientific studies." Without Humboldt's benevolent interest, Liebig asserted, he would have been lost in that sprawling metropolis, where it was difficult for young students to mingle socially with men of distinction. Humboldt introduced him to Gay-Lussac, Thénard, and others, and as he became increasingly impressed with Liebig's ingenious studies in organic chemistry, he resolved then and there to procure a professorship for him in Germany. And through Humboldt's help Liebig was finally installed at the University of Giessen, where he wrote his epochal work on *Organic Chemistry in Its Application to Agriculture and Physiology* (1840). In dedicating it to Humboldt, Liebig acknowledged his admiration and his profound gratefulness to a man "who proved himself to be the most zealous and industrious scholar of the century." Humboldt came to be justly known in the annals of this science for having promoted one of the great founders of modern chemistry.

The desire to recognize talent at the crucial moment

when it struggled for recognition, then help lift it to a useful professional station and sustain its recognition with unfailing friendship, was one of Humboldt's most endearing traits. For some time past he had tried his best to locate Friedrich Gauss, the mathematical genius, in Berlin. In that winter of 1824 Alexander begged his brother to promote Gauss to a professorship at the University of Berlin. Aggravated by a negative reply, Humboldt promptly dedicated the fourth part of his American works to Gauss.

I have not grown so indifferent to the glory of Germany as not to have indulged in a feeling of exultation over the great work that you so happily accomplished. When I returned to Europe [in 1804] I made my first and only request to the King of Prussia on your behalf. It is from no want of effort on my part that you are not now enjoying a brilliant position in my native city.

The mental climate of Paris continued to depress Humboldt. The resurgence of nationalism, the reliance on military power, and the ministerial despotism had all but anæsthetized the French Assembly. It was all extremely annoying to a man who had chosen Paris for its traditional liberties. Reading the *Journal des Débâts* in one of the boulevard cafés, he was startled to see how little freedom was left to the press.[4] Such symptoms of sickness of the body politic did not prevent Humboldt from studying them with morbid curiosity. He would not miss a single phase of Parisian life, would question the physicians who attended the dying Louis XVIII, and later would mock

---

[4] George Bancroft, the American historian and diplomat, visited Humboldt in 1820, finding him much concerned over the political trend toward reaction. Later, in 1847, Bancroft reported that Humboldt's liberal views had not changed.

at the "sickening spectacle" of the pompous crowning of Charles X in the Cathedral at Reims.

The German geographer Karl Ritter reported on September 17, 1824 that he had met Humboldt at Arago's home:

I found six or eight guests there already; toward eleven [at night] Alexander von Humboldt finally appeared, and everybody was eager to hear his reports, for nobody here is as good an observer as he. He had seen everything, was up at eight in the morning to make his visits, had been informed at once of the King's [Louis XVIII's] death, had spoken with all the doctors . . . and attended the lying-in-state of the corpse. That day he had been in Saint-Germain and Passy, and had talked to so many public officials that he returned bursting with anecdotes, which he related with much wit and humor." [5]

It was as if Humboldt had deliberately intended to witness at close range the end of a monarch and a new turn in history. Observing and registering were all that he, as a foreigner, could afford to do. When he was asked, the following year, to intervene on behalf of the independent Central American states in Vienna and St. Petersburg, he refused by referring to his various writings, which he claimed bore witness to his political beliefs. He feared being compromised by political ostentatiousness, as had happened to Madame de Staël when she was temporarily banished from France. Subsequently he would take advantage of her distinguished circle, forgiving her, as it were, for her

[5] George Bancroft noted in his diary on May 28, 1821 that he met Humboldt in the home of the French writer and politician Benjamin Constant when General Lafayette was present. "The more I see of Mr. de Humboldt, the more I admire him; he does understand the art of talking to perfection. He is at home on every subject that is started. . . . In politics he is decidedly liberal, and can manage a politicial discussion even with the great masters of political wisdom."

demonstration of courage. It would seem likely, though there is no way of proving it, that Humboldt championed Chateaubriand's fight for freedom of the press, for he was an avid newspaper-reader and always maintained high regard for free public debate. But Humboldt would not match the political courage of his friend Arago, partly because he was a foreigner in Paris and partly for the sake of his own comfort. This trait irritated many of his friends, and must have shocked his brother, who was courageous enough to quit his political career when the reactionary trend in Berlin became unbearable.

Humboldt, preoccupied with his scholarly work, was ready to hide his liberal convictions and go "underground" with his badge of the French Revolution, for the sake of such protection as he, a free-lance scholar, required from the men in power. He realized that Europe had turned the clock back at the Congress of Vienna, and that Paris exhibited the danger signals of new political unheavals. Those symptoms forced him to a major decision: either to suffer the consequences of political unrest and the attending uncertainties of old age in Paris, or to return to Berlin. Ever since his Berlin visit in 1824, he had played with the idea of returning, and would seem to have been emotionally prepared to do so on account of his brother. By 1826 he knew that the British government would not oblige him with the means of carrying out his plans, and he also surmised that the new Tsar, Nicholas I, might be prepared to renew his predecessor's invitation to come to Russia. One of the Tsar's emissaries had indicated as much in Paris, and if, as Humboldt had reason to expect, the Tsar invited him to Russia, it seemed likely that Berlin would make a better starting-point than Paris. Could he not profit from the family relationships between the Romanovs and the Prussian royal family? Was Friedrich Wilhelm III not the father-in-law of the new Tsar?

In the fall of 1826 Humboldt reconnoitered his chances in Berlin. This time it was the King's turn to make a final offer to his Royal Chamberlain, whom he had come to like and respect for his great knowledge and kindly disposition. The King promised him an annual pension of five thousand thalers, support for occasional travels, and permission to spend a few months every year in Paris—a condition that some maintained Humboldt insisted upon. It was as nearly ideal a solution as he could have wished, though he may not have been fully aware of his future obligations at court. In any event, Humboldt had seen enough of court life to realize that it would provide a stage not only for himself, but also for such friends as might come to seek for influential protection.

How difficult it was for Humboldt to accept the King's proposal is evident from a passage in a letter he wrote to Gauss on February 16, 1827:

It is a great decision for me to give up part of my freedom and of the scholarly pursuits that have provided me with wonderful intellectual experiences over the past eighteen years. But I do not regret what I have done. On my last visit in Germany I felt much impressed by its intellectual life. The prospect of living near you and being able to join those who share my admiration for your great and varied talents was an important motive in my decision. I shall not be found wanting in my intention to be useful and always to seek your counsel.

Caroline foresaw that her brother-in-law would have to spend much time in the King's company. "In the end one tires of everything that is without love, and so it is with

Alexander when he finally got weary of Parisian life. He
hopes to win a bit more leisure here." She had seen him
only very briefly, for, as usual, Alexander had lost no time
in visiting various officials and renewing acquaintance-
ships. Before Caroline knew it, her brother-in-law was on
his way to Paris to prepare for his final transfer to his native land.

He would stop over at Weimar to see his brother, who
was visiting there. Goethe told his friend Eckermann on
December 11, 1826:

Alexander von Humboldt was here this morning for a few
hours. What a man he is! I have known him for so long, and
yet he amazes me all over again. One can truly say that he has
no equal in information and lively knowledge. Whatever one
touches, he is everywhere at home and overwhelms one with
intellectual treasures. He is like a fountain with many spouts
at which one may simply fill one's pitchers—forever refreshing
and unfailing. He intends to stay for a few days, and already
I can feel as if I had lived through years.

The friendship of these two men was evidently as close
as ever, notwithstanding the differences of their scientific
ideas. Goethe had noticed with some anguish how Humboldt's geologic viewpoints had departed from Werner's
concepts, which the poet championed out of sheer sympathy for their precept of gradual, non-violent changes in
earth history. That nature should have need of convulsions
like mountain upheavals and volcanic catastrophes, as
Humboldt claimed, was foreign to the wisdom of Goethe's
old age. The poet's scorn at Humboldt's Huttonian view is
evident not only from passages in *Faust* but in his *Xenien:*

All of them are equally despised,
New Gods as well as idols.

Yet if there was a friend who could lay claim to Humboldt's approach to nature as a work of art, it was Goethe. It was he who had inspired the naturalist with a belief in science as a step that could prepare the investigator to turn seer. "The general principles enlarge our spiritual existence and put us in touch with the entire earth," Humboldt had written in his *Views of Nature*. Detailed analysis, necessary as it was, seemed useless unless it led to a perception of principles operating harmoniously. And harmony was what Goethe most emphatically envisioned, a philosophic concept of the universe akin to the central ideas of Taoism and Brahmanism. To be cosmically oriented was, for Humboldt, to give human existence a new perspective, to lift it to a plane on which individuals and nations might come to value each other in the secure knowledge of an all-pervading unity, a macrocosm. The study of physical phenomena was important only if through them one could listen to an echo from the cosmos. Without this philosophic orientation, Humboldt claimed, science was bound to turn into a mere scramble for utilitarian knowledge, tempting man to adopt in nature a competitive role for which human equipment was altogether too limited. But how was he to make people understand his vision? He must inevitably address himself to an audience and give a course of lectures. Such happy thought may have spurned Humboldt to hasten his preparations for the move to Berlin.

Packing up his belongings in Paris could not have been much of a job. He had never owned the furnishings of his home. Even his library consisted at that time of only the most necessary reference works. His American collections were scattered among scientific institutions in Paris, Madrid, and Berlin. He need only take a few mementos—a stuffed eagle from the Andes, some rock and mineral specimens from Chimborazo, and his notebooks, manuscripts, and published works. And what sense would there have been in getting depressed over farewell visits with his friends when he had happy prospects of seeing them soon again? Naturally, he would miss the circles of Arago and Gérard, "the very center of my existence in Paris." But much as the human heart may fortify itself on such occasions by all manner of comforting expectations, it is bound to miss a beat over the severance of accustomed ties. Paris had been his choice. It had nourished him for almost twenty years. His life would never be the same again.

By happy chance, Humboldt would leave Paris in the company of his niece Gabriele's husband, young Baron von Bülow, who had just been appointed Ambassador to the Court of St. James's. Toward the middle of April 1827 they left for London, where Humboldt may have wanted to obtain final advice about his project for India. It seems certain that he cut short his visit in England when he realized how hopeless his chances were.

Back in Berlin in May, he was suddenly confronted with the chores of finding an apartment, buying furniture, and settling down with one servant, Karl Seifert. That his apartment should have been in the none too fashionable northern part of the city is understandable: it was halfway between the scientific institutions and the Oranienburg Gate, which led to Tegel. He never minded walking, and was so accustomed to it that he used to accompany friends to distant addresses late at night and then entice them to return with him to his quarters for the sake of continuing an interesting chat. On such nights his servant, Seifert, would make him comfortable, bring him a glass of wine, and ask for his schedule for the following day.

The manservant of a bachelor of fifty-seven can be expected to play a significant role if, as in Humboldt's case, the master is of an absent-minded scholarly disposition. And Seifert's role came to be important to a grotesque and truly embarrassing degree. He was a stocky young man in his early twenties, and if his record betrays an eminently practical and even cunning character, nevertheless he had a way of reading poetry and talking glibly about art. To have chosen as famous a man as Humboldt for a master required some courage on Seifert's part, the more so as his employer had a disquieting reputation of forgetting to pay his bills and of delaying payments during a temporary ebb of liquid assets. But it could hardly have escaped Seifert's notice that Berlin was buzzing with all sorts of rumors about his master, that Humboldt had returned to Berlin to become a power behind the throne, a formidable influence on a weak King.

The rumor-mongers and Seifert must have been surprised to read the public announcement of Humboldt's lecture course to be given in the largest concert hall in Berlin. The story went that everybody was welcome to attend his lectures free of charge. Many doubted Humboldt's earnestness, his ability to entertain a mixed audience of burghers, merchants, students, and society, but they would surely attend for the fun of seeing an eccentric explorer. And many Berliners looked forward to a chance of practicing their traditional wit on a lecturer who was said to speak better French than German. A few learned men had attended some of Humboldt's scientific discourses at the university and had been transported, it was claimed, by the lecturer's appeal for liberty of thought such as had enabled the ancient Greeks to progress so remarkably in art and science. By all accounts, a Humboldt turned lecturer would provide good entertainment.

When Humboldt began his lectures in the concert hall of the Singakademie on December 6, 1827, the house was packed. The stalls were filled with royalty, government officials, and society women, the orchestra crowded with a motley of burghers, professors, and students. For its social mixture it was the most unusual audience Berlin had ever seen. To everybody's surprise, the lecturer spoke German fluently, and what he had to say at first about the æsthetic experience of nature studies was by no means so erudite as one might have expected from a man so learned and famous. It was at all times profitable, he reminded his audience, to accept nature's company with a sense of wonder and pure enjoyment, and no commonplace experience to let oneself be transformed by the delicious fragrance of a morning in the woods or the murmur of a waterfall. Had the greatest painters and poets of all ages not profited from such inspirations? To have it confirmed by Humboldt was reassuring, and it prepared the audience to follow their teacher on his sweeping survey of earth and universe. How had the Greeks and their successors shaped the concepts of nature? What had Copernicus and Galileo, Leibniz and Laplace, found out about stars and celestial mechanics? They had revealed an orderly universe, a cosmic design shared by an earth whose atmosphere and surface forms reflected the lawful pattern. Its mountains and volcanoes, its seas and minerals and living creatures, were not haphazard creations, but a gigantic unity whose component parts existed by virtue of interrelatedness.

Amazing how this Humboldt had seen it all so clearly, the arrangement of life zones in high mountains, as on Chimborazo, and how he could relate volcanic catastrophes to a geologic destiny that linked continents! The lecturer had been there, on the Amazon, on Mexican snow peaks, and in the Alps; had witnessed in the company of Laplace, Faraday, Werner, and Goethe the birth of new sciences. In steaming jungles and on the wind-bitten uplands of the Andes he had met Indians and found them human, even civilized, to the point at which they fashioned such religious symbols and monuments as the Incas and Aztecs had known. Speaking of races, Humboldt reminded his audience that "in claiming the unity of the human race we resist the unsavory assumption of higher and lower races." To be sure, some peoples were exposed more than others to higher education and cultural ennoblement, but "there are no inferior races. All are destined equally to attain freedom" (*Cosmos,* Vol. I).

The sixteen weekly lectures were a resounding success. They made science popular in public instruction, which till then had been dominated by literature and art; they were a challenge to anybody's ignorance of man's place in nature. Even Berlin's most influential newspaper conceded that "the dignity and charm of the lecturer arose from a unique combination of an attractive subject matter and the deep erudition of a teacher who never failed to make the best use of his seemingly inexhaustible store of knowledge." In a letter to Goethe, Wilhelm reported: "Alexander is really a *puissance,* and has acquired a new kind of fame by his lectures. They are admirable. He is more than ever his former self, still hampered by a kind of shyness, an unmistakable anxiety traceable in his manner of addressing the public."

In another letter Wilhelm reported to his son-in-law Hegemann on January 10, 1828:

The lectures are rather strenuous for Alexander; though he earns much applause and real fame. It is hardly possible to read better than he. . . . So far as I have been able to hear, everybody feels the same way. I hardly think that envy could find any fault with him. Taken together, the two courses—the one at the university and the one in the concert hall—were attended by fourteen hundred, or at least thirteen hundred, people. Few, however, go to both courses. The King is not always present. Today, for instance, he was absent. Alexander is going to publish, and has already started writing the lectures down. You will be simply amazed.

And Caroline, in her precise way, wrote to her friend the Russian General Rennenkampf:

My brother-in-law's lectures render in bold outline an all-embracing painting of nature, the relationships between our earth and the planetary system as far as we now know it. It touches on the results of countless diligent researches and observations, the experiences and visions of hundreds of years, all so clearly explained.

Goethe received his report from his friend Zelter, and must have recognized his admired Humboldt in the terse description:

Before me stood a man of my liking who gives what he owns without knowing to whom, a speaker devoid of tricks and nebulous thoughts. . . . Where he might err, one would feel obliged to believe him with the greatest pleasure.

But many found reason to censure Humboldt. The philosopher Hegel felt slighted because of Humboldt's sarcastic remarks about Hegelian "fantasies of nature." Hegel would always remain for Humboldt the "philosopher who had smuggled historical Christianity into philosophy." Much worse, and rather dangerous for Humboldt's position at court, were the rantings of certain politicians and generals who could see nothing in Humboldt but a dangerous apostle of freethinking and atheism who was determined to undermine the precepts of religious tradition. A lesser danger was felt by a lady who was rumored to have asked her tailor for an alteration of her evening dress so that it should have its upper sleeves equal to two dimensions of the star Sirius!

Almost fifteen years later, Humboldt wrote to a friend: "The little I achieved in the Singakademie before a mixed audience (King and bricklayers) protects me from the charge of having objected to a popularization of science. With knowledge comes thought, and thought imbues people with earnestness and power." Knowledge was a public trust to be shared by those who cared to be informed, not a privilege reserved for academicians. But when his publisher Cotta asked Humboldt for immediate publication of the lectures, he answered that not even the most lucrative proposals could entice him to that. It was one thing to lecture ex cathedra, quite another to commit yourself to print. To be published, the lectures would have to be weighed carefully, worked over, and provided with such proper quotations of sources as he had given in his other writings. Nevertheless, on the basis of his lecture notes, he would prepare a book on physical geography. The letter to his publisher had hardly left when Wilhelm saw his brother at work outlining what later came to be the first volume of *Cosmos*, the encyclopedic survey of nature that would engage Humboldt for the rest of his life.

The lectures extended into the spring of 1828, and were fittingly commemorated by a committee composed of Lichtenstein, the rector of the university, Leopold von Buch, the geologist, and Schinkel, the architect, who presented the speaker with a medal especially designed for the occasion. Its ornaments—allegories of the Triumph of Apollo surrounded by the signs of the zodiac—prompted Humboldt to the humorous remark: "After such a comparison [with Apollo], nothing is left to me but to die."

For asserting that science was as capable of enriching the cultural life of nations as literature and the arts, Humboldt's lectures attracted much attention all over Germany, especially among those who, in 1822, had organized the German Association of Naturalists and Physicians (*Versammlung deutscher Naturforscher und Ärzte*). This association was the ideal medium for the propagation of Humboldt's views on nature and science. Rector Lichtenstein and the King agreed with Humboldt that the association should be invited to hold its next annual meeting in Berlin.

As could be expected, the proposal was received with much enthusiasm all around. Humboldt was elected acting president, and invitations were issued with prompt dispatch. The first to be invited was the mathematician Gauss at Göttingen.

Permit me, my admirable friend [Humboldt wrote to Gauss on August 14, 1828], to renew my plea for you to add glamour to the meeting and be my house-guest. The hotels here are bad and easily filled. True, I can offer you only one—but a very

spacious—room, with a view on a nice garden, but you are welcome to receive visitors and occupy the adjoining rooms. You
may breakfast and take lunch and dinner with or without me
at any time you may desire. If you should bring a friend along,
I could put him up quite easily in a neighboring house. You
will have a coach at your disposal. All this can be left to
me. . . . Vacation time is here, and such diversion will do
you good, and your celebrated name would add such brilliance
to my native city, as I have always so greatly desired.

When Gauss arrived, he climbed the stairs to Humboldt's apartment on the second floor and may have noted
that the house belonged to Herr Glatz, by Royal Appointment Carpenter to His Majesty the King. Around the
corner stood a warehouse and a synagogue. The famous
mathematician was known to shy away from crowds and
strangers. To be dragged from lecture rooms to dinners
and receptions, to bow before the King and his English
guest, the Duke of Cumberland, to chat in French with
guests from beyond the Rhine, were to Gauss extremely
annoying chores. He was glad to hear his host refer to this
gathering as "a literary fair." Actually, though, Humboldt
was convinced that the association meeting was a grand
manifestation of intellectual unity, a wholesome experience for a nation sadly torn by political and religious
strife.

When the congress opened, on September 18, 1828,.
Humboldt was faced with a most brilliant gathering: in
the royal box the King and his family surrounded by ministers and foreign guests; the tiers of seats occupied by men
immortal in the annals of science—Gauss, Liebig, Bessel,
the astronomer from Königsberg, Geoffroy Saint-Hilaire
from Paris, de Candolle from Geneva, and Berzelius, the

eminent Swedish chemist, to name only a few out of six hundred scientists.

Humboldt stated that it was a singular distinction to address the distinguished gathering, not because it had assembled in personal acknowledgment of his own feeble efforts "to kindle the dawning light of knowledge from the abysmal depths of nature," but because it welcomed him back as one who had strayed in distant lands. He reminded his audience how the ancient Greeks had valued the enlightening force of free speech and thought. Nothing could be more inimical to science and human progress than for those who felt called upon to labor for enlightenment to submit to uniformity of thinking.

Without diversity of opinion the discovery of truth is impossible, for truth in its entirety cannot be seen and evaluated by all men at once and from one point of view. . . . Those who regard as a golden age the time . . . when diverse opinions, the disputes of the learned, shall be completely adjusted, show as little insight into the requirements of science and its ceaseless progress as those others who, in idle self-sufficiency, boast of having maintained the same views in geology, chemistry, and physiology.

Science was growing so rapidly, branching into so many fields, that he, as acting president, suggested that the assembly hold its meetings in separate sections. Little did the speaker know that his procedure was to be written into the statutes of every similar professional gathering all over the world.

In the evening Humboldt played host in the Royal Theater to six hundred guests, the King and diplomats attending, while the royal orchestra played and refreshments were served. Even Humboldt, suspicious as he was of mass gatherings, admitted that the meeting had been stimulating. How exemplary it had been must be obvious from the subsequent founding of similar scientific associations: the British Association for the Advancement of Science in 1831, the Italian Association in 1839, the American Association for the Advancement of Science in 1848, and in 1872 the French Association. But by having made the meeting into a brilliant social event, Humboldt may have contributed to a tendency for the association to degenerate somewhat over the next twenty years into what he himself scornfully called a "theatrical spectacle, where in the midst of endless feasting the vanity of learned men finds ready gratification." It is in this sense that one should interpret a passage of a letter to Gauss in which Humboldt confessed that a "few hours' talk with you, my dear friend, will be more highly prized by me than all the meeting of the so-called natural philosophers who move about in such immense masses and with such a mania for feasting." This attitude, strange as it must seem for a man who had craved society all his life, was to disappoint many who expected Humboldt to take an active and leading part in the development of the German Association. Its committee would ask Humboldt time and again to participate in the annual conventions, always to be turned down with excuses that he was too old or too busy to accept the invitation. As his position at court developed into an influential office, he may have felt satisfied by his unrivaled power for arbitration of all cultural affairs.

When the association members dispersed to return to their occupations, a few may have sensed that Humboldt did not regard himself as completely settled in Berlin. He may have spoken to men like Gauss or Liebig of prospects for more exploration. He had another plan up his sleeve. He was, in fact, waiting with a tingling sense of anticipation for a message from St. Petersburg.

14

By Coach to Central Asia

THE MAILS FROM St. Petersburg had suffered the usual
wintry delays. Bogged down by ever mounting snowdrifts
and frozen rivers, Russian coachmen found it hard to catch
up with the relays for Berlin and Paris. As ferrymen
pushed the mailcoach across frozen streams, diplomatic
couriers were seen to drown their worries in vodka. Deliv-
eries were difficult at all times, for the post roads were
muddy the rest of the year. In December 1827 it was especially urgent for the mails to get through in time: Count
Georg Cancrin, the Russian Minister of Finance, had
given special orders for safe delivery of a certain pouch in
the Prussian capital.

For Cancrin it could hardly have been difficult to convince Nicholas I that it was a good time for Humboldt to
visit Russia. The Tsar fully understood the reasons. Back
in 1811, shortly before Napoleon had launched his ill-fated
campaign against Russia, the Tsar's predecessor, Alexander
I, had invited the famous explorer. In August 1827 Cancrin
had asked Humboldt for an opinion on the feasibility of a
platinum currency in Russia, and had added on that occasion that Humboldt might find it "quite interesting to
visit the Ural Mountains." As far as the platinum project
was concerned, the reply had been discouraging, for in
Humboldt's judgment such a monetary standard could not
be profitably maintained against the silver currencies of
other nations.

"I hope," his letter continued, "to use my first spare time

to learn Russian so that I may be able to read the new mining journal that brings so many interesting articles." And in a postscript the writer called attention to the fact that the letter was not in his own handwriting because he did not want to bother His Excellency with the illegible script. "By sleeping on rotting leaves I contracted rheumatism in the forest of the upper Orinoco. It is my greatest wish to present myself in person to you. The Ural and the Ararat, even Lake Baikal, appear to me like attractive visions."

It would be an easy thing, Cancrin advised the Tsar, to entice Humboldt to do some exploring where it was most needed: the Urals, with their gold and platinum mines, and the little-known regions, the steppes and mountains, bordering on China. Naturally, the Baron must be given some choice in his travel routes, but in view of his mining experiences it would be of the greatest interest to have him look into as many mines as possible. One would have to take account of Humboldt's scientific interests and treat him generously—like a visiting dignitary.

Listening to his Minister, the Tsar may have had his own thoughts. In previous years Russia had failed to push its influence westward. Had it not been for Metternich and the English, Russian troops might have been used for intervention in Spain and in Italy. What had come of the international army that Alexander I had proposed at the Congress of Aix-la-Chapelle, and what indeed of his Holy Alliance? It was evident that Russia had been denied a seat in the council of nations despite her valiant help in wiping Napoleon's tyranny from the map of Europe. Russia must strengthen its position, must explore its mineral riches and the trans-Volga regions as far as Siberia. Russia was in dire need of experts like Humboldt. Already she had invited mining engineers from Germany and France. How very timely Count Cancrin's advice was!

In December 1827 Cancrin dispatched two letters in which he assured Humboldt that the Russian Emperor would be glad to grant all necessary financial aid and assistance. The Ural region was most important, more so than Siberia and Lake Baikal. "Traveling in Russia is easy, rapid, and safe in the highest degree," he blandly assured the Baron,

but outside of the big cities and the road to Moscow one must provide for a cook. For travel you will want a carriage and a *britska* (Polish cart with springs). Too much luggage is not advisable, and Your Honor should carry none but the most necessary instruments. I shall provide you with a mining official able to speak various languages, and a courier for ordering horses and other commissions. . . . I shall not fail to send instructions to all governors and mining officials, with orders to put you up. Customs will be instructed to facilitate your entry into Russia. You may speak German as far as Norva, whence it is an easy trip to St. Petersburg.

To travel east across the vast steppes to Siberia and meet caravans from China! Cancrin need not ask him twice—of course he would go, provided that he was not to start before the spring of 1829. He would give up his visit to Paris meanwhile to work on the first volume of *Cosmos*. "Your Excellency," Humboldt answered Cancrin,

asked me for a candid opinion on the financial aspects of my journey. I have spent all of my inheritance (100,000 thalers), and as I used it all up for scientific purposes, I say this without fear of being censured. . . . I would wish not to spend more than my own pension of from 2,500 to 3,000 thalers. These could be used for the trip to St. Petersburg and back . . . and

what I might spend otherwise would have to come out of the
Imperial Treasury. I have no intention of profiting from this
journey, but must avoid spending more than I can afford. I
would come in my own French coach and with a German
servant (a hunter who ought to be made comfortable for the
sake of his health), and with Gustav Rose, professor of chemistry and mineralogy, a very unassuming but very well-
informed young man. I like to be comfortable, and cherish
cleanliness where it is possible, but am cheerful and content
when confronted with unavoidable miseries. I do not crave
preferential treatment, but am very receptive to friendliness.
I have spent my life in foreign lands under difficult circumstances, and have given no reason for others to complain about
uncautious behavior . . . I still walk very lightly on foot,
nine to ten hours without resting, despite my age and my
white hair. . . . I feel it my duty and wish to serve your government as far as my limited knowledge in mining and technological subjects permits, and to report more on products and
institutions than on people. . . .

This frank letter prompted Cancrin to reply that Russia
would never permit Humboldt to spend money of his
own.

Humboldt was still sprightly in his fifty-ninth year,
walking up to ten hours a day, as on his last excursions
around Teplitz, whither he had followed the royal family
in the summer of 1828. One day he was sitting by the roadside chipping rocks with his geological hammer when he
heard a carriage pass by. Completely absorbed by his
work, he barely looked up when somebody reached over
his shoulder to press a coin in his hand. Absent-mindedly
he accepted it and, turning around, saw a liveried man run
for the Queen's coach, which had been waiting at a distance. That same evening Humboldt, in dark-blue dress

coat, presented himself, coin in hand, to a Queen who a few hours earlier had mistaken him for a tramp.

In discussing the Russian itinerary with fellow scientists in Berlin, Humboldt suddenly decided to invite Professor Christian Gottfried Ehrenberg to accompany him. Ehrenberg had studied micro-organisms in lakes, and could be expected to continue his brilliant research in Russia, where the Caspian Sea and Lake Baikal would give him unrivaled opportunities. And Ehrenberg's medical training would come in handy for the expedition in case of illness. The mineralogist Gustav Rose would give Humboldt a helping hand by collecting minerals and making geologic observations. Seifert was to be handy man, valet, and hunter combined.

With Ehrenberg and Rose to take care of earth studies, Humboldt would feel free to devote himself to magnetic observations. The subject of earth magnetism continued to hold his interest. Had André-Marie Ampère not suggested that a magnet is due to electric currents circulating within the molecules, and had his friend Arago not induced an artificial magnetization of steel needles by wrapping them in an electrified wire coil? If magnetism was a form of electricity, further surveys of the earth's magnetic fields would be more important than ever. To extend the net of such observations into central Asia seemed all the more promising for the chances they offered to relate magnetism to mountain structures and mineral deposits. It was not that Humboldt foresaw clearly what in our age has come to be so important—the usefulness of magnetic methods for geologic studies—but that he must have envisioned such relationships when he decided to equip himself with the latest instruments: an inclinometer of Gambey's construction, an Earnshaw chronometer, and a tent free from iron. This tent was to be his field laboratory on the Russian trip, and he would be careful to place it away from habitations so as to eliminate any disturbing influences of metal.

These preparations indicated a new scientific attitude commensurate with the progress of science since Humboldt's American travels: he would concentrate on magnetic studies. Gone were the days when he and Bonpland could take care of a host of scientific studies. He would surely collect plants on this trip, but only where new flora could be seen in relation to interesting geographic features. What with the Russians insisting on a study of mines, it would be a hurried journey, considering the enormous distances to be covered before the Siberian winter would begin. That Humboldt should have planned such a short trip is understandable only in view of his plan to follow it up with other travels in Asiatic Russia. He was to all appearance prepared to follow in the footsteps of his countryman Peter Simon Pallas (1741–1811), who had been called by Catherine the Great to explore the regions between the Crimea and China.

In the midst of exciting preparations came the shocking news that Caroline's illness had taken a critical turn. She had attended her brother-in-law's first lectures, but somewhat later had suddenly showed symptoms of cancer, which the doctors considered incurable. In March 1829 Humboldt stood by her bedside watching her beauty fade in a valiant struggle, her large, dark eyes still lively, her mind touchingly absorbed by Alexander's new travel plans. She weakened rapidly, and died on March 26. What Caroline had meant to Alexander none but he could have known. Except for his mother, she was the only woman who had ever come close to him, touching his remoteness with a patient sympathy like a delicious scent for him to remember on his restless wanderings. Was it not Caroline who had tried to draw him into her family, first at Jena when she had given birth to her second child, and then again in Paris?

In Humboldt, Caroline's death may have evoked memories of his friendship with Haeften, the young officer whom he had feted in the castle at Bayreuth. Two days after Caroline's death, Humboldt wrote to his friend Haeften's widow:

My precious friend! The sufferings of my poor sister-in-law are at an end. She passed away quietly the day before yesterday, on the 26th. In my brother's and my own name I pass this mournful news on to you, convinced of your deepest sympathy. Her doctor, Rust, had noticed the symptoms of her dreadful disease for over a year. . . . She was really ill only since December, and in between was gay and always ready to participate in everything human, art in particular. . . . I had gone with the King to Potsdam, and while there received the news of her death by special courier. She will be buried, according to her wish, in the park at Tegel, under the beautiful oak trees. . . . My brother has aged greatly. The suffering of her loss all but finished him. She was the common bond of our family. . . .

The flowers on Caroline's grave had scarcely faded when Humboldt ordered the carriages to be packed for the trip to Russia. But for Caroline's illness, he would have left one month earlier, but now he would wait no longer, much as his brother Wilhelm needed his comforting presence. St. Petersburg, the Urals, and Siberia beckoned from afar, sufficient reason to forget grief and death, cruel as it must have been for Wilhelm—the only person left in Humboldt's life who really mattered.

On April 12, 1829 the Humboldt party bade farewell to Berlin. In the first carriage—Humboldt's own—were Ehrenberg, Rose, and His Excellency the newly titled Privy Chancellor of the King,[1] dressed in a winter coat, wrapped in blankets. A second carriage followed, with Seifert anxiously watching trunks and boxes strapped to the roofs and luggage racks. The weather was beastly all the way to the Vistula, with howling snowstorms and sleet. The ferryboat was pounded by drifting ice. At Königsberg they stopped for two days to visit the great astronomer Bessel, famous for his determinations of the earth's periodic aberrations of rotation and revolution, and inspected his observatory. Rose and Humboldt took notes of the university's mineral collections. The icy roads to Memel were enough to discourage any traveler: at one point the carriages had to be dug out of snowdrifts, and shortly before reaching the border town, drift ice, accumulated in a lagoon of the Baltic Sea, blocked their progress for several days. To a man like Humboldt such momentary obstacles were welcome opportunities to get out his instruments and measure the magnetic intensity, while Ehrenberg collected shells on the icy beach.

After a few days the carriages reached the Russian border station where, to everybody's surprise, customs officials waived all the red tape of examination and Humboldt was delighted to receive his official travel permit. Months in advance Cancrin had seen to it that the travelers were

---

[1] In 1852 Humboldt wrote to his friend Berghaus: "I need not ask you especially not to add anything to my name like the pestilential Excellency, Privy Chancellor, Baron, and such German misdemeanors."

given all possible aid. He would no doubt have done something about the dreadful state of the post road had it been in his power. The crossing of the Dvina River near Riga gave everybody a real taste of things to come. The carriages were ferried across on sailboats, their ice-coated wheels slipping perilously, while the waves splashed in a howling blizzard of sleet and snow. A Russian courier was waiting on the other bank, ready to gallop off in the direction of St. Petersburg to arrange for fresh carriage horses at intermediate relay stations. Humboldt would have liked to spend more time in the ancient Hanseatic towns of Riga and Dorpat (Tartu, in Estonia), with their historic monuments and geological collections, but he had to hurry. The carriages rolled on, fourteen times to be ferried and once to be pulled out of a swampy hole. On May 1, 1829 St. Petersburg appeared. The coaches clattered past the marble palace of the Hermitage, the Tsar's Winter Palace, and the Admiralty, finally stopping at the gate of the Prussian Embassy.

My journey was exceedingly fortunate and pleasant [Humboldt had written to his brother en route] . . . My health is splendid, the travel company agreeable. We have no occasion to open the medicine chest—Ehrenberg's four cubic feet of medicaments. . . . It would be too tiresome to report on all the festivities at Dorpat. They drove me around in a coach-and-four; visits with professors from eight in the morning until nine in the evening, when the university feasted us with a magnificent dinner. . . . My carriage stood it all, not a nail missing. Once a horse smashed the shaft with a kick of its hoof. Seifert has proved himself most active and helpful.

The long-expected guests found themselves the center of attention in the Russian capital. At the Museum of Natural History, Humboldt was introduced to Russia's fabulous riches: a diamond from Persia as large as a child's fist, topaz crystals the size of a young man, a platinum nugget weighing twenty-one pounds! He visited the art gallery of the Hermitage with its matchless collection of pictures by Rubens, Rembrandt, and Spanish masters. Not far from it was an open market crowded with visitors for Easter week, Russians in long, dark-blue coats, with their ruddy faces framed by furs, exotic-looking traders from Astrakhan and Persia.

Everywhere the reception was overpowering.

I seem to be surrounded wherever I go [Humboldt wrote to his brother on May 10]. It is impossible to be treated with greater distinction or with more generous hospitality. I dined nearly every day with the Imperial family in their strictest privacy—covers being laid for four—and I have spent the evenings with the Empress in the most delightful freedom from ceremony. The heir apparent also entertained me for dinner, so that he might remember me, I was told, in years to come. . . . The Minister of War gave me a collection of maps, all published by the government printing office. . . . Our new [Russian] carriages are most beautiful, and cost 1,200 thalers each. Everywhere I go they offer me money like hay and anticipate every wish.

But the thought of his bereaved brother put him in a melancholy mood:

We have come so close to each other over the last years that every feeling for you fills me with loving tenderness. How well I can understand your present position and your motive for retiring from social superficialities! If I should return by November, I shall certainly share your long evenings with you every fortnight or so. . . . Nature can be so soothing to the

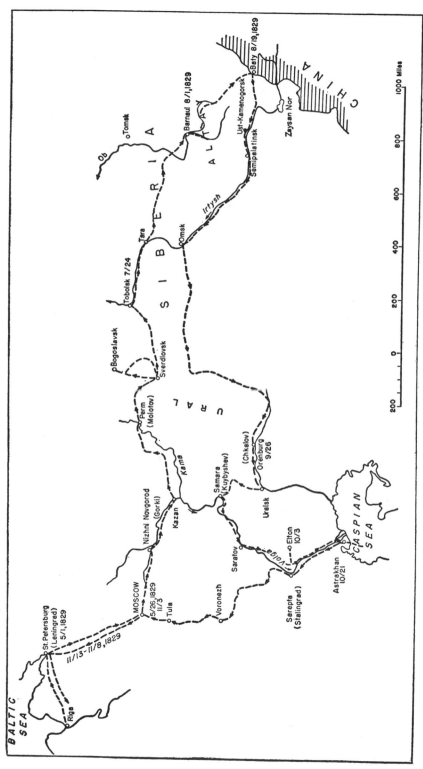

HUMBOLDT IN RUSSIA AND CENTRAL ASIA (1829)

tormented mind, a blue sky, the glittering surface of lake water, the green foliage of trees may be your solace. In such company it is even possible to forget the reality of one's personal existence. It lends wings to our feelings and thoughts.

How was he to impress his brother with his own brand of religion, a poet's certainty of the healing experience of merging with earth and sky? The thought of his bereaved brother would continue to haunt him on this journey, would make him long for the person who had always been a restful calm in the whirling eddies of his life. Not to worry his brother, he must carefully avoid the slightest hint of impending dangers. He had never known physical fear except on that day when the jaguar confronted him in the jungle. The Russians would see to it that nothing should interfere: they were much too eager for him to carry out his exploration plans, to study mines and magnetism, land forms and vegetation.

On May 20 the party left St. Petersburg for Moscow, where Humboldt was greeted by his old classmate from Freiberg, Gotthelf Fischer de Waldheim, "who is called Excellency, driving about in a fine carriage and enjoying a pension of 7,000 francs. We are continually the object of attention with the police, government officials, Cossacks, and guards of honor. Unfortunately, we are scarcely alone a moment. We cannot take a step without being led by the arm like invalids. I should like to see Leopold von Buch in such a position!" Russia was not like the Amazon or Mexico, where he had traveled anywhere he liked, at ease with himself and his companions and never suspected of doing something he was not supposed to do.

Beyond Moscow they could not rely on hotel accommodations. The mail stations were simple houses with one room reserved for overnight guests. Meals were prepared by their own Russian cook in the family kitchen. In larger towns the party was billeted by the chiefs of police in the homes of well-to-do families. A few days after leaving Moscow, mattresses were at a premium, and Humboldt ordered Seifert to purchase some. The carriages were drawn by three or four horses harnessed abreast and kept galloping most of the time, the coaches swaying and thundering over the wooden pavings of villages. The coy little timber houses clustered like forgotten sheep around village churches, also of wood. The scenery was bathed in Russian spring weather, rolling fields and birch trees bright with fresh green, and the Volga River in a mighty flood inundating the famous bazaar of Nizhni Novgorod (Gorki). The town, with its church spires and convents rising behind an ancient wall, had been an ancient bulwark against Tatar invasions. It was too early in the season for the Chinese fair, which was held in July, but the city fathers sent delegations to welcome the travelers with a ceremonius offering of bread and salt. Humboldt greeted an old acquaintance from Paris, Count Polier, who begged to join the party on its way to the Ural region.

The carriages were loaded onto a Volga barge for the river journey to Kazan. It had been equipped with a canvas awning, a table, two benches, and an improvised brick stove. By June 1 the party was on its way, the barge floating past embankments lush with poplars, oaks, and lindens. The Volga was in high flood, a mile wide at places, with islands of luxurious vegetation rising from the muddy waters, and the boatmen chanting their mournful songs all day long. Four days later they landed at Kazan, then a city of fifty thousand inhabitants. a fascinating place with all the ancient glamour of the Orient, mosques, and Tatars wearing turbans and long, colorful cotton gowns. Humboldt visited the palace of a Mongol princess, entered a mosque in stocking feet, and drove out to the ruins of Bulgar, an ancient stronghold dating back to the seventh century. Here at Kazan had been the stronghold of the Golden Horde from the Kirghiz Steppe. From here Timur Lenk (Tamurlane) had directed the historic raids into Poland and Hungary. To collect the mementos of Timur's reign, ancient Mongol coins and manuscripts, was to taste history in its most colorful moments. This was Asia's outpost, intoxicating to Humboldt with the prospects that beckoned on the eastern horizon. The university and museum at Kazan offered chances for installing a magnetic observatory and a training center for mining geology.

From Kazan the coaches rolled on to the Ural mountains, toward Perm (Molotov) and Yekaterinburg (Sverdlovsk). On the road they passed gangs of prisoners exiled to Siberia, men and women walking unshackled, as was customary for minor offenders. Much later, on the way to Tobolsk, the coaches overtook long lines of prisoners marching, each convict tied to a long rope. Such gangs were flanked by wild-looking Bashkir guards, whose bows and arrows were objects of ethnological interest. Gustav Rose reported in his diary that the Siberian exiles were rather well treated, fed and housed in rest-houses specially built for this purpose.

For such episodes one must turn to Rose's account of the journey, as Humboldt was too cautious ever to describe his impressions of the Russian people. He must have known in advance how sensitive the government was to critical comments; he had assured Cancrin in a letter:

It will be self-understood that we confine ourselves to observations of an inanimate nature, and avoid everything connected with government or the condition of the poorer classes. Statements made by foreigners unacquainted with the language are usually held to be incorrect, and when referring to subjects as involved as the rights of social classes, such opinions can only irritate without producing any beneficial results.

One suspects that this change of attitude on Humboldt's part toward reporting on social conditions resulted as much from unpleasant experiences with the Spanish government as from a realization that his political opinions on Russia were not wanted. And a traveler who felt muzzled was not likely to keep a diary if, like Humboldt, he intended to return.

A man like Rose was in a much better position to report candidly, but even he failed to render detailed accounts of episodes that could be expected to shed an unfavorable light on his or Humboldt's opinions. "A Siberian journey," Humboldt wrote in one of his letters, "is not so pleasant as one in South America. . . . Since Kazan we have not seen a single inn. One sleeps on benches or in the carriage. But life is tolerable, and I must not complain."

When they arrived at Nizhni Tagil, in the central Ural, the mountain divide that marks the geographic border with Asia had already been crossed. At Berezovsky, Humboldt watched the mining of gold and platinum from river sands. Nearby, his magnetic needle registered, by irregular deviations, the presence of magnetite deposits. The incredible riches of the Urals in iron, copper, gold, and platinum had made many a family wealthy—as, for example, that of Prince Demidov, who lived near Berezovsky in a château gaudily furnished with French brocades and silver chandeliers. In its pompous interiors, Russian servants in embroidered blouses and high boots passed refreshments, caviar, and champagne, music being played by a balalaika orchestra on the terrace.

A few days later the Humboldt party was barely able to extricate itself from forest swamps, but as it reached the summit of Belaya Gora, Rose reported how he and Humboldt saw the vast steppe of western Siberia stretching monotonously to the horizon.

A Russian companion, the engineer Helmersen (later a general), described Humboldt as walking with his head bent forward, dressed in a frock coat of dark brown or black, a white scarf around his neck, and wearing a round hat.

On excursions he never rode horseback. When the carriage was unable to proceed he would walk, climbing high mountains without any signs of fatigue, clambering over rough terrain like one accustomed to fieldwork. His meals were always moderate, even after the most tiring march, when the Russians would oblige him to accept their lavish hospitality with mountains of food and a never ending choice of liquors.

Helmersen reported an incident of this trip. Humboldt's carriage had stopped at a relay station on the Bashkirian steppe when a native was seen running up to the coach wildly gesticulating and shouting. Planting himself in front of the naturalist, the Mongolian delivered a long harangue in Turkish dialect, not a word of which was understood by any member of the party. The torrent of words having stopped, the amazed Humboldt turned to Helmersen asking: "What does this *gentleman* want?" An interpreter was called. It then appeared that on the previous night the complaining herdsman had been robbed of his horses, and on hearing that there was a great man arriving *who knew everything*, he had come to inquire who the bandits were and how he might retrieve his animals. No sooner had this touching tale been related than the local police appeared to arrest the intruder. Humboldt, laughing heartily, begged that mercy might be shown this unfortunate son of the steppe.

At Yekaterinburg a week was spent in packing rock and mineral specimens. By July 17, fourteen boxes had been handed over to the Superintendent of Police for shipment to St. Petersburg and Berlin, where they arrived in good shape. The most exciting incident of the trip to the Ural mines was the discovery of diamonds. Humboldt had predicted it when he told the Tsar that he would not leave Russia without having located diamonds in the Urals. He had carefully studied the first reports of gold and platinum deposits in Russian mining journals, and had noticed on that occasion a curious geologic analogy with similar occurrences in Brazil, where diamonds had been found in association with such precious metals. En route, Humboldt had frequently discussed the matter with Count Polier, who happened to own gold fields on the eastern slope of the Urals. Polier must have trembled at the thought that diamonds might be found on his estate, and on reaching the Ural mines he watched Humboldt day after day, expecting to pick up useful information.

With visions of diamonds dancing in his confused head, the Count vanished suddenly. At his estate he ordered his German overseer, Schmidt, instantly to search in the gold-bearing river sands nearby. Four days later a miner appeared with the first diamond, of one and one-half carats. Within a week others of greater size were found. Humboldt did not learn about the discovery until he returned to St. Petersburg, where he was handed a parcel containing a diamond that the Count presented to him in tribute to the man whom he rightly regarded as the discoverer of Russia's first diamond field.

The road to Tobolsk in Siberia was covered in record time, the carriage horses galloping way into the night and stopping on but few occasions, as on the Tyumen River, where fossil mammoth bones were seen on the embankment. Tobolsk was the seat of a Governor General, whom Humboldt reminded that in 1761 a French astronomer, the Abbé Chappe d'Auteroche, had there observed the transit of Venus. Following such traditions, Humboldt claimed his right to set up his instruments for some astronomic observations of his own. The Governor was so impressed by his distinguished guest, and so concerned over his welfare, that he ordered his adjutant to watch the Humboldt party in all their occupations. From then on, Humboldt was surrounded day and night by a special suite consisting of the Governor's adjutant, several Cossacks, and a physician.

Tobolsk had been largely settled by exiles of German extraction. Among them was a physician, Dr. Albert, whose professional duties called him every year to visit Mongol settlements in the steppes nearby, chiefly to attend women suffering from venereal diseases. It turned out that this doctor was a nephew of Lotte Werther, who had been immortalized by Goethe's first novel. So delighted was this Siberian doctor over Humboldt's friendship with Goethe that he played host to the party. As a farewell present he gave Humboldt a collection of valuable ancient manuscripts. Less comforting was the prospect of traveling through a district feared by all travelers because of its mosquitoes. If they proved to be more vicious than the Orinoco species, Humboldt and his companions were willing to wear the contraptions Dr. Albert had invented: clumsy leather caps with a net of horsehair attached for facial protection. These caps turned out to be less blissful than the doctor had foreseen, for Rose reported that they proved to be instruments of torture, whose suffocating effects he would gladly exchange for insect stings.

The party rolled off in a cloud of dust. Within a week it hoped to reach the foothills of the Altai Mountains, but on the second day the travelers were checked by a country doctor who warned them not to proceed farther: the road would lead through settlements infested by the Siberian brand of plague. After much consultation it was decided to go on, taking all the necessary precautions. None of the servants was allowed to touch villagers, and for days nobody was permitted to drink anything but clear well-water. From Barnaul, on the northern slope of the Altai, Humboldt wrote to his brother, on August 4:

One travels—or rather flees—across these monotonous grasslands as over an ocean, sailing on land as it were, in which we covered 140 miles in twenty-four hours. We suffered greatly from heat, dust, and yellow mosquitoes . . . the insects on the Orinoco can hardly be worse. At noon the temperature registers only 85 degrees in the shade, but the nights are terribly cold—down to 36 degrees. . . . As we reached the majestic Ob River, a frightful storm raged out of the Kirghiz Steppe. We camped on the river. The night was lit by huge campfires, which reminded me of my days on the Orinoco. As it started to storm and rain, we were at least relieved from the suffocating mosquito caps and insects. We crossed the Ob at two o'clock in the morning, and spent two days at Barnaul seeing the silver smelter. . . . The Governor of the province of Omsk owns a wonderful collection of Chinese, Mongolian, and Tibetan manuscripts. Unfortunately, our party increases constantly, thanks to the excessive but kindly protection, for our safety. Not only did the Governor General of Tobolsk give us his adjutant, with four Cossacks, but tonight there appeared all of a sudden, with his entire suite, the commander in-chief, who is to accompany us along the border as far as Omsk. . . . Now that we have penetrated Asia for over a thousand miles, the vegetation gradually has assumed a Siberian character, but as trees characterize a landscape I must confess that the banks of the Ob remind me in that respect a little of the shores of the Havel and Tegel lakes. As for large animals, I mention only large tigers, very similar to the Bengal variety, which are killed in the Altai only in defense. The presence of these beasts at such northern latitudes is very curious indeed.

On August 4 the party left Barnaul and traveled in light native carriages to another mining district Schlangenberg (Smeinogorsk), thence proceeding along the banks of the Upper Irtysh River. At Krasnoyarsk they passed the last Cossack villages, and on August 19, 1829 reached the Chinese border. "At one o'clock we arrived at the Chinese frontier post," Rose reported in his travelogue, "of which there are two on each bank of the Irtysh River, Mongols on the left and Chinese on the opposite bank, both commanded by Chinese officials. In midstream lay an island where Cossacks supervise fishing."

The Chinese official was a young, slender man who had recently come from Peking by cart, traveling four months to report for duty at the border station. Dressed in a blue silk gown of ankle length, he wore a pointed cap ornamented with peacock feathers—a ceremonial sign of his rank. He ushered the party into a Kirghiz tent, and Humboldt and his companions sat down on carpeted boxes. Then tea was offered, and Humboldt addressed the Chinese official with a few Russian sentences, a Mongol serving as translator. What might be the object of the honorable visitor's travel, the representative of the Son of Heaven asked Humboldt, and when the visitor had satisfied him, the Chinese official, rising with all the dignity of a mandarin, handed two Chinese books to Humboldt as a present. As it turned out later, these books were an eighteenth-century novel.

The mandarin's bodyguard could not have looked very different from Marco Polo's companions: Kirghiz cavalry armed with swords, bows, and arrows, their eyes popping at the sight of Humboldt's pencil. Who but the Emperor of China might ever have seen such a utensil? To the mandarin it semed the most priceless thing in the world, and he was quick to ask for the favor of owning one. With much ceremonious bowing, Humboldt presented his pencil to the mandarin. So overcome was he with the precious gift that it was some time before he could be persuaded to accept Humboldt's real gift: a piece of valuable blue cloth.

This Humboldt had come to see: the ramparts of Asia, ice-covered mountains above the desert, and the tents of Kirghiz nomads, their flocks of sheep and horses grazing on the plains. Favored by clear weather, Humboldt and Rose climbed to some vantage point whence he could see the snowy ranges and surrounding steppes. Nearby lay Lake Zaysan Nor, and south the great Gobi Desert, mysteriously hidden in a dusty haze. At night the muffled sound of drums came from a lama temple, its walls black against the steppe, almost silvery in the moonlight sparkle of sand. The night wind whistled under the stars. Sand crept gingerly into the tents with a snake-like motion, and the jackals pierced the darkness with their wailing cries. Soon ducks and geese would rise from the lakes and rivers, winging southward toward the Ganges. Here, in central Asia, caravans had linked China with the Black Sea coast when history was younger and Alexander the Great's trail lost somewhere in Bactria.

15

The Dual Role of Serving Science and Kings

A FESTIVE CROWD had gathered in the Moscow Academy of Science to shake hands with the man of the hour. Grand dukes and generals, blazing with medals, rubbed elbows with academicians, who carried their gala uniforms, swords, and three-cornered hats with unaccustomed aplomb. At the top of the staircase stood Humboldt, shivering from a cold draft, his dark-blue frock coat pointedly modest save for the Star of the Order of St. Anne—the Tsar's first token of gratitude. Hundreds filed past, shaking hands with the white-haired explorer, who bowed affably, trying to catch the polite words that the Russian guests addressed to him and his companions in French, German, and Latin.

At last he was allowed to enter the lecture hall. When the rector of the university had finished reading the proceedings in Russian, comprehensible to all but the honored guests, Humboldt was addressed in a poetic oration as the "Prometheus of our time"—the harbinger of knowledge and culture. For minutes his thoughts were back in the Urals and the Altai Mountains. When would he ever be able to catch his breath? It seemed incredible that in twenty-five weeks he should have covered 9,600 miles by coach. He had crossed the Volga River ten times, the Siberian Irtysh eight. His party had used as many carriage horses as Timur's cavalry might have employed on one of their historic raids. By the time Humboldt returned to Berlin, he would have traveled 11,500 miles—almost half of the earth's equatorial circumference.

And now these endless speeches and orations! If only he would be allowed to read his report! At last, the evening session having been extended beyond the allotted time, Humboldt gave his brief summary in French. He had spread the net of magnetic observations over the remotest regions, where no data on earth magnetism had so far been obtained. Now it was the task of the Russian scientists to supplement his pioneer labors by establishing observation stations all across Russia as far as the Pacific. Humboldt foresaw an international union to pool all data on earth magnetism, and this, in fact, was realized a few years later, becoming the first international co-operative research organization. Humboldt reminded his audience how difficult it would have been for him to obtain an overall picture of Russia's geology but for the aid of his companions, Rose and Ehrenberg. Thousands of mineral and rock specimens had been collected, diamonds discovered in the Ural, and temperature readings obtained from lakes, streams, and soils.

On the return journey from Siberia, he had stopped over at Astrakhan, on the Caspian Sea, where he had rented a steamboat to gather samples of water for chemical and microbiological analysis. The largest inland sea had furnished Ehrenberg with unrivaled data for a miscroscopic study of fresh-water life; a new science—limnology—might result from such labors. But, above all, central Asia had furnished novel geographic and geologic observations with which to round out his studies in Europe and America. "It was one of the great moments of my life," Humboldt wrote to his brother. If only the Russians had not smothered him with attentions! Even at the Academy reception in Moscow he was not allowed to feel at ease. When Ehrenberg and Rose had spoken briefly, the rector dragged Humboldt to a showcase to admire at length a plait of hair from the head of Peter the Great.

"My journey across nearly every part of European Russia," he wrote to his brother on November 29, 1829, "has so enlarged my social relationships, and so greatly increased the chimerical notion of my usefulness to everyone that I feel quite overcome by the amount of drudgery imposed upon me by this position." The Tsar had invested him with a high decoration and had sent him a priceless vase of malachite from the palace and a sable coat worth five thousand rubles. He thanked Humboldt for his life-giving influence, which was bound to bring immense cultural progress to Russia. But pleasant as the Emperor's gifts were, they could hardly make up for the restrictions imposed on Humboldt's Russian travels. They had smothered an explorer's most precious requisite: the ease to move about and the liberty to report freely. As it turned out, the reign of Nicholas I was tyrannical and ill disposed to political reforms. Later the Tsar took exception to Humboldt's mission to Louis-Philippe's court in Paris, when the Prussian sovereign attempted to establish closer relations with France's liberal-minded monarch. There had been plans for Humboldt to return to Russia, and the Tsar had invited him shortly after his return to Germany, but Humboldt refused to accept. How deeply annoyed he was by the Tsar's political orientation is evident from his letter of May 22, 1843 to Berghaus, saying how great an effort it had been for him to dedicate the three volumes of his

Asie Central to the Emperor. "It was an unavoidable step, as the expedition was accomplished at his [the Tsar's] expense. The Emperor sent me his portrait. I should have been better pleased to have had no answer at all, or only a formal acknowledgment."

Humboldt had no sooner returned to Berlin, late in December 1829, than he found himself embroiled in a most unpleasant scandal. By using his reports on Mexican mines, an English mining consortium had attempted to sell shares for millions of pounds sterling. Newspapers alleged that it was all Humboldt's doing, this having enticed thousands of ignorant investors to support a speculative business venture. Nothing could have been more damaging to the man whom everybody in Russia expected to exercise great discretion about his observations in the Ural mines.

"It is not my fault," Humboldt assured Cancrin in a letter of April 3,

that my data on the riches of Mexican mines, published fifteen years ago, should have lured innocent people into investing millions. I made it clear from the very beginning that I will have no part in this fraudulent deal. For this reason I turned down the position of director general and consultant in Europe, and declined to accept free shares (which would have amounted to twenty thousand pounds sterling). I also refused the gift of a large golden *tabatière* from those who had enriched themselves by having felt tempted through my writings. In short, I did everything to keep away from their project. . . . I did not write a line in reply save for a brief rectification of certain exaggerated figures published in German newspapers, which might quite easily have been ascribed to me, though I never let anybody, not even newspapers, publish anything without my signature.

To assure Cancrin and the Tsar of his scholarly intentions, Humboldt sent Cancrin the four volumes of a new edition of his works on Mexico. A few weeks later he learned from St. Petersburg of the attempted theft of valuable precious stones from the Imperial collections, which might have led to unpleasant rumors about Humboldt's recent visit if the thief had succeeded in reaching the treasure.

News of Humboldt's return to Germany spread like wildfire and reached the octogenarian Goethe in February 1830, when his friend Zelter reported: "Alexander von Humboldt came back to Berlin, and is visible but to few people. He is like a boiling kettle. At second hand one hears marvelous things that I would rather have directly from him. But who understands when somebody talks with enthusiasm?" The winter weather being what it was, Humboldt, suffering from a painful boil, found few occasions to visit his brother at Tegel. But Wilhelm was frequently in town attending to his new duties as president of the Museum Council.

The old Château of Tegel had finally been rebuilt after Schinkel's plans, and with its additional rooms it would seem to have offered the owner a new chance for enticing Alexander to live there. It was an ideal place for solitude and study, and when spring came, Wilhelm hoped fervently to see more of his brother. But Alexander found himself in constant demand by the King, who wanted him every other day for lunch or dinner—court duties that eliminated all prospect of living at Tegel. Whether Wilhelm had heard of Alexander's future travel plans or not, he seemed determined to see his roaming brother more firmly anchored in Berlin. Ever since Alexander's ill-timed departure for Russia, Wilhelm had pulled wires to have his brother appointed Director General of all the Berlin museums. The King agreed, knowing that no man could fill this position more adequately than his Chamberlain.

When Wilhelm good-naturedly came forth with this suggestion, Alexander flew into a rage. "I should have relinquished my life in Paris and returned to my country *merely* to become director of a picture gallery . . . and busy myself with subjects diametrically opposed to everything that earned me a wholesome reputation in the world? That would be too humiliating. . . . I would sooner quit the country than be exposed to such hazards!" He would accept no other official position than the Privy Councilorship of the King, whose advisers, he suspected, had meant to place him in cold storage as a museum director. From now on he must be the King's right hand in all matters involving science and liberal arts. To be the King's confidant, an advisory power behind the throne, to act as spokesman for a world about to enter the age of science, and in the sovereign's entourage to enjoy security to complete his studies—that and no other object interested him. Posterity would understand this compromise with a monarchical order, provided that he lived long enough to complete his labors: his reports on Asia and his project for writing *Cosmos.*

At this point Humboldt was prepared to stake his hard-won reputation on longevity, a life span sufficient for him to set forth his natural philosophy in the grandest possible perspectives. Science should on no account be permitted to deteriorate by adopting materialistic and utilitarian aims. In giving new directions to cultural life, neither Arago in France nor Faraday in England might accom-

plish what Humboldt felt to be his singular mission. And
to justify his compromise with court life, he must gamble
on life expectancy. Such a gamble obviously involved
sacrificing all further plans for exploration, forcing Humboldt to come to grips with the painful problem of rooted-
ness in a sort of soil that was both fertile and secure. "The
Russian journey has changed my outlook on life more than
any other of my explorations. It made me more serious
and conscious of my age." He must preserve his nervous
energy as well as he could and devote himself to the tasks
ahead.

In May 1830 it became evident that Friedrich Wilhelm
III was determined to make the most of Humboldt's position at court. First, his Privy Councilor must accompany
the Crown Prince to the opening of the Polish Parliament
at Warsaw; afterwards he must bring the Empress of Russia to the King's summer residence in Silesia. There he met
his brother, who in that region owned an estate that had
been the King's gift in recognition of his diplomatic services. The summer was unexpectedly cut short by alarming
news from Paris: a revolution had forced Charles X to relinquish the throne to Louis-Philippe. If there was one
person in the King's entourage acquainted with the Orléans family, it was Humboldt, who was promptly commissioned to proceed to Paris to report on political events.

Before leaving Berlin, he wrote to Arago: "I shall bring
my German lectures on astronomy and physical geography
along so that we can discuss some chapters. I maintain an
ambition to concentrate my energy on them. They are the
life's work to which I must devote most of my time." But
the visit to Paris had been planned long in advance of the
Revolution, and when Humboldt left Berlin on September

28, 1830, he meant to adhere strictly to the period of four months which had been granted him in his contract with the Crown. As it turned out, he did return in January, but only for eighteen days, and then to hasten back to Paris, where he stayed until the spring of 1833.

Befriended by Louis-Philippe and his family, Humboldt found ready access to an inner government circle in which his friends Arago and Guizot occupied important positions. For him life in Paris society had always been a source of interesting information, so that his scientific labors could not have suffered much from evenings reserved for his diplomatic mission. And his servant Seifert proved to be up to all tasks when confidential dispatches to Berlin had to be dictated or messages delivered. Arago had furnished Humboldt with quarters at the Observatoire, to be used as a study and reception room for visitors. A suite at the Hôtel du Jardin des Plantes served as a separate bachelor establishment. Humboldt saw much of Arago, discussing his manuscripts and the arrangements for a careful checking of all magnetic, astronomic, and barometric data collected on the Russian trip. Its results were quickly presented in a first volume: *Fragments de géologie et de climatologie asiatiques*, (Paris 1831). The haste in which it was prepared makes one suspect that Humboldt intended to impress his friend Cancrin in St. Petersburg with his industry and usefulness, for in the same year (1831) the Tsar invited the author to return to Russia. Because of Humboldt's obligations in Paris this offer was so singularly ill-timed that he shelved the plan—if, indeed, he considered it seriously at all.

Humboldt's first report on Asia, being the first scientific treatise on the remote regions of the Ural and the border-

lands with China, excited much interest in Europe. If his
American travels had earned him fame as a second Columbus, the Asiatic studies caused people to regard him as
another Marco Polo who had lifted the curtain from a portion of the world which everybody had considered practically inaccessible and utterly mysterious. More than that,
to naturalists the book was a sensation for its bold concepts
of Himalayan mountain-making. When Goethe received
his copy in the fall of 1831, he wrote to his friend Zelter
in Berlin:

> The extraordinary talent of this exceptional man is really
> best revealed by his oratorical style. . . . Few people are
> actually capable of being convinced by mere reading, but
> many will readily yield to the force of spoken words, and in
> this respect his [Humboldt's] treatises are real oratory, de-
> livered with impressive facility, so that one is tempted to com-
> prehend the impossible. That the Himalaya should have risen
> 25,000 feet from the earth, and appear as solid and proud as if
> nothing had happened, is beyond my comprehension. It would
> require a total reorganization of my cerebral system—a pitiful
> thought—if space could be found for such marvels. . . . Must
> one probe into everything?

Once more the eighty-two-year-old sage of Weimar had
been rocked by Humboldt's novel ideas. When Goethe
died, in March 1832, Humboldt lost his most inspiring
friend.

In the spring of 1833 the author of this epochal work
returned to Berlin in the proud certainty of at last having
completed his huge American works. The *Examen critique
de l'histoire de la géographie du Nouveau Continent* appeared in 1834, in Paris. One can imagine what it must
have meant to Humboldt to see it complete after twenty

years of writing and editing. He must have put the finishing touch on this volume while he was completing his preliminary Asiatic studies and at the same time planning the first volume of his *Cosmos*, for which his German publisher Cotta had offered him a contract in 1828. What energy and mental discipline! A man in his early sixties dividing his literary labors in such a fashion that he was able to pick up a bundle of manuscript dealing with the voyages of Amerigo Vespucci, then return to astronomic or magnetic data from Sibera—and carry on his crowded social schedule into the bargain. Small wonder that such fabulous physical and intellectual powers excited the admiration of his contemporaries. Many may have asked themselves whether Humboldt was really one or several persons. His writings exceeded in output the literary works of any contemporary naturalist, and would in time to come rival the voluminous labors of Leibniz and Buffon.

And now, in March 1833, he was prepared to start with the most ambitious of all his writing projects: *Cosmos*.[1] In writing to his publisher, Georg Cotta, he mentioned

the most important work of my life, the sketch of a physical description of the universe. . . . This work, for which your noble father contracted with me on March 12, 1828, has unfortunately been delayed by my expedition to northern Asia and the Caspian Sea. But precisely this journey contributed immeasurably to an enlargement of my views, also enabling me to render them more vividly in a manner that has earned my nature descriptions so many favors. I am working now with much love over this physical portrayal of the universe. . . .

[1] According to Humboldt the word *cosmos* was used first by Pythagoras, meaning world order, earth and universe combined. In Humboldt's definition it denotes the entire material world.

A few months later Cotta was delighted to learn from a friend that Humboldt had showed him in Berlin a considerable portion of a new manuscript, part of which he had read to the visitor. More reassuring still was the news from Humboldt's own letter of June 22 that he did not "contemplate any travel to Italy, France, or Spain (I mean travels prompted by myself) until I have completed, or at least finished, part of this work." A most astonishing passage follows in the same letter. In it Humboldt implores his publisher, for God's sake, to think over whether he really wants to pay him the munificent sum of five thousand thalers on the completion of this work. "The physical description can hardly be good business for you or comparable to such income as you are obliged to pay to Schiller's and Goethe's heirs." Cotta should think it over carefully, he wrote, and not let himself feel bound by the old contract.

I am writing so candidly, and really contrary to my own interests, because I feel honor-bound to do so. I stand very much isolated in Germany, and am without the slightest trace of another contact with publishers! . . . I cannot help myself, what with all my obligations to the King: frequent trips with His Majesty, on which I carry as many as twenty or thirty paper boxes of manuscript. In July and August I must play travel companion for the King in Bohemia, where the Austrian Emperor will join us. Afterwards I must go with the King to witness a military spectacle at Magdeburg . . . and later threatens the (nomadic!) Association meeting at Breslau.

More than ever the King had come to depend on his Councilor. Ailing and irritable, he may have regarded Humboldt as a combination of nurse and secretary, expecting to be entertained by reading, conversation, and the presentation of visitors. There were moments of desperation when Humboldt complained to his friends of being torn between his conflicting duties to the King, his manuscripts, and his brother Wilhelm, to whom he had to administer cheerful thoughts, for Wilhelm's health was rapidly declining. In March 1834 Humboldt mentioned this unfortunate turn of events for the first time, admiring his brother's fortitude in fighting off melancholy moods evoked by a deforming arthritis. The brothers would sit in the park at Tegel discussing classic writers or the mystic philosophy of Meister Eckhart, of whose piety Humboldt once said that it touched him like a mild breeze of spring.

In March 1835 Wilhelm was reported critically ill, and Alexander hastened to Tegel, carrying with him a bundle of manuscripts that he had promised to return to his publisher in Paris. He found Wilhelm in a coma. "I did not think that my old eyes could have shed so many tears. It lasted for eight days. Pity me," a letter to his publisher Gide in Paris continued. "I am the unhappiest of men. My brother died the day before yesterday, at six o'clock." And to Wilhelm von Schlegel he reported on April 19:

We saw the noble soul die for ten long days and nights. He passed away with the composure and cheerful acceptance of one blessed by great mental talents. . . . In moments of consciousness he would recite thirty to forty verses in Greek from the *Iliad* and Pindar or from the hallucination of Thekla by Schiller. He worked on his large linguistic book on the very day when a bloodletting prevented apoplexy. He leaves two works that should not necessarily be considered as separate: (1) on the languages of the Indian Archipelago, the South Sea

Islands, in their relationship to Sanskrit, and (2) researches on linguistic structure and its influence on the cultural growth of nations. . . .

So grief-stricken was Alexander that for weeks he felt loath to accept invitations and buried himself in his studies. No loss could have been felt with greater anguish. Although Wilhelm had been his severest censor, Alexander had loved him all the more for his integrity; he was surpassed by none of Humboldt's friends for the soaring flight of his ideals and the warmth of his affections. The survivor must labor in the shadow of his brother's death; he determined to memorialize him. Varnhagen von Ense, the husband of Humboldt's old friend Rahel Levin, would publish Wilhelm's writings: the philosophical essays on art, statesmanship, and classic literature, to be followed by a special edition of the linguistic studies, which, in Alexander's estimation, "assisted so powerfully in the development of a new universal science of language, in which differences of structure are traced back to types founded upon the intellectual constitution of mankind."

And yet for Humboldt to deliver a memorial address for his departed brother at Leipzig, on the occasion of the bicentennial of Leibniz's birth, would not do. He excused himself by saying that his eulogy would of necessity be contrained by moderation, and "constraint annihilates freedom, without which it is impossible to produce anything satisfactory." He was to commemorate his brother in the first volume of *Cosmos,* whose closing passage quoted Wilhelm's faith in humanity:

If we want to single out one idea that emerged from history with ever increasing force, it is the concept of humanization:

the tendency to break down barriers of prejudice and religion, and the belief in mankind as one large community capable of evolving its inherent capacities. This, then, is the ultimate goal of society, one in which man himself recognizes visions of indefinite expansion.

Now, at sixty-six, Humboldt would go on living with the sense of dedication which his brother had shown. Without him, Tegel would never be the same, and yet Humboldt would return there often to enjoy the company of grandnieces and grandnephews and the friendship of Wilhelm's oldest daughter, Cabriclc, and hcr husband, of whom he was to see quite a lot at court. And as if fate had meant to make up for his lonely hours in the Berlin apartment, good old Seifert had finally found himself a wife and installed his own household nearby. There was a gay festivity whon thoir firot child wao christcncd Alexandra Caroline, a name to be toasted because it so happily united the memory of the master's departed sister-in-law with his own. In years to come, the child would often sit on Humboldt's lap, her fingers toying with her godfather's picture books or playing hide-and-seek with the white-haired man whom she would always remember as a kindly tutor. When her mother dusted books in Humboldt's study, little Alexandra helped, placing them back on the lower shelves, where she would remember them first for their bindings and later for their strange titles. And of a sudden her father, Seifert, was off again to accompany the white-haired uncle to faraway Paris, where French ladies drove about in splendid coaches and soldiers talked about a shooting war. Returning from his last trip in the fall of 1835, her godfather had brought her a doll from Paris and some wonderful-smelling perfume for a lady, his niece

Gabriele, who lived near the King. It was all very exciting to the little girl when her godfather and her daddy left for Paris in a coach, her father sitting in the carriage waving and leaving her to cry a little—Alexandra thinking of the long road and the horses galloping toward France.

Shortly after New Year 1839, Alexandra was old enough to listen to her godfather's talk about Paris, and while she could not understand everything, it comforted her, and it did a lot of grown-ups, that he had tried his best to avert a war. He had, the story went, met a man in Paris by the name of Samuel F. B. Morse, who had shown him the telegraph. These were exciting times, when people had started to ride in a train of iron carriages pulled by a snorting monster called a locomotive. Railway travel would at least make it easier for the white-haired uncle to move around, or would he perhaps stop moving?

At times the King's carriage would drive up before the house to take Humboldt for a ride to Potsdam. There he must attend parties with the royal family and its guests, who listened to him by the hour, the first lady embroidering and the King standing by the window looking a bit bored. And there were other days, not all to Humboldt's liking, when he was asked to read stories to the King's grandchildren. Meals at court were rather simple, and so was entertainment, dictated as they were by the puritanical tastes of a King who had never learned to fit his role.

Ever since his morganatic marriage with a young Countess Harrach in 1824, Friedrich Wilhelm III had been happier. He had acquired a taste for cheap variety shows in Berlin, relishing them for the break in a routine that demanded adherence to a rigid schedule: signing of decrees and letters, receiving ambassadors, listening to his ministers, and entertaining cousins from England and princes from other parts of Germany. A visit of the dukes of Orléans and Nemours in 1836 had caused quite a stir among Berlin society, especially as it was rumored that Humboldt paid these French aristocrats generous attention, and that he, in fact, had engineered the Duke of Orléans's marriage with a Princess of Mecklenburg.

For Humboldt, *rapprochement* between Prussia and France was the order of the day, the more so as Louis-Philippe had allowed himself to be surrounded by advisers who eyed the German side of the Rhine with considerable envy. On no account should France be encouraged in such ambitions, for Humboldt visualized quite clearly that a war of *revanche* might revive the Holy Alliance, in which case Russia would have a chance to renew her claims for participation. The new Duchess of Orléans came to be Humboldt's staunch friend, and corresponded with him for many years, seeking his advice in many perplexing situations. That the reception of the French princes had not been what Humboldt had hoped did not discourage him in the least in trying to influence Friedrich Wilhelm III in the matter of improving relationships with France. But the King was getting old, and at last died in 1840.

"It is my fate to survive everybody, my family and kings"—and Humboldt might have added Jefferson and Madison, Gallatin and Beethoven. Of these illustrious men, Beethoven could have meant little to a naturalist so unresponsive to music as Humboldt was. That he consented to listen to Chopin's playing at a soirée given by Prince Radziwill in Berlin was mere politeness. All the more astonishing it is that a few years later Humboldt

placed the names of Mendelssohn and Meyerbeer on the
first list of honors that Friedrich Wilhelm IV conferred on
a number of German and foreign men of science and art.
It was fortunate for the author of *Cosmos* that he was
able to interest the aging King and his oldest son in his
latest work. As early as the fall of 1834 Humboldt had
sent an outline to Varnhagen von Ense.[2] "I have the crazy
notion," he wrote,

to depict the entire material universe, all that we know of the
phenomena of universe and earth, from spiral nebulæ to the
geography of mosses and granite rocks, in one work—and in a
vivid language that will stimulate and elicit feeling. Every
great and important idea that glows in my writing should here
be registered side by side with facts. It should portray an
epoch in the spiritual genesis of mankind—in the knowledge of
nature. But it is not to be taken as a physical description of
earth: it comprises heaven and earth, the whole of creation.
Fifteen years ago I had started writing it in French, and called
it *Essai sur la physique du monde*. In Germany I had originally
thought of calling it *The Book of Nature*, after the one that
Albertus Magnus wrote in the Middle Ages. But all this is uncertain. Now my title is: *Cosmos, Sketch of a Physical Description of the Universe, after the enlarged lectures in the years
1827 to 1828. . . .* I realize that *Cosmos* sounds very ponderous and that it is not without certain affectation . . . the
main drawbacks of my style are an unhappy disposition to

[2] By sending Varnhagen von Ense his first outline, Humboldt won
the co-operation of a man in whose literary judgment he could trust, for
his friend had made his reputation as a biographer and chronicler of his
time. The correspondence between Humboldt and Varnhagen von Ense
is one of the most revealing sources of reference for the old age of the
great naturalist, more intimate than his letters to Heinrich Berghaus, the
geographer, to Gauss, and to the diplomat Baron C. J. von Bunsen, whom
Humboldt cherished for his extraordinary versatility of mind.

poetic forms, lengthy participial constructions, and too great a concentration of several ideas and feelings in one sentence. I believe, however, that I can manage to counterbalance such radical evils by expressing myself simply and with occasional generalizations. A book on nature should produce the impression that she herself elicits. . . . My manner of writing differs from that of Forster and Chateaubriand, for I have always attempted to write truthfully, descriptively, and actually scientifically, without losing myself in the dryness of pure knowledge.

And his knowledge of regions in different parts of the world was seen intimately linked to humanity's history and its various cultures. "The influence of nature's physical traits," Humboldt wrote in *Cosmos,* "on the moral nature of people, the secretive mutual interaction of sensual and super-sensual, lends to nature studies a special challenge as yet little appreciated." For man to feel integrated with nature was to obtain a true balance of life, was to avoid that measure of artificiality which made for exaggerated values of a literary and political sort. Humboldt's philosophy demanded no such allegiance to an idealized norm as the romantics had claimed, but a more realistic one that created values through the consciousness of acting a part in the universal whole. Knowledge of how plants and other organisms live, how their grouping and specific traits reflect the integration of physical and organic factors, was to give a more universal understanding of human capacities. In this sense knowledge was not meant to be a tool for power, but the deepest enjoyment of life. Because of this Humboldt envisioned a special science to orient people through the higher consciousness of their participation in the cosmic design. Such an experience embodies the *"prin-*

ciple of individual and political freedom forever rooted in the equal rights of a unified humanity" (*Cosmos*, II). This attractive practical philosophy might well have made educated people better conscious of their common purpose, rather than of their differences. It might have prevented the excesses of colonialism and eased class struggles. But no matter how uniquely fate had endowed Humboldt to present this portrait of the universe to a mankind tempted by the privileges accruing from mechanized power and nationalistic objectives, Europe would not claim the portrait as its own. A more materialistic orientation, ushered in by Darwin's *Origin of Species* and followed by the ideas of Karl Marx, Sigmund Freud, and a host of scientists and inventors, was destined to replace Humboldt's visions with other values.

Yet in the field of science, which continues to dominate our life for better or for worse, one cannot fail to recognize a philosophic striving for universal interpretations of nature. For what is Sir James Jeans's concept of the "expanding universe," or Albert Einstein's "unified-field theory," or, for that matter, the atomic theory, but renewed attempts at understanding the harmony of matter? Seen in this perspective, Humboldt's philosophy need neither be lost nor outdated, for it would seem to stem from a lasting desire in man to derive orientation from a knowledge of his position in nature. Humboldt's life was one of exploration in the most exalted sense of the word, and it may well be that the essence of his views of nature—namely, the interrelatedness of man and the universe—could still help modern science and science-education to yield to a better integration of knowledge than excessive specialization presently admits.

16

The Troubles of a Protector

HISTORICAL INCIDENTS CAN create patterns of behavior which a less gifted personality may find worth imitating if his station in life will permit it. Friedrich Wilhelm IV of Prussia lacked the genius of his forebear, Frederick the Great. Nor was he so placed as to earn laurels on the field of battle. But he was sensitive to the shadow of his forebear, so sensitive that within a few weeks of his father's death he had found in Humboldt a Voltaire of sorts to install at the very place where the great Frenchman had spent so many years, the small garden palace of Sans Souci near Potsdam. The new King had watched the fame of his father's councilor grow until it began to overshadow that of all other contemporaries, and now that fate had placed this extraordinary man at the zenith of his reputation, the King was determined to make him the focus of his attention. At forty-five, Friedrich Wilhelm IV was provided with a family of his own, and was tolerably happy with a Queen whose Bavarian origin and royal upbringing at Munich had brought the court a kind of southern charm. He was of a romantic disposition and rather brilliant mind, and if some regarded him as emotionally unstable, nobody could deny that he promised many things.

As for Humboldt, the King could hardly wait to appoint him a member of the State Council and to give him guest rooms in the park at Sans Souci, and later in the Town Palace at Potsdam. The King furnished Humboldt's quarters with potted palms and fern that the botanist Will-

denow had previously cultivated from South American
seeds. Simple draperies and pictures of tropical scenery
served to imitate a jungle tent replete with camp bed.
For Humboldt's sake the Amazon must come alive in Potsdam's feudal setting! In so romantic a nest the occupant
proved hardly the type to be coddled by surroundings.

At seventy-one Humboldt would not take orders lightly,
as he proved when he asked the new sovereign to excuse
him from attending meetings of the State Council. He was
much too busy, working as he still did until half past two
in the morning, fighting against all the disturbing interruptions that he could not avoid despite his own clever
ruses. It was infinitely more to his liking to return to Paris
on a brief diplomatic mission. A year later, in May 1841,
the King let him go, welcoming him back again in November. Thereafter, in 1842, the King took Humboldt to London for the christening of the future Prince of Wales, later
Edward VII.

The King had been warned of Humboldt's liberal beliefs by members of his entourage. The case of Göttingen
University had showed him where Humboldt stood on the
issue of constitutional rights. In September 1837, seven
professors were expelled by Ernst August, King of Hanover, for their vehement protests against his abrogation of
the rights of free speech. That Humboldt's friend Gauss
should have lost his appointment aroused the old Jacobin
to bitter accusations against the tyrant at Hanover: "What
barbarity! The villains propose to disband the universities,
but they will not succeed in doing away with that old-
established institution. . . . Many in the so-called upper
classes of society," he wrote to Gauss, "are utterly insensi-
ble to the nobility of mind so evident in the sacrifice of all

material advantage to the voice of conscience." But he consoled himself in the thought that such incidents were necessary for the rise of freedom in a country politically lethargic, as was Germany.

Meanwhile he interfered at Hanover for the reinstatement of the professors, but failed because of the overcautiousness of his diplomatic maneuvers. Who else in Europe could have appealed as strongly to the conscience of intellectuals? Who might have come forth with a more ringing manifesto for freedom than Humboldt? In this respect he failed just as he had showed weakness on occasions when Metternich's heavy hand had stifled the hopes of liberal patriots. Was he afraid of losing his cherished power at the court of Berlin? A few months before the dismissal of the professors, Humboldt had attended the centenary celebrations of Göttingen University as a guest of honor. On that occasion the students had greeted him with a torchlight parade, and Humboldt had lauded the free development of intellectual life in German universities. In the case of the dismissals, Gauss naturally felt Humboldt's caution as a shocking letdown, though he may have excused it when Humboldt wrote on December 19, 1850:

Public praise has a depressing effect upon me. I am fully aware that longevity requires patience, and that it increases fame. But in a disturbed world such as I have seen since 1789 I have always sustained the firm conviction that a fancy uniform must never prevent me from defending the eternal principles of political freedom and constitutional institutions, a faith that I continuously expressed in my writings, speeches, and friendships.

He maintained his faith in liberty, but in the case of the Göttingen professors he had showed himself reluctant to live up to it. No doubt the King had a hold over Humboldt, restraining him on occasion with the gilded shackles of court life, playing on the inner insecurity of a man who craved his protection. In the circus of court life Humboldt was the lion tamed to jump, snarling defiantly as he did so, his mental fangs bared—but jumping. And he had to suppress whatever thoughts and hopes he may have maintained, hiding his inner self much as he had hidden it in his boyhood days when nobody, not even his mother, had encouraged him to feel secure in his enthusiasm for nature.

Such weakness was made up for by Humboldt's generosity toward friends. Among them was one who deserves a very special place for his lasting services as an immigrant scientist in the United States: Louis Agassiz (1807–73). Meagerly supported by poor parents, young Agassiz had struggled hard to gain recognition through research on fishes, and he needed a job. At once Humboldt had gone to his aid, asking his geologist friend Leopold von Buch to join him in efforts to secure a foothold for the young Swiss. Once established, Agassiz sent Humboldt his publications; when visiting Paris in 1832, he implored his influential protector to help him secure a German publisher for his writing on zoology. A few days later Humboldt sent him one thousand francs to ease his fears and anxiety. "One might well despair of the world," Humboldt wrote to Agassiz's mother, "if a person like your son, with knowledge so substantial and manners so ingratiating, should fail to make his way." The book on fishes deserved to be circulated and subscribed for, and Agassiz, not knowing how to address kings in proper style, received Humboldt's suggestion: "Your Royal Majesty, deeply moved, I venture

most humbly to lay at your feet my warmest thanks for the
support so graciously granted. . . ."

In Paris, Humboldt repaid Agassiz's visit. "After a cordial greeting," Agassiz reported,

he walked straight to my books, a small shelf containing a
few classics, the cheapest editions I could afford to buy in the
bookstalls on the quais, some works on philosophy and history, chemistry and physics, his own *Views of Nature,* Aristotle's *Zoology,* Linnæus's *Systema naturæ* . . . and a German
encyclopedia. . . . I shall never forget, after his look of mingled interest and surprise at my little collection, his half-
sarcastic question as he pounced upon the great encyclopedia:
"What are you doing with this ass's bridge?"

Shortly afterwards Humboldt invited Agassiz for dinner
in a restaurant near the Palais Royal, "and for three hours,
which passed like a dream, I had him all for myself. How
he examined me, and how much I learned in that short
time! How to work, what to do, and what to avoid, how to
live, how to distribute my time, what methods of study to
pursue. It was not sufficient for him to cheer and stimulate
the student; he also wanted to give rare indulgence to a
young man who could allow himself few luxuries." Such
attention from a famous man thirty-seven years his senior
might well have turned a poor student's head, but not
Agassiz's. A year later he was happily married and on the
road to fame.

The friendship continued, and was kept alive by Humboldt's perpetual interest in Agassiz's work. His letters to
the young Swiss naturalist are uncommonly long and full
of ardent friendship.

Your letters [he wrote on August 15, 1840, from Berlin] continue to be always warm and affectionate. I receive few like

them. Since two thirds of the letters addressed to me (partly copies of letters written to the King or the ministers) remain unanswered, I am blamed, charged with being a parvenu courtier, an apostate from science. This bitterness of individual accusations does not diminish my ardent desire to be useful. I act oftener than I answer. I know that I like to do good, and this awareness gives me tranquility in my overburdened life.

Was it that through Agassiz Humboldt recalled his own *Sturm und Drang* period, years when he had sought the friendship and protection of men of affairs and influential scholars? Agassiz needed only to mention his desire to accompany the Prince of Canino to the United States, and Humboldt would ask the King for a grant of fifteen thousand francs to help Agassiz carry out his project. When nothing came of it, Humboldt continued to encourage his young friend in his plans to go to the United States. True enough, Agassiz's theory of glaciation did not please Humboldt at first. Good-naturedly he wrote:

But I am only a grumbling, rebellious subject in your kingdom. Do not be vexed with a friend who is more than ever impressed with your services to geology, your philosophical views of nature, your profound knowledge of organized beings.

And when Agassiz finally sailed for Boston in September 1846, one of the last greetings he received was Humboldt's note written from Frederick the Great's Sans Souci:

Be happy in this new undertaking, and preserve for me the first place of friendship in your heart. When you return, I shall be here no more, but the King and Queen will receive you on this historic hill with the affection which, for so many reasons, you merit.

At Sans Souci, where Humboldt sometimes stayed overnight, he would sit into the early hours of the morning coping with an ever swelling tide of correspondence.

It is not that I lack the good will to reply [he wrote to Wilhelm von Schlegel on June 12, 1843]. But understand, please, that I dispatch to both hemispheres some three thousand letters a year—all handwritten without the aid of a secretary—and that I never go to bed before two o'clock at night, only to sit at my desk again at six. Under such conditions I really can claim some lenience. I hasten to reply only in cases . . . where I can really hope to do some good. . . . Add to such a plight *my firm intention not to relinquish my literary career so that nobody can mistake me for a courtier.* . . . Just now I have published over a hundred sheets—three volumes of my studies on Inner Asia, which I correct myself. Each sheet must travel twice from Paris to Berlin, Königsberg, and Silesia. Amid this singular confusion of my life I am now writing—in German—the biggest of all the works I am able to produce: *Cosmos*. . . .

The work on Asia was his *Asie Centrale, recherches sur les chaînes de montagnes et la climatologie comparée* (Paris, 1843). This geography of Asia incorporated not only the results of his Russian expedition, but also a complete survey of everything known from ancient historical and contemporary sources, those of the Himalayan region included. The infinite care with which he had prepared this impressive new opus is evident from the manner in which he rendered geographic nomenclature: Chinese place names appeared both in Klaproth's mode of transcription and in Chinese characters; Indian place names in English transcription, with Sanskrit spelling wherever it was available. It would be difficult to find among modern gazetteers a more exemplary mode of preparing such a treatise. Consideration for other peoples' customs came to Humboldt as naturally as his spontaneous desire to offer help where it was needed.

Now that he was placed so favorably to help others, it often happened that the King was asked to confer a medal here or a new appointment there, to make a grant for Niebuhr's archæological expedition in Egypt, for new astronomical instruments at a university, or to show leniency toward unfortunate men who had been placed in desperate circumstances because of political or personal conflicts. When the poet Heinrich Heine asked Humboldt to intervene on his behalf so that he, the exiled, might be allowed to seek medical treatment at Hamburg, Humboldt responded promptly. That he did not succeed in this instance was owing to the obstinate insistence of the King's ministers that Heine recant his diatribes against German customs.

With the advancing years Humboldt became the sole arbiter for important cultural affairs, the *deus ex machina* of an age that saw significant advances in natural science and liberal arts. And the King, for all his romantic disposition, proved himself capable of relying on Humboldt's advice, especially in the eight years before the Revolution of 1848. This "romantic on Cæsar's throne," as the philosopher David Friedrich Strauss called him, reactivated life at court by drawing scholars, artists, and writers to Sans Souci. There Humboldt would read frequently from the writings of Chateaubriand or Jefferson, show reports of exploration, or explain the latest advances in astronomy.

The historian Leopold Ranke reported that on one occasion Humboldt entered the King's salon and, after a brief exchange of pleasantries with the assembled guests, pulled out a newspaper and posted himself under a chandelier. While the Queen proceeded to take up her knitting, the King and his guests listened to Humboldt read a lengthy article about political tolerance from his favorite French paper, the *Journal des Débats*. Such efforts at enlightening his sovereign were prompted by a desire to inspire the King with such moral principles as freedom from prejudice, forbearance, and magnanimity rather than with specific political ideas and party programs. As Humboldt was expected to spend several evenings a week with the royal family, he found himself often in a quandary over the best entertainment. In such predicaments he sometimes turned to Tieck, the dramatist, or to outstanding actors for the reading of classical plays.

Such duties at court were rather a light burden compared with the King's annoying habit of sending his mail courier late in the evening to Humboldt's home just when he had settled down to write a few pages of *Cosmos*. He must look over the King's private correspondence "for careful revision and lenient criticism" of his private letters to potentates, ministers, and petitioners. So accustomed had the sovereign become to Humboldt's daily company that he complained bitterly to his entourage when his Councilor did not appear for lunch. How Humboldt managed to parry the King's barrage of questions is difficult to guess, for the monarch pestered him with problems like the origin of patricide, torch dances, and hieroglyphic script, and the ancient population of Rome. Although exceedingly well informed about history, Humboldt found himself often pressed to get the correct answers posthaste from such of his learned friends as the astronomer Encke or the archæologist Curtius. While complaining about these disturbing obligations, Humboldt was wont to console himself by saying: "After having pursued my literary labors amid the deafening noise of the New World [in the jungle], disregarding mosquito stings, I believe it possible to write amid the confusion at court and a crowd of court officials."

The first friction with the new King came over the bill to regulate the social and economic status of Jews. Always eager to aid in the emancipation of the oppressed, Humboldt promptly argued, in 1842, against the hypocritical attitude of lawmakers who claimed to fulfill the divine will, allegedly expressed in the Old Testament, for the separation of Jewish nationals. "The history of the Dark Ages," Humboldt snorted, "shows to what extremes such interpretations may be carried." Years later he succeeded in influencing the King and his cabinet toward an amendment to grant intellectuals of Jewish origin full participation in academic life.

No matter how long he had labored for the freedom of Negroes in America, his pleas at conferences fell invariably on deaf ears, and his hopes for the abolition of slavery were again to be defeated when John Charles Frémont lost his campaign for the Presidency of the United States. How unspeakably happy he was when, at long last, in 1856, he was able to report to his friend Böckh: "I have accomplished the project I have so long sought to bring about—namely, the Negro law: every slave will from now on become free upon touching Prussian soil"! But the dreadful vision of a political conflict in America remained. It made him wish to die before a civil war might rend that nation apart.

If people could only be made to understand how unifying were the matters of the mind, and how nature herself operated by co-operation! Class prejudices and political hatreds would then disappear. Was the universe not one large example of a coherent system, and did its energies not accomplish order by integrated action? For mankind to separate itself from this higher order simply because it suited the ambitions of some powerful groups would never do. He must continue to hold up his own portrait of the universe to these confused people, and must go on writing his *Cosmos*, his vision of nature.

And when his impatience over stupid political and court affairs would rouse his temper, there were always a few open-minded friends to understand his scorn. From Sans Souci dates many a letter or brief note written in French, Hebrew, or Sanskrit. Such languages were employed for strictly confidential notes containing sarcastic remarks on members of the court or society, and were addressed to Rahel Levin, Alexander Mendelssohn, or perhaps a member of the Beer family, whose illustrious son was Giacomo Meyerbeer, the composer.

Yet neither social life nor fame had hardened Humboldt to the sufferings of people in humble and tragic circumstances. In October 1843 he sent the director of the Berlin museums twenty thalers for the widow of a museum attendant who was in dire need of firewood for the winter. A few months later Varnhagen reported in his diary that Humboldt was laid up with illness, which had led to rumors of his death, whereupon the sculptor Rauch received a request from an anatomist at Dresden for Humboldt's skull. When Humboldt was informed of this, he remarked: "I need my head for a little while longer, but later I would be only too happy to oblige the gentleman."

At this stage one might think of this busy old man as having been much too preoccupied to find time and energy to bother about students who approached him for help. Yet sometimes Humboldt, an avid reader of professional journals, felt so struck by a paragraph as immediately to toss off a note of appreciation to its author. On one such occasion, in 1842, the septuagenarian wrote to a young mathematician, Gotthold Eisenstein, whose contribution to a mathematical journal had attracted his attention. A few days later Eisenstein presented himself at Humboldt's apartment, a young man in his twenties, poorly dressed, his face pale, his melancholy eyes expressing a kind of shy helplessness to which Humboldt was drawn instantly. Son of a small Jewish tradesman in Berlin, young Eisenstein somehow had managed to study mathematics, and as Humboldt talked to him about theories of higher calculus and problems of spherical trigonometry, he realized at once that the young visitor was a genius.

From then on, Eisenstein was a frequent house-guest, and was introduced to distinguished men at the Berlin Academy. Seeing how terribly poor Eisenstein was, Humboldt supported him, and two years later obtained for him an annuity of 250 thalers from the King. Determined to lift this young genius to a secure position, the fatherly protector sent Eisenstein to Gauss, at Göttingen. So impressed was the famous mathematician with Eisenstein that he wrote to Humboldt that he would be glad to sign his own name to some of Eisenstein's brilliant contributions. Unfortunately, the young man was afflicted by a melancholy disposition that detracted from his studious zeal, though not from Humboldt's esteem.

As Eisenstein continued to suffer from poverty and

yearly postponements of his hope of securing an academic position, Humboldt's compassion grew. The King was constantly approached for small grants, the Minister of War petitioned for Eisenstein's early release from army service. In October 1846 Humboldt wrote to Eisenstein:

My affection for you is not merely grounded on your remarkable gifts. My heart is drawn to you by your gentle, amiable character, and by your proneness to melancholy, to which you must not yield, I implore you for Heaven's sake. You must not continue to avoid all society. . . . Make an effort to see me once a week, distract your thoughts by music, theater, art. . . . I should indeed rejoice were my hearty sympathy affording you any relief . . . letting you feel how highly I prize your friendship.

The trouble was that young Eisenstein thought himself a second Newton, as he later said in a summary of his works which Humboldt had asked him to prepare when applying for a professorship at Heidelberg. When this failed to materialize, Humboldt continued to support poor Eisenstein partly from his own pocket, partly through renewed grants from the King's purse. When Eisenstein became suspected of liberal views, after the Revolution, even these grants were suspended—a fact that did not prevent Humboldt from writing more and more letters to influential people imploring them to do something for his friend and depriving himself of money otherwise badly needed to pay his own bills. So infuriated was Humboldt over the callousness of people who could have helped Eisenstein out of his misery that in 1851 he wrote to his friend Dirichlet, the mathematician: "Eisenstein is dying, allowed to perish for lack of bread, with the most scandalous indifference. . . . My remonstrances are ridiculed, and I am sent to Jericho! . . . These are strange times in which I am bidding good-by to the world!"

At last Eisenstein was elected a member of the Academy of Science, but soon after he was found to be consumptive. In 1852 he was hospitalized, Humboldt paying for his nursing. "In him [Eisenstein] was exhibited an active mind in a sickly body, a wonderful creative faculty in a life passed wholly amid sorrow." The banker Mendelssohn would have contributed money to send Eisenstein to Sicily for recovery, but it was too late. Humboldt wrote in utmost grief to the young man's parents that the last grant due their deceased son would be used for funeral expenses. Gauss's comment on Humboldt's action was "One of the most wonderful jewels in Humboldt's crown is the zeal with which he lends his assistance and encouragement to genius."

But was this not more than simple encouragement? To his friends and to the King, Humboldt had written countless letters imploring them to do something on behalf of his unfortunate friend. By so doing he had exposed himself to an almost humiliating degree. This was surely not mere encouragement, but a reawakened passion for identifying himself with a man of great creative talent. Once more, as on so many previous occasions, Humboldt had fallen in love with the creative phenomenon of genius, desiring to partake in its productivity and, in this instance, to shield it from calamity. Eisenstein's melancholy disposition and illness invoked Humboldt's compassion to a point at which the protector felt called upon to play the role of savior—or mother. In attempting to settle his friend's condition, Humboldt battled against the injustices of frailty and prejudice. Once the suffering friend had become a symbol of all human torment, nothing could stop Humboldt's attempts to save genius from an end as tragic as it was undeserved.

Whether Eisenstein actually was a genius is beside the point, though in this connection it is certainly fascinating to recall that F. W. H. Myers in his *Human Personality* (Vol. 1, pp. 80–1) cited a case of a young mathematician incapable of solving a simple proposition in Euclid at a time when he was able to excite Gauss with mathematical complications that would have occupied most men for a lifetime. It must suffice that in Humboldt's estimation Eisenstein was a genius, and genius, once recognized, automatically elicited the image of a sovereignty of the mind to which homage was due. Many of Humboldt's friends may have felt like ascribing such determined action to senility, but what could have been more youthful than the urge to give succor to a talented youth of humble Jewish origin and save him from an undeserved doom? The obstinacy with which Humboldt pursued this case suggests that he was by no means an all-powerful influence behind the throne.

Despite all the growling about the desiccated atmosphere of Berlin, Humboldt seems to have relished soirées and a few musical entertainments. The house of Prince Radziwill was a focus of musical culture, the home of the Mendelssohn family a meeting-place for artists, writers, and men of affairs. If Humboldt forced himself on one occasion to listen to a Paganini concert, it was to please his nieces. As in Paris, Humboldt's company was cherished not solely for his status as an "institution" of society, but also for his witty gossip and story-telling. "It served the purpose equally well," his friend Berghaus remarked, "if it was a piece of general news or town gossip . . . he could play with it as he pleased, turn and twist it in such a manner that wit, irony, worldly wisdom, and versatile genius were welded together with a little spite and knavish bonhomie." Humboldt's sarcasm was usually aimed at a pietistic circle around the King or at society folks who were ever ready, Bible in hand, to spread their venom in a whispering campaign. For this sarcasm he was feared and hated, was called a Jacobin, an atheist, a vain courtier. If a number of academicians came in for a spray of his bitter feelings ("sexless, poisonous insects," Humboldt called them on one occasion), it was because of the growing irritations of his confused life.[1]

In Paris, on the other hand, which he visited again from September 1842 to February 1843, and from December 1844 to May 1845, Humboldt felt as much at home with Arago as in the intimate circle of Louis-Philippe, and at the Tuileries or Versailles. On such occasions he may have sported the red button in his buttonhole to prove his gratitude for the decoration and rank of officer of the Legion of Honor. It is unrecorded whether he ever wore the grand cordon of the same French decoration, the highest bestowed on statesmen or friendly potentates, which Napoleon III conferred on him six years before his death. This Francophile son of the Prussian capital was rarely seen to wear decorations, of which he had more than any other contemporary scholar.

If he came to be embroiled in the struggle for such dis-

---

[1] Professor Francis Lieber of Columbia College, New York, reported a visit to Humboldt in 1844. Humboldt told him that he had entertained the King by showing him drawings of the New York aqueduct. The King's interest had prompted Humboldt to discuss classic examples of aqueducts with the King for an entire week.

tinctions, it was really the King's fault: in 1842 he appointed Humboldt Chancellor of the Peace Class of the Order of Merit (*pour le mérite*), which Friedrich Wilhelm IV founded. It is difficult to say whether or not the Chancellor truly enjoyed this added responsibility, for he complained about the bickerings of prospective candidates and the chicaneries of certain men at court who objected to his placing the composer Mendelssohn or Liszt or Sir John Herschel on the first list. In those days the Peace Class of the Order of Merit was meant to be something like the Nobel Prize in our time: a singular distinction for meritorious accomplishments in the realm of culture. Humboldt saw to it that this order was conferred on many of his own friends, including Gauss, Bessel, Arago, Faraday, and the French painter Ingres.

But with all his fame, his far-flung correspondence and duties, this Chancellor, this Excellency and member of the State Council, was not living in clover. He generally worked late at night over his *Cosmos*, only to retire in his new apartment near the Oranienburg Gate thinking of how he could pay his servant Seifert. Never a good manager of household affairs, and always recklessly generous with aid to deserving students, Humboldt would often wake up on the tenth of the month to find his monthly allowance spent. His pension from the King was wholly insufficient to make ends meet. The rent for his apartment and the cost of carriage visits to Potsdam and Tegel took one third, living expenses another third; charities and postage (a costly item for one who wrote some three thousand letters each year and mailed a flood of manuscript copy and proofs) swallowed the rest, leaving no money for Seifert and for interest on debts that Humboldt had contracted and would continue to contract with the Mendelssohn bankers. On such occasions, which happened chiefly in Humboldt's last years, Seifert must find a Jewish money lender and persuade him to lend a small sum, with Humboldt's library as security. In these later years the master of the house did not know whether he owned his books or his furnishings any longer. He owed Seifert back pay for many years. As early as 1842, he drew up a will naming his servant sole heir to his belongings. At last he saw no way out but to petition the King for help:

Sire:
With these lines, the first I have penned to you since the approach of my death, I venture most humbly to solicit a last favor from Your Majesty. Since the ruin of my fortune in scientific undertakings and the publication of a costly work, I have unceasingly endeavored, with much anxiety, to discharge the heavy obligations under which I labored when I was summoned to Berlin by his late Majesty. In the unfortunate year 1848 alone, I was asked to pay 11,000 thalers, the greater part of which was demanded by business transactions. Notwithstanding my industrious use of nightly hours, it is most uncertain whether I shall be able before my death to discharge my debt to the banking house of Mendelssohn, to whose kind forbearance I have remained indebted for the last seventy years. In order to free myself of the tormenting anxiety of using up the small sum that Seifert, my loyal traveling companion to Russia, will inherit upon my death, I throw myself in this solemn hour with every confidence at the feet of Your Majesty with the request that you will come to the aid of one who has so often pleaded for others, and by your royal gift to an old man extinguish the debt still due the house of Mendelssohn, which I hope will not exceed one year's income. The

mere expression of my wish has consoled me. For one who for so many years has enjoyed the privilege of intimate companionship with Your Majesty, and with your noble-minded and generous consort, the Queen, there is no need to fear in taking so bold a step.

With every expression of grateful and respectful homage,
I remain Your Majesty's faithful and devoted servant,
Alexander von Humboldt

To be sure, the King would help him—but the anxiety remained and took a tragic turn. Years before, Humboldt had petitioned the King for a salaried position for Seifert. When granted, it left Seifert still dissatisfied. Had he not attended his master on every occasion, in Russia, Paris, London? Had he not watched over him, packed his trunks, supervised his social schedule, and attended to a thousand commissions? Clearly, Humboldt must understand that the salary of a royal castellan—eight hundred thalers a year— would never suffice, even if His Excellency paid his salary punctually, as he had agreed to do, but of late had not done.

Was Seifert threatening his master with blackmail, or was it that he foresaw an early end to his opportunities for making the most of his relationship with the man whom many thought as famous as Napoleon Bonaparte? At last Humboldt responded to Seifert's pressure by writing the following:

My dear Seifert:

In order to protect you from any aspersions that might possibly be cast upon your well-proved honesty and loyalty, I wish to certify by this letter (since by God's providence I may suddenly be removed) that I have given to you and your heirs, in acknowledgment of your valuable services, the sum of 2,688

thalers, this being the cash value of my Order of the Red
Eagle in diamonds, recently paid to me at my request by
the Comptroller of the royal household. Herewith I repeat
the statement of my will, as of May 10, 1841, deposited at the
criminal court, that I bequeath to you and to your heirs all the
goods in my house, such as gold medals, chronometers and
clocks, books, maps, pictures, engravings, sculpture, instruments, sable furs, linen, the small amount of plate, beds, and
all the furniture, under the condition, quite painful to me, that
should the King not liquidate my debt to the house of Alexander Mendelssohn . . . you will endeavor to meet my liabili-
ties by the sale of the "Chalcography," worth more than 2,500
thalers. This you will no doubt do from your feelings of honor
and respect to my memory. I may yet be so fortunate as to
meet my debts by the results of my nightly labors. . . .

Quite obviously, Seifert had threatened the old man,
tortured him with demands until he agreed to sell his most
valuable decoration. The servant having turned master of
the house, nobody was allowed to see Humboldt without
having been scrutinized by Seifert, who, for all we know,
may have demanded entrance fees. The hold this devilish
man had over his master had in the course of time been re-
inforced by his daughter Alexandra, who came running
into Humboldt's study like a whirlwind, showing the old
man how well she did in school, pressing a doll into his
lap, and looking at her godfather with all the innocence of
a child. Accustomed to such charming scenes, how could
Humboldt have done without Seifert, the man who had
made it possible for him to make one more visit to Paris
at the age of seventy-nine?

He had returned to Berlin in January 1848 quite shaken
by the seething unrest in the French capital. Sinister fore-

bodings were in the air. A revolution was brewing. Why, even in Berlin there were rumors of political demonstrations. If only the King had heeded his warnings! But Friedrich Wilhelm IV had other things to do. He had, in fact, run amuck with his romantic mania for reconstructing medieval architecture all over the land, building castles when the very soil under his feet was burning with demands for freedom. This King had started well, but he was a madman, full of fears for the monarchy, a nature complicated in its mixture of generosity, pietism, and mad eccentricities. He was likely to call his generals to the palace for a Bible lesson or, at another time, to debate endlessly the urgent matter of constitutional reforms. These he hated on principle. To fire the nation with enthusiasm for the final completion of Cologne Cathedral, to reside like a medieval knight in a castle on the Rhine, when time was running out to save his name before the judgment of history!

What good was it for the King to have Humboldt appointed a member of the State Council when he preferred to listen to politicians and generals, of whom none saw the handwriting on the wall? By the winter of 1847–8 the nation was seething with political unrest, knocking at the King's door with legitimate demands for action.

By March 1848 public sentiment had reached the boiling-point. A crowd began to gather around the King's palace in Berlin, shouting demands for representative government and the abdication of the monarch. Like rivulets, they gathered from all corners of the city, massing for a decisive demonstration. When bricks began to fly through the windows of the heir apparent's apartment, it looked as if the palace would be stormed at any moment. Fearing for his life and the fate of his family, the King gave the order to fire on crowds already fortified by barricades. Come what might, he would not abdicate. Suddenly the King recalled the troops and offered himself and the Queen as hostages to the leaders of the revolutionary movement. Said the historian Leopold Ranke: "He gave the impression of one who had flunked his examination." While the heir apparant fled to England, the King submitted to the demands of a parliamentary committee.

On March 18, when street fighting began, Humboldt was in his apartment. A gang of workers demanded entrance in search of arms. Why, he asked, did they want to disturb the peace of a scholar seventy-nine years old? The intruders, baffled when he introduced himself, withdrew with apologies, asserting that they were well aware of his sympathies and had no wish to disturb him. To spare him further annoyance, they are alleged to have posted a guard in front of his house. Whether this story is true or not, its very existence suggests that Humboldt enjoyed considerable popularity among the people of his native town. For years it had been rumored that he had pleaded with the King for release of persecuted individuals and for liberal reforms in government. That he was a staunch friend of this King who had failed so dismally to heed political warnings, few, if any, of the liberal leaders understood. The truth was that Humboldt had grown old. He was weary of human strife, and loathed being drawn into revolutionary turmoil, not only because he must harness his remaining strength for *Cosmos*, but also because of a deep inner revulsion against violence of any sort. Had he not seen the great ideals of the French Revolution come to naught? The bloody upheavals in Latin America, with their never ending political unrest, had dampened his enthusiasm for republican forms of government.

He consoled himself with the thought that, after all, "centuries are but seconds in the development of the human race. . . . The ascending curve is formed of smaller curves, and it is exceedingly uncomfortable if one happens to live in one of the recessional oscillations." However great Humboldt's reluctance to be drawn into political manifestations, his reputation was that of a liberal with radical leanings. On January 4, 1848 the Duchess of Dino (formerly Talleyrand-Périgord and Sagan) noted in her diary:

There is some truth in Madame de Lieven's remarks about Humboldt. I do not assert that he is absolutely radical, but his liberalism is of a very advanced type, and in Berlin he urges the Princess of Prussia along the path that she does not always follow with sufficient prudence. Humboldt, however, is too clever to compromise himself, and though he makes himself conspicuous to some extent, he is at bottom a relic of the few remaining elements of the eighteenth century.

The writer of these lines, it may be noted in passing, was an astute observer of social life in the highest circles, capable of reflecting accurately the opinions of the Berlin court. When, on March 21, political parties rallied for a parade in favor of German unity, and the crowd called for the King, a cry was raised for Humboldt, who suddenly appeared on the balcony of the palace, acknowledging their sympathy with a silent bow. Had the people sensed that he was one of them? If some still doubted where Humboldt stood, they would soon have occasion to find out.

The following day, on March 22, 1848, a funeral procession for the heroes of the Revolution turned into a mass demonstration for liberty and national unity. Factory workers and students carried banners, and out in front was Humboldt. This time he marched alone—no kings or titled persons near him—his body bent forward as he walked bareheaded, a cold wintry wind playing with his white hair, thinking perhaps of that remote day in 1790 when he and Forster had stood on the Champ-de-Mars in Paris, where it all had started.

17

American Tribute to an Aging Friend

AS BLOOD WAS spilled in street fighting in Berlin, Paris, and Vienna, the news from the capital of the United States was hardly less stirring to Humboldt than the people's call for freedom. The Treaty of Guadalupe Hidalgo (1848) had sealed a crushing defeat for the Mexican Republic.[1] The Star-Spangled Banner was waving from settlements along the California coast, fluttering from Sutter's Fort, where gold had been struck. To Humboldt such news must have been like the rumbling of a distant earthquake. Had Jefferson not foreseen it all forty-four years before, when, at Monticello, he had discussed the future of America? What had then been the vague vision of an American Empire stretching from coast to coast had now become political reality.

By September 1848 Humboldt had received a copy of the Mexican peace treaty. More exciting still, the same mail had contained newspaper clippings from the *National Intelligencer* (Washington), with the first authentic news of the California gold fields. The reports of a certain Ed-

[1] Humboldt's attitude toward this event was reported in a letter George Bancroft wrote, on January 28, 1848, to President Polk: "In Paris I met Alexander von Humboldt, and he gave me leave to say to you, how greatly he was pleased with it. The amount of territory you demand [of Mexico], he deemed to be legitimately due to us, and the tone of moderation that prevails through the message won for it his cordial, unhesitating adhesion. His opinion is of value; for having been honored with Mexican citizenship, the bias of his partialities is for Mexico."

ward F. Beale, and another from the U.S. Navy Agency
at Monterey, spoke of a mad gold rush near the Sacra-
mento River. One thousand men were said to be digging
near Sutter's Fort, where a day's labor had produced ten
thousand dollars' worth of gold. "I am afraid," Humboldt
wrote to his friend Berghaus, "that the discovery of the
rich gold fields in California will at first have unfortunate
effects on its colonization. Adventurers, pickpockets, and
rabble of all sorts will migrate there, even from Europe,
and thus delay the development of agricultural settlements
for a long time to come."

Much as he had wanted California to be added to the
American Union, Humboldt was not pleased to think of
the beautiful Pacific coast as a playground for greedy adventurers. They would cross the continent westward via
the Great Salt Lake in Utah, where John Charles Frémont
had extended his explorations from Oregon. For a while
Humboldt put his writings of *Cosmos* aside as he looked
over maps of North America and studied Frémont's *Report of the Exploring Expedition to the Rocky Mountains
in the year 1842, and to Oregon and North California in the
years 1843–44.*

Just then, in 1848, Berghaus, the geographer and editor
of a geographic journal in Berlin, prepared a new map of
North America. Humboldt assisted him by furnishing certain official data recently received from Washington. Frémont had named a large stream, the Ogden River, and a
mountain range in Nevada after Humboldt, and had verified the position of a salt marsh (Humboldt Sink) in Utah
at the very place that Humboldt had designated on his
Mexican map. From Saskatchewan to Tennessee, surveyors
and settlers would name villages, towns, and counties after

Humboldt (see Appendix D). Now that California, Arizona, and Texas were about to join the United States, a new generation of Americans remembered him. His name would for all time be linked to the great American West, to desert mountains, streams, and pioneer settlements on the prairies. Forty-four years after his visit with Jefferson, everything seemed to come true: a railroad would link St. Louis with the Mexican border and the California coast. This thought evoked memories of days when he had drafted the Mexican map, envisioning an overland coach express from New Orleans across Texas to San Luis Potosí.

How long was life, and how much of it he had spent in coach travel! Carriage drives to Bogotá and Callao, to Washington and Paris, and to Siberia! And the fears of pirates and British men-of-war out there near Tenerife, the frightful storms in the Caribbean. Soon he would be traveling in a railroad carriage from Berlin to the King's residence at Potsdam, and any day his native city would turn into a railroad center. Why was he singled out to live so long? To complete his *Cosmos*, to be sure, and to witness the conquest of time and space by rail, steamboat, and telegraph.

Samuel F. B. Morse came to his mind. He had met Morse in 1838 at Gérard's studio in Paris, and at the meeting of the French Academy of Science he had congratulated Morse on his invention. Afterwards he had taken Arago and Gay-Lussac along to see Morse's exhibition at the Institut de France. These Americans were bent on speeding up life—were, in fact, fulfilling one of his most cherished dreams: to make the world safe for travel and communication, to link oceans and continents, perhaps to create a family of nations. To make California prosperous, Americans must dig a canal at the Isthmus of Panama. When that would happen, the engineers might perhaps remember his 1826 article in which he had discussed the various possibilities for such a project. How well he remembered Goethe's enthusiasm over the Panama and Suez canals, and Goethe's wanting to live longer so that he might experience the thrill of it all!

The telegraph had come to speed up news, but was it practical for rapid communication of weather reports? The French had been the first to inaugurate this service. "What good would it do," Humboldt asked his friend Berghaus, "when it can only increase the general confusion?" If Morse came to Berlin, Humboldt would introduce him to the King, as he actually did, years later, when Morse asked him for his picture. Everybody pestered him and Seifert with requests for mementos. In such a predicament, Daguerre's method was a real godsend, making it so easy to oblige visitors with portraits. Soon everybody would be taking pictures of flowers, landscapes, and people. He must admit that it was a painless procedure to sit before the camera dressed in a frock coat and wearing a decoration. But on such occasions to choose the right medal was a terrible nuisance, for he rarely ever wore his "tinsel hieroglyphs." His friend Berghaus saw him wearing a star on only two occasions.

Seifert would bring him the cardboard box from his study, and he would go over them, discarding the broad silk cordon of the Legion of Honor and the Star of the Order of St. Anne. These gifts of Napoleon III and the Russian Tsar conjured up embarrassing thoughts of tyrannical and boastful rulers. And how painful to recall the moment when he had returned the Order of the Red Eagle with diamonds—in order to pay debts. But his favorite decorations were still there: the Order of Merit and the Star of the Order of the Black Eagle. *"Suum cuique"*—to each his own—was the motto. What could he call his own? His books were mortgaged; his furniture was promised to Seifert. Had he ever wanted to own anything? His brother had always amassed things, books and manuscripts, Greek and Roman antiques, and land. At eighty Humboldt had less perishable things on his mind: the people's cry for liberty, America, and *Cosmos*.

By 1850, prominent Americans came to pay their respects. Visitors like Edward Everett and George Ticknor came from Boston; Judge Charles Patrick Daly from New York; and Benjamin Silliman from Yale College. Accompanied by his young son and George Jarvis Brush, Silliman, the eminent mineralogist and founder of the *American Journal of Science*, came in the summer of 1851 to knock at Humboldt's door.

"A plain house in a quiet part of the city," reported Silliman:

he met us with great kindness in his library, a room of considerable size. He was not engrossing but yielded to our suggestions. . . . He has perfect command of English and speaks quite agreeably. There is no stateliness or reserve about him, he is as affable as if he had no claims to superiority. He conversed with an exceedingly musical voice, is animated and amiable, he stoops a little, has brilliant eyes, is of light complexion, his features and stature round but not fat, his hair thin and white, his conversation brilliant and sparkling with ideas. He was well acquainted with the *American Journal of Science*, with Col. Frémont, and Prof. Bache's coastal survey. He traced for us a canal project on a map, across the Isthmus at Darien. He told us that he had spent three weeks with Jefferson at Monticello in 1804, who entertained him with an extraordinary project regarding the ultimate division of the American continent in three great republics, involving Mexico and the South American states. He made some very interesting remarks about the present state of Europe, and on the impossibility of keeping down moral power by physical force. In his library hung a portrait of the King and of his brother Wilhelm, the antiquarian and philologist.

After the visit, Humboldt sent Silliman a letter in which he wrote:

I have moral reasons to fear the immeasurable aggrandizement of your Confederacy, the temptation to abuse power, dangerous to the Union. . . . I am not less impressed by the great advantage that the physical knowledge of the world, positive science and intelligence, ought to derive from this growth . . . it superimposes, not without violence, new classes of population upon the aboriginal races now rapidly nearing extinction.

The approaching near-extinction of the American Indians was a bitter pill for Humboldt to swallow, the more so as the much admired Frémont had condoned Kit Carson's ruthless shooting of Indians on his Rocky Mountain expedition. It was a shocking thought for one who had inspired Gallatin to write a treatise on the American aborigines to inform the government of the necessity for integration of the Indian element. Humboldt could hardly have overlooked certain compromising incidents in Frémont's life, such as the court-martial provoked by his rash handling of the California campaign. If Humboldt admired Frémont, it was for his achievement as an explorer and his firm stand on the all-important issue of Negro slavery. As presidential candidate Frémont had spoken against Van Buren's policies, pleading for abolition, and that in Humboldt's estimate sufficed to recommend Frémont for the Order of Merit. In sending the medal, Humboldt concluded his letter with a sentence the Federalist Party would remember: *"La Californie, qui a noblement résisté à l'introduction de l'esclave sera dignement representée par un ami de la liberté et des progrès de l'intelligence."* [2]

Quite unexpectedly, in January 1853 a visitor was introduced, a robust young man who had just returned from years of travel in Brazil and the upper Missouri region: Balduin Möllhausen (1825–1905). He had arrived at Hamburg with a load of live American animals for the Berlin Zoo, and was full of stories of the Duke of Württemberg's ill-fated expedition to Fort Laramie, where the party had barely escaped scalping. So delighted was Humboldt with this visitor that he invited him to stay as house-guest. It must have pleased the host enormously to see how interested young Möllhausen was in Seifert's daughter, Alexandra Caroline. Attractive, and having grown up under the tutelage of the famous Humboldt, this girl had all the charms a man like Möllhausen might have looked for in a prospective mate. And now that romance had so unexpectedly come to his own home, the eighty-four-year-old Humboldt would do everything to bring it to a happy end. When, in April 1853, Möllhausen sailed for the United

[2] George Bancroft, who had visited Humboldt in 1820 and 1847 in Paris, said of him on the occasion of the Humboldt centenary in 1869: "Humboldt was always the friend of young America. He measured his regard for us, not by any merits we might have, but by the goodness of his heart. He, who knew our continent so well, knew the relations of the United States toward every part of it . . . wishing especially that California and all the tract of land which now belongs to us on the Pacific might come to us."

States, he carried in his pocket not only his appointment as topographer to A. W. Whipple's memorable expedition to locate the route of a railroad to the Pacific, but also Humboldt's letters of recommendation—and, still more important, Alexandra's promise to be his wife.

While in Arizona and California, the young explorer would send his love letters to Humboldt's diplomat friend Baron Leo Gerolt, in Washington. Gerolt, on special request from Berlin, forwarded them in the diplomatic mail pouch to the lovesick girl. When Möllhausen returned the following year laden with plant and rock specimens for Humboldt to study, a marriage was celebrated, and Alexandra's godfather toasted their happiness in French champagne. A year later the offspring of this blissful union was christened Alexander Möllhausen. His godfather, Humboldt, looked down from his Olympian age of eighty-six on a new generation about to usher in the age of science. By that time Humboldt had almost completed his report [3] to Lieutenant (later Major General) Whipple on the geology of Mount Taylor and the San Francisco mountains in the Zuñi country near Flagstaff, Arizona. Balduin Möllhausen came to be known as the prolific writer of American Indian love stories, travel lore, and poetry (forty-five large works in 157 volumes, besides eighty novelettes in 21 volumes!) which earned him the sobriquet of the German Cooper. Long after *Uncle Tom's Cabin* and *Hiawatha* had fired the imagination of countless emigrants, Möllhausen's books sustained this sentimental tradition.

[3] This report was sent from Humboldt's quarters in the town palace at Potsdam in the form of a four-page letter, on August 18, 1855. A postscript assured Lieutenant Whipple that "because of my great age I write illegibly, and I have asked Mr. Möllhausen to translate it [from French] into English for publication."

Three years later, in 1858, the Secretary of War, John B. Floyd, wrote to Humboldt from Washington, D.C.:

Never can we forget the services you have rendered not only to us but to all the world. The name of Humboldt is not only a household word throughout our immense country, from the shores of the Atlantic to the waters of the Pacific, but we have honored ourselves by its use in many parts of our territory, so that posterity will find it everywhere linked with the names of Washington, Jefferson, and Franklin.

The letter was attached to an album composed of nine maps, showing the various localities named after Humboldt.

His name a household word in the United States? Perhaps Agassiz's lectures or Frémont's political campaign speeches had spread its fame, but such factors would hardly have made for nationwide popularity. It is more likely that thousands had come to revere and love him as the author of *Cosmos* and *Views of Nature,* then available in English translations. The first two volumes of *Cosmos* appeared in 1845 and 1847, and could not possibly have been better timed in the light of that great migration which drew thousands of politically troubled men and women to the United States. Whatever teachers and writers like Agassiz and Prescott may have drawn from Humboldt's works, it was *Cosmos* that aroused a new generation of Americans. Replenished by emigrants, doctors, artisans, tradesmen, and adventurers, this new agglomeration of Europeans carried Humboldt's gospel of nature to America. Once transplanted, it was bound to spread, riding as it were on waves of migration to which the example of Humboldt's daring exploits lent, if not directed, sentimental inspiration. An author so infused with natural philosophy and so vigorously determined to popularize natural science was bound to produce echoes in many who felt inspired by grand and unspoiled scenery in the United States, where lakes looked like oceans, and valleys like primordial chasms, and where deserts conjured up visions of Biblical lands.

Such were the intangible factors in making Humboldt a household word. And Agassiz was there, in Boston, to remind his generation what it owed to the author of *Cosmos:*

This mode of treating his subjects, emphatically his own, has led many specialists to underrate Humboldt's familiarity with different branches of science, as if knowledge could only be rendered in pedantic forms and a set phraseology. . . . To what degree we Americans are indebted to him, no one knows who is not familiar with the history of learning and education in the last century. All the fundamental facts of popular education in physical science, beyond the merest elementary instruction, we owe to him. The first geologic cross sections, the first sections across an entire continent, the first average of climates illustrated by lines, were his. Every schoolboy is familiar with his methods now, but he does not know that Humboldt is his teacher. How few remember that the tidal lines, the present mode of registering magnetic phenomena and ocean currents, are but the application of Humboldt's researches, and of his graphic mode of recording them.[4]

Was it so surprising that, around 1850, American tourists went to Europe eager to get a glimpse of the legendary Humboldt, sometimes to return to their homes with a

[4] From Agassiz's address in commemoration of Humboldt's birthday delivered in Boston, 1869.

plaster copy of the bust that the sculptor Rauch had made of him? For he was not easy to see, terribly busy as he then was, trying to finish his last great literary work. Rather than allow visitors to distract him, he would take time off to look through the great reflector he had helped to establish in the Berlin Observatory, once more to reassure himself of Moon and Saturn, cosmic nebulæ and double stars, then to rush home and cover page after page describing the starry heavens. "Where the ordinary mind is tempted to fix the stars on the crystal-like vault of heaven, the astronomer widens the distance of space by charting our universe, and he makes us see innumerable other worlds in a sudden apparition of luminous celestial islands. This sudden feeling of magnificence . . . is the *Magic of the Infinite* that moves us so deeply on an ocean, on mountain peaks, and by the clarifying power of great telescopes."

To countless readers the author of *Cosmos* spelled magic: the very grandeur of distant spiral nebulæ, of mountain ranges born from ocean depths, of tropical luxuriance and momentous explorations. It was an encyclopedic compendium of nature written for a generation still unequipped with museum exhibits, natural-history books, and popular libraries. It surprised the author not a little to know how popular his *Cosmos* was, for much of it was couched in scholarly terms and richly documented with bibliographical references. If the scholarly manner of writing was not magic, it was at least awesome and at the same time reassuring as to the accessibility of the source materials. To read *Cosmos* is to experience something akin to the performance of a master organist who draws his registers so skillfully as to burst all architectural bounds, dissolving them by the force of harmonies. And this grand

orchestration of knowledge rang out like a warning to
know and respect nature's harmony, manifest in celestial
spheres and the smallest of organisms.

"Communion with nature awakens within us perceptive
faculties, faculties that have long lain dormant. It makes
us understand at a single glance the influence exercised on
the realm of intellect by physical discoveries, and how a
judicious application of mechanics, chemistry, and other
sciences may lead to national prosperity."

That such welfare would eventually lead to the formation of national power complexes which, by their conflicts,
might outbalance the benefits of science to society was
none of Humboldt's concern. He conceived of himself as
standing on the threshold of the age of science, and he
foresaw its fateful impact on humanity and was acutely
aware of the temptation for science to turn utilitarian,
when its real aim should be to rid mankind of ignorance
and confusion. The fact-finder and tool-inventor could in
Humboldt's estimation be regarded as valuable only if
their labors led to ideas binding all peoples together and
orienting them through integration toward a higher natural order. Seen historically, Humboldt's philosophy of
science is more directly related to the classic traditions of
Greek and Renaissance scholars than to those of his own
time, in which Goethe exerted more influence over Humboldt's natural philosophy than any other contemporary.
What gives Humboldt's philosophy unique stature is its
forceful emergence from the romantic medium of his age.

Was it so surprising to author and publisher that the
public craved this work, that for a time its sales began to
rival those of the Bible? "In the history of book-publishing
the demand is epoch-making," Humboldt's publisher,

I. G. Cotta, wrote in 1847, and this news came from the firm that had published Goethe's and Schiller's works in numerous profitable editions.

Book parcels destined for London and St. Petersburg [continued the publisher's report to Humboldt] were torn out of our hands by agents who wanted their orders filled for the bookstores in Vienna and Hamburg. Regular battles were fought over possession of this edition, and bribes offered for priorities. . . . This race by booksellers, unheard-of since the first editions of Schiller and Goethe . . . is overwhelming proof of a demonstrative desire of the public to read the second volume of your immortal work. Never was such success more deserved, nor could it appear more satisfying to the author. . . . This, your most honored Excellency, must, in my humble judgment, be worth your having lived for. . . .

The author knew too well that he was living on borrowed time, and that by continuing to write the third and fourth volumes of *Cosmos* he was cheating death. He would survive them all, Arago and Gérard in Paris, his own nephews and nieces. "My life is a painfully torn and laborsome one," he wrote to Gauss in April 1847,

in which only the hours of the night are granted me to do some work. You may ask why I, with my seventy-seven years, don't try to change my position. Human life is a complicated problem. One is handicapped by sentiments, traditional obligations, and foolish hopes. . . . My physical strength is miraculously preserved, but this winter unfortunate family events might well have shaken my health. . . . These few, and for you rather uninteresting, lines have no other purpose but at long last to recall the memory of a man [Gauss] who in my estimation stands higher for mental power and nobility of character than anybody among the contemporaries.

By the time young Möllhausen's marriage was consummated, Humboldt had become an almost legendary figure in Berlin. People would watch him in the streets walking to bookstores and museums with bent gait, strangers greeting him respectfully and whispering to one another: "There goes old Humboldt." At Potsdam he would take short walks to the top of a favorite hill, resting on a bench and enjoying the park-like scenery. On one such occasion he found the place occupied by a young man who boasted of having seen much finer views. When Humboldt tactfully inquired where this might have been, the stranger brazenly alluded to Chimborazo! Amazed, Humboldt asked who had accompanied him on that occasion? Two fellows called Humboldt and Bonpland and a young Spaniard—all of them much too feeble to have reached the summit. And in what year might this have been, Humboldt asked. At this point the young man engaged the old gentleman in a fruitless argument over the precise date of the climb. It ended abruptly when Humboldt introduced himself, and within seconds the young lout had vanished in the shrubbery.

At another time, a favorite general of Friedrich Wilhelm IV cornered Humboldt at the royal dinner table with the remark: "Your Excellency probably goes to church very often these days?" Humboldt replied "You are very kind, sir, for showing me the way by which I could make my fortune."

A Fourth of July dinner in Berlin had prompted the secretary of the United States Legation, Theodore S. Fay, to invite Humboldt, and Fay noticed that the honored guest looked a bit tired. "Doesn't this fatigue you?" Fay asked. "Not at all," replied Humboldt, "I can bear a lot"—and he continued to relish the occasion. Shortly afterwards Fay visited Humboldt in his apartment and, as he entered, saw the old man with a letter in his hand. Flinging it on the table, Humboldt trembled with indignation as he exclaimed: "Here is a man who charges me with not believing in God." Is it surprising that this accusation of atheism infuriated him? While it is true that Humboldt did not belong to a church, he was nevertheless religious in a sense his friend Goethe had defined when he said: "Whoever owns art or science is religious, but a person not owning either had better take to religion."

In these years Humboldt's position at court had come to be irksome. Since the Revolution of 1848, Friedrich Wilhelm IV had harbored deep resentments against all liberals, whom he suspected of republican plots. Nevertheless, the King continued to rely on Humboldt's advice in cultural matters, which his councilor maneuvered unobtrusively with great skill. So accustomed was the royal family to Humboldt's presence, and often so bored by his lengthy discussions of literary subjects, that the King would doze off in his chair with Humboldt standing by the fireplace reading or talking. Because the aged guest never felt comfortable with room temperatures below seventy-seven degrees, his own apartment at the palace was always heated in advance. But the King was showing signs of mental trouble. Subject to religious hallucinations, he would suddenly appear in Humboldt's room, his face distorted, begging to be calmed down. Being accustomed to walk alone in the park at night, and suffering from shortsightedness, the queer monarch was arrested on one occasion by his palace guard and on another night was found dazed at the foot of a tree where he had bumped his head. By 1858 it had become obvious that he could play his kingly role no longer. When his younger brother was named regent, Humboldt was seen less frequently at the palace. He had known so many rulers in his lifetime—the Bourbons and Napoleons in France, Victoria in England, two tsars of Russia, and four of his own Prussian kings, not to speak of minor European royalty—that he must have felt a bit weary of them all.

Despite occasional bouts of stomach trouble and a severe attack of grippe, the sage had felt well enough to advance his writings, even to fulfill his duty as a voter. On September 28, 1855 Humboldt wrote to Bunsen:

Yesterday I sat for three hours as a voter. In the years 1848–50 I belonged to the Carpenters' Union; yesterday I voted with sixty mail-carriers—as I live opposite the Post Office. It is by no means irrelevant that people of the working class should exercise the right to vote and enjoy equal rights with the aristocracy, the waiter, and the Orientalist Stahl. As long as such institutions as primary elections exist, not everything is lost.

His energies were unabated, smoldering like subterranean fires that continue to radiate heat in all directions long after the fiery lava grows cold. He saw no reason to relax when so many people all over the world wrote him about affairs that demanded instant attention. It was impossible to satisfy all, considering an annual flood of letters rising to 3,800 a year! Of course, he could have engaged a secretary (provided somebody else would pay), but Humboldt loathed intermediaries, saying that the personal touch of handwritten answers was needed. Even if he replied to only half of the letters he received, it is probable that he wrote from twenty to forty letters daily.

People had come to regard him as omniscient. Many well-meaning souls offered to run his household, recommended remedies for his ailments, asked him for opinions on mountain-climbing, mining, flying, where to settle in the Americas, how to get jobs with the government, when to sell their paintings to the King or present petitions for annuities.[5] Visitors came from all corners of the world: Catlin, the painter of American Indians, the brothers Schlagintweit fresh from Tibet and the Himalayas, the archæologist Niebuhr from Egypt—all wanting to be introduced at court or at some museum, engaging his precious time for hours on end. One day in the summer of 1856, a man arrived from New York, Bayard Taylor, the publicist and traveler, bent on interviewing Humboldt for the *New York Tribune.* To him we owe one of the liveliest descriptions of a visit with the celebrated author of *Cosmos:*

> While in Berlin he lived with his servant, Seifert, whose name only I found on the door. It was a plain two-story house, with a dull pink front, and inhabited . . . by two or three families. The bell-wire over Seifert's name came from the second story. I mounted the steps until I reached a second bell-pull, over a plate inscribed "Alexander von Humboldt." . . . A stout square-faced man of about fifty, whom I at once recognized as Seifert, opened the door for me. . . . He ushered me into a room filled with stuffed birds and other objects of natural history, then into a large library. . . . I walked between two long tables, heaped with sumptuous folios, to the further door, which opened into the study. There was a plain table, a writing desk, covered with manuscripts and letters,

---

[5] At last, a few weeks before his death, Humboldt felt, if reluctantly, prompted to stem the incessant flow of well-meaning inquiries by publishing in newspapers requests that the public refrain from writing to him.

the little green sofa . . . maps and pictures on the drab-
colored walls.

Seifert went into an inner door, announced my name, and
Humboldt immediately appeared. He came up to me with a
heartiness and cordiality which made me feel that I was in the
presence of a friend, gave me his hand, and inquired whether
we should converse in English or German. "Your letter," said
he, "was that of a German, and you must certainly speak the
language familiarly, but I am also in the constant habit of
using English." He insisted on my taking one end of the green
sofa, observing that he rarely sat upon it himself, then drew
up a plain cane-bottomed chair and seated himself beside it,
asking me to speak a little louder than usual, as his hearing
was not so acute as formerly. . . . The first impression made
by Humboldt's face was that of a broad and genial humanity.
His massive brow . . . bent forward, overhung his chest like
a ripe ear of corn, but as you looked below it, a pair of clear
blue eyes, almost as bright and steady as a child's, met your
own. . . . His wrinkles were few and small, and his skin had
a smoothness and delicacy rarely seen in old men. His hair,
although snow white, was still abundant, his step slow but
firm, and his manner active almost to the point of restlessness. . . . He talked rapidly with the greatest apparent ease,
never hesitating for a word, whether in English or German,
and, in fact, seemed to be unconscious which language he was
using, as he changed five or six times in the course of the conversation. He did not remain in his chair more than ten minutes at a time, frequently getting up and walking about the
room, now and then pointing to a picture or opening a book to
illustrate some remark.

When Taylor mentioned that he planned to go across
the Kirghiz Steppes to central Asia, Humboldt commented
that fifty miles gave you the picture of a thousand, but
that the people were exceedingly interesting. "He had seen

their ceremonies, and was struck with their resemblance to those of the Catholic Church." When the visitor noted a live chameleon in a glass case, Humboldt remarked: "He can turn one eye towards heaven, while with the other he inspects the earth. There are many clergymen who have the same power." Taylor mentioned that he had seen Washington Irving before leaving New York. Humboldt had met Irving in Paris, and when his visitor reminded him of Irving's advanced age, Humboldt was surprised. "I have lived so long that I have almost lost the consciousness of time. I belong to the age of Jefferson and Gallatin, and I heard of Washington's death while traveling in South America."

Seifert reappeared and reminded his master that it was time, whereupon Taylor prepared to leave. "You have traveled much, and seen many ruins," Humboldt said. "Now you have seen one more." "Not a ruin," Taylor replied, "but a pyramid," and pressed the hands that had touched those of Frederick the Great, of Schiller, Goethe, Pitt, Napoleon, Cuvier, Chopin—"in short of every great man Europe produced for three-quarters of a century." As Taylor was ushered out, Seifert pointed to an elaborate piece of bead-work in a gilt frame. "This," he said, "is the work of a Kirghiz princess, who presented it to his Excellency when *we* were on our journey to Siberia." There was a ring, and a servant came in to announce a visitor. "Ah, the Prince of Ypsilanti," said Seifert. "Don't let him in, don't let a single soul in, I must go and dress his Excellency."

A year later, in October 1857, Taylor visited Humboldt again in his quarters at the King's palace in Potsdam, noting that Humboldt's step was not so firm as before, and that he looked a little paler. Small wonder that the eighty-eight-year-old man seemed worn out, for Humboldt had spent sixteen hours proofreading the fourth volume of *Cosmos!* "I am unconscious of any mental fatigue," the old gentleman said smilingly, and showed his visitor a map whose fine lettering he read without glasses. Eight months before, he had suffered a slight stroke, which had prompted the King to reassure him that he need not worry about debts: he, the King, would be glad to take care of them.

"My strength is dwindling," Humboldt reported to Bunsen on December 12, 1857. "I am not ill, but plagued by skin irritations. It is by no means pleasant to experience a gradual loss of the phosphorus of thought, or a loss of weight in the brain, as the new school would say. But I do not lose my courage for work." This kept him alive; this struggle to complete *Cosmos;* he must keep wading through piles of manuscript, notes on polarization and thermal dynamics, Faraday's magnetic induction, Liebig's latest researches in organic chemistry, Sir Charles Lyell's geologic concepts, and Darwin's zoological reports.

Almost twenty years earlier, he had asked Darwin for temperature readings of the Pacific and observations on color changes in ocean waters. Darwin had been happy to oblige him, writing on November 1, 1839:

That the author of these pages [the *Narrative of Travels*], which I read over and over again, and have copied out, should have so honored me, is a gratification of a kind which can but seldom happen to anyone. . . . I beg to return you my sincere thanks for your very kind letter: it was an honor I scarcely ventured to hope for. . . . When I left England I was a mere amateur naturalist and from want of knowledge, not seeing the purport of such researches, I neglected them. The study of this work inspired me to regard the structure of natural science much more humbly.

In July 1858 the author of *Cosmos* had progressed so far with the final volume that he wrote a preface, touching and admirable for the following paragraph:

At my great age it would be understandable were I to ask for the indulgence of my readers, the more so since they have received my labors so enthusiastically. But considering the scientific ambition that fired me from my earliest youth, I can see no reason for not treating my work with greater diligence than ever. The distribution of the five volumes [the fourth had appeared in two parts] is all the greater for their translation into nine different languages. However, it is quite unavoidable that in the wealth of facts . . . certain errors should have crept into my text, partly through my own fault and partly through that of translators.

Persistent rumors that Humboldt was confined to his home because of illness so alarmed his publisher that he anxiously inquired about his health. On November 3, 1858 the ninety-year-old man replied reassuringly: "I am sending you in the next few days a new batch of manuscript so that you may appreciate the capability of my industry. My bravest hopes go even beyond the completion of *Cosmos.*"

Time was ticking away relentlessly. He was weakening. One more winter had come, its snow falling like a heavy curtain difficult to lift for a glimpse of another spring. Fate had generously granted him the utmost limit of life that he might hope, a last span in which to complete *Cosmos.* There was still so much to do: a more detailed account of rocks, plants, climates, and ocean currents! Writing at intervals about the geologic foundations of the world, he had just finished describing granite rocks seen on his Russian journey when he suddenly paused. It was March 2, 1859. As if by sudden inspiration, he decided to add his customary notes and references to the first eighty-five pages of the last volume. His conversation with earth and universe could not go on much longer.

On April 19 Seifert was sent to dispatch this manuscript to the publisher. Two days later Humboldt took to his bed, exhausted and feverish. Relatives and friends came to cheer him by pointing to the spring weather. The flowers in the park at Tegel were waiting for him. But his final appointment with Cosmos was at hand. The end came on May 6, 1859, at half past two in the afternoon. He could rest at last.

The Prince Regent had ordered a state funeral and on May 10 all of Berlin was on its feet to accord last honors to the illustrious man. House-fronts were draped in black as multitudes flanked the streets where the funeral procession was to pass. It formed at eight in the morning in front of Humboldt's apartment house. Ahead of the cortege walked four royal chamberlains, one carrying a red velvet cushion with the insignia of Humboldt's decorations. The hearse, drawn by six horses and led by grooms of the royal stable, was accompanied on each side by twenty student delegates carrying palm leaves. Azaleas and laurel wreaths covered the coffin, behind which walked Wilhelm von Humbolt's descendants and relatives, their somber mourning contrasting with the long, colorful gowns of the Knights of the Order of the Black Eagle, the glittering uniforms of the ministers of state, and the diplomatic corps. Six hundred students were flanked by uniformed standard-bearers marching to the tune of Chopin's Funeral March. Behind them walked eight ministers of the Evangelical Church, followed by all the members of both parliaments, the Academy of Science, university professors, members of the Academy of Arts, the directors and teachers of all schools, the magistrates, and municipal delegations. Thousands of citizens of Berlin and neighboring towns terminated the procession as it moved to the Cathedral. At its entrance stood the Prince Regent and members of the court. Of a sudden, all church bells began to ring. Choirs chanted as church dignitaries found words to bless what had been a flame of knowledge.

The following day they laid Alexander von Humboldt at rest in the flowering park at Tegel next to his brother and Caroline.

Appendix

A. *EXPLANATORY NOTES ON* COSMOS

THE PRINCIPAL AIM of this extraordinary work was to portray the physical order of earth and universe so that such knowledge might become common property and, beyond specialization, help in the understanding of nature for both æsthetic enjoyment and the liberation of human energies. What with the start of specialization in science and the one-sided emphasis on literary values in the culture of his period, Humboldt recognized in the rational understanding of the universe a challenge for mankind to gain orientation through personal participation in an integrated order of cosmic proportions.

In his introduction to the first volume Humboldt stated his aim when he wrote:

The most important aim of all physical science is this: to recognize unity in diversity, to comprehend all the single aspects as revealed by the discoveries of the last epochs, to judge single phenomena separately without surrendering to their bulk, and to grasp nature's essence under the cover of outer appearances. In so doing, our endeavor passes the narrow confines of the sensual world so that we may hope to master the crude substance of empirical knowledge by the binding force of ideas. . . . The purpose of this introductory chapter is to indicate the manner in which natural science can be endowed with a higher purpose *through which all phenomena and energies are revealed as one entity* pulsating with inner life. Nature is not dead matter. She is, as Schelling expressed it, the sacred and primary force. . . .

The philosophy of *Cosmos* comprises four prolegomena:
1. The definition and limitations of a physical description of the world as a special and separate discipline.
2. The objective content, which is the actual and empirical aspect of nature's entity in the scientific form of a portrait of nature.
3. The action of nature on the imagination and emotion as an in-

centive to nature studies through media like travel descriptions, poetry, landscape painting, and the display of contrasting groups of exotic plants.
4. The history of natural philosophy, the gradual emergence of concepts pertaining to the cosmos as an organic unit.

By introducing his subject in the form of a general "portrait of nature" (Volume I), Humboldt appealed to the sense of wonder about worlds in outer space: the Milky Way, cosmic nebulæ, and planets. From the stellar world, the reader is then led to our Earth, in which geologic and atmospheric dynamics are seen to influence the life and groupings of plants, animals, and people. Volcanoes and mountain ranges signify by their origins a dynamism of their own, reflected even in the growth of mineral particles lending their nourishing substance to plants. Vegetation is an organic precipitate of earth and atmosphere, uniquely revealing the integration of solar, earthly, and organic energies. All organisms are subject to physical agencies, among which wind and ocean currents have aided migrations of many life forms, the races of mankind included.

This portrait of nature is enlivened by historical anecdotes and travel incidents: the boy Galileo dreaming of measuring the earth's shape as he observed the swinging motion of church chandeliers; the encounter on the Orinoco with Indians who unknowingly observed electricity by rubbing dried cotton and bamboo fibers against each other.

From this general and objective approach to nature, the work proceeds to the subjective realm: the sensual perception of natural phenomena as experienced by poets, painters, and students of nature through the ages (Volume II). Such reflections on the imagination are valued as means for intensifying the experience of nature. The Delphic festival of the ancient Greeks, Homer, and Euripides are quoted along with Roman sources like Pliny the Elder to illustrate how the ancients ascribed human feelings to plants, animals, and physical energies. Chinese temple gardens and Dutch landscape artists— in fact, the entire range of artistic experiences of nature—are cited to illustrate the point. And behind it all is Humboldt's pleading for more botanical gardens and nature museums (at their best with round architecture!) in which visitors may look at replicas of landscapes (dioramas). There follows a history of the cosmic concept of unity, as distinct from the history of natural science, with references to Strabo's expectations of land between western Europe and eastern Asià, and to Cardinal Nicholas of Cusa (Nicolaus Cusanus), who, one hundred years before Copernicus, believed the sun to be the center of the planetary system.

The first volumes had sketched this portrait of nature in a general manner. The next three were meant to substantiate Humboldt's ideas by a more detailed account of scientific studies. Again they are rendered in historical perspective and provided with copious and detailed bibliographical references and comments. The third volume is a survey of astronomical knowledge, beginning with Aristotle's idea of world order resulting from unified energies of matter, and ending with Sir John Herschel's classification of stars. In treating these subjects, Humboldt took pains to underscore the historical traditions of astronomy, so uniquely equipped to provide for man's orientation in space. A description of the planet Mercury, for instance, begins with the sentence: "If one recalls how since earliest times the Egyptians occupied themselves with Mercury (Set-Horus), and the Hindus with Budh [Sanscrit name for knowledge], and how under the smiling skies of western Arabia star knowledge in the tribe of the Asedites was exclusively concerned with Mercury . . . one must be astonished that the dying Copernicus complained about his inability to have observed this planet. The Greeks had already singled out this planet for its strong, sparkling light." A discussion of meteorites evokes memories of his own observations in America and Europe, then leads to a classified account of these messengers from space on the basis of the latest chemical studies, proving the interrelatedness of terrestrial and cosmic substances.

As in all of these descriptions, one is impressed with Humboldt's diligence in obtaining the latest and most authoritative information, which he took infinite pains to assemble from technical literature and by private correspondence.

The fourth volume is one of the most interesting because of its detailed summary of the earth's physical properties as known at the time. It begins with magnetism, its distribution and varying properties, and proceeds to an account of geophysical methods for studying the size and shape of the earth, the relationship of magnetism to polar lights and geologic phenomena. The description of these electromagnetic properties leads to the fascinating drama of earthquakes and vulcanism. In stressing the deep-seated impulses of seismic disturbances as the result of a general cooling of the earth's crust, Humboldt admits that local tensions, occasioned by internal collapse of rock structures in volcanic regions, do create localized earthquakes of great intensity. All major earthquakes and volcanic eruptions are traced back in history in a pioneering statistical account of terrestrial convulsions, which has remained largely unused in the progress of earth science. The detailed description of volcanoes in many regions of the earth leads to concepts of regional grouping along unstable and fractured portions of the earth's crust, with special reference to American regions. The description of volcanic rocks corresponds to the accepted and orthodox classification established by Bischof, Rose, and Lyell.

The fifth volume was meant to conclude the survey of "tellurian phenomena in their purest objectivity," its preface dating from July 1858. It begins with an account of landscape-forming volcanic and associated processes and an orthodox classification of rocks into igneous, sedimentary, metamorphic, and conglomerates. Credit is given to Füchsel and Werner for having introduced the concept of rock formations. "Werner, unfortunately," Humboldt wrote about his eminent teacher of geology, "regarded what he called geology as the *dreamy* part of geognosy," meaning that Werner neglected the dynamic interpretation of geology as given by Hutton, and more especially Lyell. In calling Werner "my great teacher, though hampered by his restricted viewpoints," Humboldt no doubt indicated how much of his geologic knowledge he owed to his own observations and the study of works by Lyell, von Buch, Murchison, and Dana.

In the midst of his descriptions of granite rocks encountered in Siberia, Humboldt died, leaving the final volume incomplete. His faithful collaborators, Professors Eduard Buschmann and Carl Bruhns, provided for the entire work a detailed index amounting to no less than 1,117 pages!

B. A BRIEF APPRAISAL OF HUMBOLDT'S MAIN CONTRIBUTIONS TO KNOWLEDGE

AS POINTED OUT in the preface, it cannot be the aim of this biographical sketch to evaluate the voluminous mass of Humboldt's works, which makes it all the more necessary for the reader to get a glimpse of the contributions with which Humboldt's name will be associated for all time. Some of Humboldt's publications have not been listed: a careful scrutiny of all would obviously require many years of study, for many still await appraisal.

1. *Anthropology*
A keen and respectful observer of native traditions, Humboldt contributed ethnologic observations on American aborigines, and on the basis of cultural affinities suggested their origins in northeast Asia. By calling attention to the magnificence of Inca, Aztec, and Maya traditions, and by collecting ancient Indian manuscripts and archæological objects, he prepared the ground not only for subsequent research, but also for an appreciation of the American Indian heritage which inspired many of his contemporaries to undertake anthropologic studies. A geographic orientation led him to recognize environmental factors in the formation of native customs, and in so doing Humboldt raised aborigines to a status entitling them to the enjoyment of human rights and political liberties.

2. *Astronomy*

First to have observed with instruments the great meteor showers of 1799, Humboldt helped to establish the concept of their periodicity, and contributed with Laplace to the knowledge of ancient calendric systems (Aztec). In *Cosmos* he wrote the first modern account of the universe in historical perspective.

3. *Botany*

In collaboration with Aimé Bonpland, Humboldt collected some 60,000 plant specimens and described some 3,500 new species. He supplied the first accurate information on rubber and cinchona trees, experimented in the field of plant physiology, and helped to create the basic concepts of plant ecology by formulating the theory of the geographic conditioning of plant distribution (plant geography).

4. *Geography*

Humboldt established principles of physiographic, political, and economic geography which laid the foundation of this science. His astronomic and barometric observations formed the basis of subsequent map-making in South and Middle America. First to introduce the term *isotherm,* he laid the cornerstone for climatology, introducing at the same time the method of geographic profiles as graphic illustrations for associated geographic features. By compiling the most comprehensive history of exploratory voyages to the Americas, he found the origin of the name America. His consideration of geographic factors in the lives of nations helped establish the basic tenets of modern geography.

5. *Geology*

Humboldt was first to recognize the relationship between vulcanism and earth structures. He called attention to geologic similarities among the Americas, Europe, and Asia. He introduced the graphic method of geologic cross-sections based on instrument-readings, and rendered the first maps and descriptions of volcanoes. By climbing Chimborazo he established an altitude record that inspired the scientific exploration of mountains, notably that of the Andes and the Himalayas.

6. Geophysics

Humboldt's magnetic surveys led to his recognition of the law of declining magnetic intensity between the poles. He was instrumental in establishing the International Union for Magnetic Studies, the first co-operative scientific organization.

7. Meteorology

With Gay-Lussac, Humboldt analyzed the chemical constitution of the atmosphere, made important observations on tropical storms, and presented the first account of air circulation in caves.

8. Oceanography

Humboldt's observations and researches on the physical properties of ocean waters enabled him to give the first graphic descriptions of oceans (Humboldt Current).

9. Physiology

Humboldt pointed the way to electrotherapy by making pioneer experiments in the electric excitability of muscle and nerve fibers, many of them carried out on his own body. First to observe the effects of high altitude on the human body, he stimulated research that later prepared the conquest of the air.

10. Zoology

Humboldt described new animals from South America (electric eel, alligator, monkey) and animal habitats. With Gay-Lussac, he made the first studies on the respiration of fishes. His observations on guano deposits in Peru inspired him to interest soil chemists in the practical use of that fertilizing substance. Through Ehrenberg's companionship on his expedition to Russia, he stimulated the science of microbiology, with special reference to fresh-water life.

C. HUMBOLDT'S HONORARY MEMBERSHIPS
IN LEARNED SOCIETIES IN THE UNITED STATES

1804. American Philosophical Society, Philadelphia.
1816. American Antiquarian Society, Boston.
1820. New York Historical Society, New York.
1822. American Academy of Arts and Sciences.
1827. Lyceum of Natural History of New York.
1834. Geological Society of Pennsylvania, Philadelphia.
1842. Academy of Natural Sciences of Philadelphia.
1843. American Ethnological Society, New York.
1856. American Geographical and Statistical Society, New York.

D. LIST OF GEOGRAPHIC FEATURES
NAMED AFTER ALEXANDER VON HUMBOLDT

Humboldt, Saskatchewan, Canada
Humboldt, Coles County, Illinois
Humboldt, Humboldt County, Iowa
Humboldt, Allen County, Kansas
Humboldt, Kittson County, Minnesota
Humboldt, Richardson County, Nebraska
Humboldt, Minnehaha County, South Dakota
Humboldt, Gibson County, Tennessee
Humboldt Bay, Humboldt County, California
Humboldt Bay, northern New Guinea
Humboldt County, California
Humboldt County, Iowa
Humboldt County, Nevada
Humboldt Current, off the Pacific Coast of South America
Humboldt Glacier, northwestern Greenland
Humboldt Mountains, range of Nanshan system, China
Humboldt Peak, Sangre de Cristo Range, Custer County, Colorado

Humboldt Peak, Venezuela
Humboldt Range, Nevada
Humboldt Reservoir, Nevada
Humboldt River, Pershing County, Nevada
Humboldt Salt Marsh, Churchill County, Nevada
Humboldt Sink, Nevada
Humboldt State Redwood Park, California

Bibliography

A. BIBLIOGRAPHY OF THE MOST IMPORTANT WORKS OF ALEXANDER VON HUMBOLDT

1793. *Floræ Fribergensis specimen plantas cryptogamicas præsertim subterraneas exhibens.* Berlin.
Observations and experiments relating to the origin of green coloring substances and species of underground plants and the physiological processes involved.

1797. *Versuche über die gereizte Muskel- und Nervenfaser nebst Versuchen über den chemischen Prozess des Lebens in der Thier- und Pflanzenwelt.* 2 vols. Berlin. French edition.
Experiments on the effects of galvanism on muscle and nerve fibers in human and animal bodies. A pioneering study in the field of electrical therapy and human physiology.

1799. *Über die unterirdischen Gasarten und die Mittel ihren Nachteil zu verhindern.* Braunschweig.

1805. *Sur l'analyse de l'air atmosphérique,* with J. L. Gay-Lussac. Paris. German edition: Tübingen.
An analysis of the atmosphere with reference to electrical properties and other atmospheric phenomena.

1806. *Ideen zu einer Physiognomik der Gewächse.* Tübingen.
Plant forms as conditioned by physical and chemical factors.

1807. *Essai sur la géographie des plantes.* Paris. German edition: Tübingen.
Plant distribution as conditioned by geographic factors. This study established the science of plant geography.

1807. *Views of Nature (Ansichten der Natur).* Tübingen. Two English and French editions.
Essays on nature studies and associated æsthetic experiences.

1811. *Political Essay on the Kingdom of New Spain.* 4 vols. London. French and German editions.
A geographic and political description of ancient Mexico, with maps and statistical accounts of mining, commerce, population census, and revenues. The first comprehensive treatise on an American nation.

1814. *Researches Concerning the Institutions and Monuments of the Ancient Inhabitants of America.* 2 vols. London. French and German editions.

Descriptions and essays on pre-Spanish antiquities and American Indian cultures. This work acquainted Europe with the cultural achievements of ancient America.

1817. *Des lignes isothermes et de la distribution de la châleur sur le globe.* Paris. German edition: Tübingen.

Presentation of a novel graphic method for illustrating the earth's temperature distribution. A fundamental contribution to climatology.

1807–39. *Voyage aux régions équinoctiales du Nouveau Continent, fait en 1799–1804.* With A. Bonpland and various collaborators. 30 vols. Paris.

Scientific results of studies in South and Middle America dealing with botany, geology, physics, zoology, map surveys, etc. The most ambitious scientific publication of the period, and the most costly.

1818–29. *Personal Narrative of Travels to the Equinoctial Regions of the New Continent.* 7 vols. London. First edition in French, Paris: 1815–26.

Travel narrative from the years 1799 to 1803, with lengthy descriptions of social conditions and native customs in the Canary Islands, Cuba, Venezuela, Colombia.

1823. *Essai géognostique sur le gisement des roches dans les deux continents.* Paris. English and German editions.

A geologic treatise on methodology, and an attempt at correlating relating rock formations of Europe and America.

1828. *Essai politique sur l'Îsle de Cuba.* 2 vols. Paris. English and German editions.

A geographic and political description of Cuba, with map and statistical data, and a noteworthy chapter on slavery.

1831. *Fragments de géologie et de climatologie asiatiques.* Paris. German edition: Tübingen.

A preliminary account of his scientific observations on his journey to western Siberia.

1836–39. *Examen critique de l'histoire de la géographie du Nouveau Continent et des progrès de l'astronomie nautique au 15ᵉ et 16ᵉ siècles.* 3 vols. Paris.

A critical study of all historical sources dealing with the early voyages and discoveries of America, with reference to the development of nautical astronomy in the fifteenth and sixteenth centuries. In this work Humboldt established the origin of the name America.

1843. *Asie Centrale, recherches sur les chaînes des montagnes et la climatologie comparée.* 3 vols. Paris.

A complete account of his studies in central Asia, with fundamental geographic and geologic contributions.

1845–61. *Cosmos, a sketch of a physical description of the universe.* 5 vols. and atlas. London. Various editions in eight other languages.

An encyclopedic description of the physical aspects of nature and its reflection in the human mind. A synthesis of unrivaled scope, by which Humboldt attempted to portray the essential unity of all natural phenomena in so far as that unity can be apprehended through general laws.

B. GENERAL BIBLIOGRAPHY

ADAMS, FRANK D.: *The Birth and Development of the Geological Sciences.* Baltimore: 1938.

ADAMS, HENRY: *The Life of Albert Gallatin.* Philadelphia: 1879.

AGASSIZ, E. C.: Louis Agassiz, *His Life and Correspondence.* 2 vols. Boston: 1886.

AGASSIZ, LOUIS: *Address delivered on the Centennial Anniversary of the Birth of Alexander von Humboldt, under the auspices of the Boston Society of Natural History.* Boston: 1869.

ARAGO, FRANCOIS: *Sämtliche Werke mit einer Einleitung von Alexander von Humboldt.* 16 vols. Leipzig: 1854–60.

BAER, JOSEPH, & Co.: *Alexander von Humboldt Katalog einer Sammlung seiner Werke, Portraits und Schriften.* Frankfurt: 1912.

BANSE, EWALD: *Alexander von Humboldt, Erschliesser einer neuen Welt.* Stuttgart: 1953.

BERNSTEIN, AARON: *Alexander von Humboldt und der Geist zweier Jahrhunderte. Virchow Sammlung,* Ser. 4, Heft 89. Berlin: 1869.

BINSWANGER, P.: *Wilhelm von Humboldt.* Berlin: 1937.

BONPLAND, AIMÉ: *Archives inédites de A. Bonpland. Trabajos de la Universita Nacional.* Vol. XXXI. Buenos Aires: 1914–24.

BORCH, RUDOLF: *Alexander von Humboldt, Sein Leben in Selbstzeugnissen, Briefen und Berichten.* Berlin: 1948.

BOUVIER, RENÉ, and ED. MAYNIAL.: *Aimé Bonpland.* Paris: 1950.

BRATRANEK, F. Th.: *Goethe's Briefwechsel mit den Gebrüdern von Humboldt (1792–1832).* Leipzig: 1876.

BRUHNS, KARL CHR.: *Life of Alexander von Humboldt.* Translated from the German by Jane and Caroline Lassell. 2 vols. London: 1873.

CANCRIN, GEORG GRAF VON: *Briefwechsel zwischen Alexander von*

Humboldt und Cancrin aus den Jahren 1827–32. Leipzig: 1869.
Catalogue of Humboldt library. London: 1865.
CERALLOS, PEDRO F.: *Resumén de la Historia del Ecuador.* Lima: 1870.
CHATEAUBRIAND, FRANÇOIS A. R.: *Œuvres complètes.* 36 vols. Paris: 1836–8.
CLEEMPUTTE, A. VAN: *La Vie Parisienne.* Vol. I. Paris: 1900.
Deux Lettres d'Alexandre de Humboldt à François Arago. Ass. Française pour l'avancement des sciences, Compte rendu, sér. 40. Vol. I, pp. 66–72.
DE VOTO, BERNARD: *The Course of Empire.* Boston: 1952.
DOVE, ALFRED: *Die Gebrüder Humboldt.* Ed. F. Meinecke. Leipzig: 1925.
DOVE, H. W.: *Die Forsters und die Humboldts.* Leipzig: 1881.
EULENBERG, HERBERT: *Die Hohenzollern.* Berlin: 1928.
EVANS, JOAN: *Chateaubriand, a biography.* London: 1939.
FOERSTER, WILHELM: *Ein Besuch bei Humboldt. Der Sternfreund,* no. 1. Berlin: 1936.
FORD, PAUL LEICESTER: *The Works of Thomas Jefferson.* 10 vols. New York: 1892–9.
FRÉMONT, ELIZABETH B.: *Recollections of Elizabeth Benton Frémont.* New York: 1912.
GAUSS, FRIEDRICH: *Briefe zwischen Alexander von Humboldt und Gauss.* Leipzig: 1877.
GEIGER, LUDWIG: *Goethe's Briefwechsel mit Wilhelm und Alexander von Humboldt.* Berlin: 1909.
GÉRARD, H.: *Correspondance de François Gérard.* Paris: 1867.
HAARBECK, L.: *Die Familie Humboldt.* Reutlingen: 1932.
HAGEN, WOLFGANG VON: *South America Called Them.* New York: 1945.
HAMY, EMIL T.: *Alexandre de Humboldt et le Muséum d'Histoire Naturelle. Nouvelles Archives du Muséum,* 4ᵉ série, v. 8–32. Paris: 1906.
——: *Lettres Américaines d'Alexandre de Humboldt (1798–1807).* Paris: 1905.
HAREN, S. F.: "Note on Alexander von Humboldt and His Services to American Archæology." *American Antiquarian Society, Proceedings,* no. 70, pp. 91–100. Worcester, Mass.: 1878.
HELLER, GEORG: *Die Weltanschauung Alexander von Humboldt's in ihren Beziehungen zu den Ideen des Klassizismus.* Leipzig: 1910.
HENNING, R.: "Die Geschichte der mittelamerikanischen Kanalidee bis zu Alexander von Humboldt," *Himmel und Erde,* Vol. XXVI: 1913.

HERZ, WILHELM: *Erinnerungen aus Paris 1817–48.* Berlin: 1851.
HODGETTS, E. H. BRADLEY: *The House of Hohenzollern; Two Centuries of Berlin Court Life.* London: 1911.
HOWE, M. A. DE WOLFE: *The Life and Letters of George Bancroft.* 2 vols. New York: 1908.
HUMBOLDT, ALEXANDER VON: *Briefe an seinen Bruder Wilhelm.* Berlin: 1923.
——: *Briefe an Varnhagen von Ense aus den Jahren 1827–1858.* Leipzig: 1860.
——: *Briefe an Christian Carl Josias Freiherr von Bunsen.* Leipzig: 1869.
——: *Briefwechsel mit Heinrich Berghaus aus den Jahren 1825–1858.* 3 vols. Leipzig: 1863.
——: *Briefe an Ignaz von Olfers.* Nürnberg: 1913.
——: "Lettres d'Alexandre de Humboldt à Marc-Auguste Pictet." Société de Géographie, pp. 129–204. Genéve: 1869.
HUMBOLDT, CAROLINE VON: [letters and biographical sketch] Ed. Hermann Hettler. Leipzig: 1933.
HUMBOLDT, WILHELM VON: *Briefe.* München: 1952.
——: *Die Brautbriefe Wilhelm und Caroline von Humboldt's.* Leipzig: 1920.
HUMBOLDT, WILHELM, and CAROLINE VON: *In ihren Briefen, 1788–1835.* Berlin: 1935.
INGERSOLL, ROBERT G.: *An Oration delivered at Peoria, Illinois, for the unveiling of a statue to Al. von Humboldt.* New York: 1910.
JEFFERSON, THOMAS, see Ford, Paul Leicester.
KAHLER, SIEGFRIED: "Alexander und Wilhelm von Humboldt in den Jahren der Napoleonischen Krise." *Hist. Zeitschrift,* 3. Folge, Vol. XX, pp. 231–70. 1916.
KLENCKE, HERMANN: *Lives of the Brothers Humboldt, Alexander and Wilhelm.* New York: 1853.
KLETKE, H.: *Alexander von Humboldt's Reisen in Amerika und Asien.* 4 vols. Berlin: 1859–61.
KOHUT, ADOLPH: *Alexander von Humboldt und das Judentum.* Leipzig: 1871.
KOTZEBUE, AUGUST F. F.: *Erinnerungen aus Paris im Jahre 1804.* Karlsruhe: 1804.
KRAMMER, MARIO: *Alexander von Humboldt.* Berlin: 1951.
KUBLER, ERNEST A.: "Von Humboldt Anniversary." *American German Review,* Vol. X, no. 6. Philadelphia: 1944.
LA ROQUETTE, J. B. M. A. DEZOS DE: *Notice sur la vie et las travaux de M. le Baron de Humboldt.* Paris: 1860.
LAMBERT, A. B.: *Baron de Humboldt's Account of the Chinchona Forests of South America.* London: 1821.

LANGER, WILLIAM K.: *The Rise of modern Europe.* Vol. XIV. New York: 1934.

LEITZMAN, ALBERT: "Eine Jugendfreundschaft Alexander von Humboldt's." *Deutsche Rundschau,* Vol. CLXII, pp. 106–26. Berlin: 1915.

——: *Wilhelm von Humboldt.* Halle: 1919.

LENTZ, EDUARD: "Alexander von Humboldt's Aufbruch zur Reise nach Südamerika nach ungedruckten Briefen an Baron von Forell." *Ges. für Erdkunde, Zeitschrift.* Vol. XXXIV pp. 311–36. Berlin: 1899.

LINDEN, WALTHER: *Alexander von Humboldt, Weltbild der Naturwissenschaft.* Hamburg: 1940.

LYELL, SIR CHARLES: *Life, Letters, and Journals.* 2 vols. London: 1881.

MACGILLIVRAY, W.: *The Travels and Researches of Alexander von Humboldt.* New York: 1832.

MADISON, JAMES: *The Writings of James Madison.* 9 vols. New York: 1900–10.

MASON, S. F.: *A History of the Sciences.* London: 1953.

MAY, WALTER: *Alexander von Humboldt und Darwin. Preuss. Jahrbuch,* Vol. CV, Heft 2. 1901.

——: *Goethe und Alexander von Humboldt. Verh. d. naturwiss. Vereins in Karlsruhe, Abhandl.* Vol. XIV, pp. 3–30. 1901.

Memoria Científica para la Inauguración de la Estatua de Alejandro de Humboldt. Mexico, D. F.: 1910.

MOBINS, MARTIN: "Goethe und Alexander von Humboldt." *Euphorion, Zeitschr. für Literaturgeschichte,* Vol. XXII, pp. 711–36. Leipzig: 1920.

MÖBUS, WILLY: *Alexander von Humboldt.* Wilmersdorf: 1948.

MÖLLHAUSEN, BALDUIN: *Diary of a Journey from the Mississippi to the Coasts of the Pacific with a United States Government Expedition.* With an introduction by Alexander von Humboldt. 2 vols. London: 1858.

MORSE, EDWARD LIND: *Samuel F. B. Morse, His Letters and Journals, edited and Supplemented by His Son.* 2 vols. Boston: 1914.

MÜLLER, CONRAD: *Alexander von Humboldt und das preussiche Königshaus.* Leipzig: 1928.

NEVINS, ALLAN: *Frémont, Pathmaker of the West.* New York and London: 1939.

ORTÍZ, FERNANDO: "Humboldt y Cuba." *Revista de la Habana,* Vol. II, pp. 155–71, 295–312. 1936.

PEACOCK, GEORGE: *The Resources of Peru.* London: 1874.

PHILIPPSON, L.: *Alexander von Humboldt's politische Ansichten.* Magdeburg: 1860.

RADZIWELL, PRINCESS: *Memoirs of the Duchess de Dino, 1841–1850*. 3 vols. London: 1909–10.

RAMIREZ, FERNANDO: "Una Visitá al Baron de Humboldt." *Diccionario Universal de Historia y de Geografía*: 1857.

RANDOLPH, SARAH N.: *The Domestic Life of Thomas Jefferson*. Cambridge, Mass.: 1939.

RAVE, PAUL O.: *Wilhelm von Humboldt und das Schloss zu Tegel*. Berlin: 1950.

RIPPY, F., and E. R. BRAUN: "Alexander von Humboldt and Simón Bolívar." *American Historical Review*, Vol. LII, no. 4, pp. 697–703. 1947.

ROBLES, ALESSIO VITO: *Alejandro de Humboldt, su Vida y su Obra*. Mexico: 1945.

PEREYRA, CARLOS: *Humboldt en America*. Editorial Madrid: 19–

RIVES, WILLIAM C.: *History of the Life and Times of James Madison*. 3 vols. Boston: 1859–68.

RÖHL, EDUARDO: "Alejandro de Humboldt." *Bol. Coc. Venezolana de Ciencias Naturales*. No. 44, pp. 153–84. 1940.

ROJAS, ARISTIDIES: *Humboldtianas, Compilación de Ed. Röhl y Prologo de Angel M. Alamo*. Caracas: 1942.

ROSE, GUSTAV: *Mineralogisch-geognostische Reise nach dem Ural, dem Altai und dem Kaspischen Meer*. 2 vols. Berlin: 1837.

SCHACHNER, NATHAN: *Thomas Jefferson, a Biography*. New York: 1951.

SELLERS, CHARLES C.: "Charles Willson Peale." *Mem. Amer. Phil. Soc.*, Vol. XXIII, pt. 1–2. Philadelphia: 1947.

SILLIMAN, BENJAMIN: *A Visit to Europe in 1851*. 2 vols. New York: 1853.

SPRAGUE, T. A.: "Humboldt's and Bonpland's Itinerary in Colombia." *Royal Botanic Gardens Kew, Bull. of Misc. Inf.*, pp. 23–9. 1926. London.

——: "Humboldt and Bonpland's Itinerary in Mexico and Venezuela." *Royal Botanic Gardens Kew, Bull. of Misc. Inf.*, pp. 20–7, 1924; pp. 295–310, 1925. London.

STEVENSON, W. B.: *Historical Descriptive Narrative of Twenty Years Residence in South America*. London: 1825.

STODDARD, RICHARD H.: *The Life, Travels, and Researches of Baron Humboldt*. London: 1859.

SYDOW, ANNA VON: *Wilhelm und Caroline von Humboldt in Ihren Briefen*. Berlin: 1906.

TAYLOR, BAYARD: *At Home and Abroad*. New York: 1860.

THOMPSON, J. P., PROF. BACHE, LIEBER, GUYOT, GEORGE BANCROFT, AGASSIZ: *Tribute to the Memory of Humboldt*. New York: 1859.

TICKNOR, GEORGE: *Life of William H. Prescott.* Boston: 1864.
VARNHAGEN VON ENSE, K. A.: *Denkwürdigkeiten des eigenen Lebens.* Berlin: 1950.
WEIGEL, T. O.: *Briefe über Alexander von Humboldt's Kosmos.* Leipzig: 1848–55.

Index